Psychology & Politics

D0874555

Psychology & Politics

AN INTRODUCTORY READER

LEROY N. RIESELBACH
Indiana University

GEORGE I. BALCH
University of Illinois at Chicago Circle

Holt, Rinehart and Winston, Inc.

NEW YORK · CHICAGO · SAN FRANCISCO · ATLANTA
DALLAS · MONTREAL · TORONTO · LONDON · SYDNEY

Preface

Much recent effort in the social sciences has been devoted to understanding and explaining the sources of human action; the social scientist seeks to discover why people behave as they do. Specifically in political science, the analyst wants to find answers to such questions as why people hold specific opinions, why some choose to participate actively in politics while others remain relatively uninvolved with public affairs, and how government officials make policy decisions. The "political behavior" approach to the study of politics, which consciously emphasizes the science in political science, seeks to specify the precise ways in which people, both leaders and followers, do act in political matters.

v

Explanation of such action has been sought by looking at social factors. There is ample evidence to suggest that laborers hold different views of the world than doctors, that Catholics are more likely to vote Democratic than Protestants, that the wealthy are more likely to have the time and the inclination to engage in political campaigning and political discussion than are the less well off, and so forth. Explanation also depends upon an understanding of the level of culture or upon the expectations to which citizens feel compelled to respond. For instance, it seems clear that much involvement in American politics, including the act of going to the polls to vote, is in response to the beliefs that in a democracy a citizen is obligated to participate.

Recently, the search for an understanding of political activity has been broadened to include the study of psychological factors. It has begun to be recognized that individual behavior reflects more than social and cultural elements: what people do and think is influenced by what they are. Put another way, this newer approach suggests that a person brings a set of dispositions, which we call personality, to a particular situation and that these dispositions will affect—but not necessarily determine—what he does in that situation. This collection of papers is intended to illustrate the range of ways in which psychological factors may influence the behavior of citizens and leaders.

The book is frankly introductory in character. It includes selections that are relatively straightforward and can be readily understood by those who are not well-versed in psychology. An attempt has been made to avoid papers that require sophistication in statistics and research methodology to be read and comprehended. To achieve these ends a number of important contributions to the study of psychology and politics had to be omitted. For those who wish to move beyond what is included here, a short bibliography is included. Since much work on this topic has been done in the American context, the selections deal largely with psychological approaches to American politics. However, the sort of analysis presented should prove enlightening in efforts to explain belief and behavior in other societies as well as in our own.

The selections follow a logical order. Part I takes up the argument, first developed in the Introduction, that an analysis of personality is highly relevant to the study of politics; suggests that this is hardly a recently discovered truth; and also outlines the conditions under which this relevance seems to be most pronounced. In Part II the socialization process, the way in which behavioral dispositions are acquired, is explored: The direct relationship between individual differences and individual attitudes and behavior is treated in Part III, while Part IV examines some implications of each of three aspects of personality—human nature, communal character, and individual differences—for larger social groupings, including political systems.

In assembling these papers, we have incurred a number of obligations which we are pleased to acknowledge here. Foremost, of course, is our debt to the scholars whose work is included here; their efforts have made clear the value of examining psychological factors in our search for an understanding of people and politics. Fred I. Greenstein and Roy E. Feldman served as reviewers, and their perceptive commentary compelled us to rethink and restate a number of points. Charles H. McCall, Jr., counseled us as we selected the papers to be included in this volume. The correspondence relating to permissions and the typing of the manuscript were handled with accuracy and efficiency by Mrs. Linda Smith. Finally, the editors of Holt, Rinehart and Winston with their cooperation and constructive criticism both eased the task of preparing the collection and made this a better book. To these people, we gladly acknowledge our debt. Responsibility for whatever errors of fact or interpretation may remain, however, should be assigned to us, as we have not always chosen to accept advice that might have further strengthened our case for the importance of psychology to the study of politics.

Bloomington, Indiana   L. N. R.
November 1968   G. I. B.

Contents

Psychology & Politics

Introduction

The story is told of the political candidate, running for reelection, who discovered that one of his long-time supporters was, on this occasion, backing the opposition nominee. With a mixture of anger and disbelief, the candidate sought out his erstwhile backer and the following dialogue ensued:

CANDIDATE: I understand you are supporting my opponent.

FARMER JONES: Yep.

CANDIDATE: Don't you remember how, in the 1930s, I arranged for the Rural Electrification Authority to bring electric power to your farm?

FARMER JONES: Yep.

CANDIDATE: Don't you remember how, after the war, I arranged for the appointment of your wife as postmistress of this town?

FARMER JONES: Yep.

CANDIDATE: And didn't I help you a few years back to get your south forty included in the Soil Bank, to your great advantage?

FARMER JONES: Yep.

CANDIDATE: Well, why are you supporting my opponent?

FARMER JONES: I remember those things all right, but what have you done for me lately?

Whatever our response to this (probably apocryphal) story, we will in all likelihood react in relation to one of the participants. We may see Farmer Jones, for instance, as a distrustful old man, or as an ingrate, or as an unprincipled opportunist, or in some other fashion. But whatever our response it will in some way be a judgment about the kind of person he is. Similarly, however impressionistically, we will reach conclusions about the candidate. The crucial point is that we do judge other people in terms of recognizable characteristics which seem typical of human beings. These typical attributes of individuals will be defined, more specifically, as *personality* in a subsequent section of this introduction.

Other examples of this human propensity to respond to the basic characteristics of people, individually or in groups, come readily to mind. In a political context, it is evident that a recent generation of Americans "liked Ike." They liked him for widely differing and often contradictory reasons, but they liked him nonetheless.[1] Some saw him as experienced, as "practical, efficient, levelheaded." Others saw him in more immediate personal terms: honest, fair, sincere, of good character generally, "above graft," and "not swayed by politics." Still others, presumably judging him as General Eisenhower, saw him as an energetic leader, an "aggressive, young, forceful, decisive, firm" man.

We look at racial, ethnic, and religious groups in like fashion. Our tendency, as deplorable as it may be, to view groups to which we do not belong in terms of stereotypes is so well known it requires no discussion. We view other nations in the same fashion: one study reveals that Americans tend to see themselves as peace-loving, generous, and intelligent while viewing the British as intelligent, hard-

[1] These characterizations of Eisenhower are drawn from Herbert Hyman and Paul Sheatsley, "The Political Appeal of President Eisenhower," *Public Opinion Quarterly* 27 (1953–54), pp. 441–460. See especially table 5, p. 456.

working, and brave and seeing the Russians as cruel, hardworking, and domineering.[2]

As these examples suggest, not only do people assign such traits or characteristics to others, but they also expect them to act in keeping with these attributes. Thus, if we see Farmer Jones as lacking in loyalty or gratitude, his change in political allegiance comes as no surprise. Or viewing President Eisenhower as honest and above graft, we can account for the appeal of his 1952 campaign pledge to end corruption in Washington. If our perspective on Eisenhower is colored by his military background, we can understand the feeling of many Americans in 1952 that he was the man to resolve the Korean conflict. In the same vein, seeing the Russians as cruel and domineering makes it easier for those who hold this view to account for the seeming hostility of the Soviets toward this country. In short, there seems to be a link between what a person is and what he does, or to put it in the terms of this book, between his personality and his behavior.[3]

This collection of papers and essays has been assembled because it is evident that the relationships illustrated in the preceding paragraphs exist and need to be understood. To put it more specifically, personality factors are becoming increasingly important for the understanding of what people believe about politics and how they act in political situations. There are two reasons for this. First, since the earliest writings in political philosophy it has been recognized that personality (that is, certain characteristics of the human organism) is *logically*[4] related to the holding of political opinions and to the engaging in certain kinds of political actions. To put it another way, observers of human behavior have noted that there is reason to expect that an individual's behavior and beliefs may be influenced in part by the kind of person he is, that is, by his personality. These observers

---

[2] See William Buchanan and Hadley Cantril, *How Nations See Each Other* (Urbana: University of Illinois Press, 1953), esp. chap. 5, pp. 45–59.

[3] It must be admitted of course that the path by which this link is reached may be the opposite of what is implied in this paragraph. That is, we may explain observed behavior after the fact by attributing certain dispositions to the actor involved. The important point, however, remains that what a person does (behavior) and what he is (personality) are related (are correlated, covary) and that knowing something about one may help us to understand something about the other.

[4] We are using "logical" in a colloquial sense here, to suggest that it is in keeping with common sense, or intuitively reasonable, to consider personality as one possible source of attitudes and behavior. We do not intend to attach more rigorous meaning to the word, such as might be used in the philosophy of science.

have also noted that political systems are organized, maintained, and changed in accordance with the needs of the human organism.

Second, there exist *empirical,* factual grounds for believing that a man's outlook and activity are colored by his personality. A number of researchers have discovered that knowing something about a citizen's personality will in fact permit some understanding of what attitudes he is likely to hold, how he is likely to act in certain situations, or how he will respond to particular kinds of events. In short, it is reasonable to expect personality to influence behavior and there is evidence to support such an expectation. Let us examine each of these points in greater detail.

THE LOGICAL RELEVANCE OF PERSONALITY

To illustrate the assertion that it is logical to see individual personality as one of the sorts of factors which may shape political opinion and behavior, it will be profitable to examine some of the ways in which students of politics think about their subject. One approach which often, either explicitly or implicitly, underlies the study of political behavior is the stimulus-organism-response (SOR) model, or as it is sometimes called, the environment-predisposition-response schema.[5] This view sees behavior as a function of factors outside the individual mediated through elements of his own makeup. In other words, this formulation pictures beliefs and actions as, in some sense, the resultant of forces (stimuli or environment) generated outside the person (for example, by institutions, group memberships, events, and so on) interacting with attributes of the individual (organism) himself. Behavior is affected by both sociological and psychological factors; it is a response to some external force (for example, a war, a political campaign, or family difficulty) as perceived by the individual or to some internal "drive" or "need" (for example, anxiety and status striving), or to some combination of the two. What should be clear here is that personality is seen as a possible determinant of behavior.

The same thing can be seen if we examine a second, more recent, approach to political life, known as "field theory." This approach conceives of the individual as a biological and human entity existing

---

[5] See Bernard R. Berelson, Paul F. Lazarsfeld, and William N. McPhee, *Voting* (Chicago: University of Chicago Press, 1954), pp. 277–304; Robert E. Lane, *Political Life* (New York: Free Press, 1959), pp. 5–7; and James C. Davies, *Human Nature in Politics* (New York: Wiley, 1963), pp. 1–30, for discussions of the SOR approach.

within social and cultural environments.[6] It suggests that to understand behavior it is necessary to look at the individual and at the situation in which he finds himself at the time he must choose among alternative behavior possibilities. Field theory attempts to take into account all major forces which may shape what a person thinks, says, or does.

In the first place, each individual exists within a given culture, that is, within a "system of norms shared by the members of society" and which includes "the prescriptions and proscriptions indicating how things should be done or should be appraised."[7] As Americans, we live within a culture which directs us to behave politically in certain expected ways. To cite one example, our culture impels us to participate actively in politics; we are expected, as "good citizens," to vote, to know something about the issues, to contribute financially to the "party of our choice," and so forth. A person's political behavior, then, may be determined to some extent by the culture in which he lives.

Beyond the dictates of the culture, an individual's beliefs and behavior are bound up in the network of social groupings of which he is a part. He may belong to some primary groups—those of which he is more than merely a formal member, in which he is an active participant, and with whose members he interacts on a personal and relatively spontaneous basis. Many Americans, for example, are deeply committed to, and heavily involved in, church, ethnic, labor union, veterans', and many other types of voluntary associations. Beyond these more immediate memberships, individuals are members of secondary, or categoric, groups. They do not meet face to face with their fellow members, but belong by virtue of their own position in society—their socioeconomic status, adherence to some religious denomination, employment in a particular occupation, and so forth—to broad class, religious, occupational, and other groups. What is important here is to note that a person may develop ways of thinking and acting which are appropriate to his membership in groups of this sort. He may learn how to approach a topic from his fellow members or he may feel social pressure to adjust his views and behavior and make them more consistent with group standards, thus protecting his own status within the group. In either case, however,

---

[6] A recent and thorough explication of the field theoretical position is J. Milton Yinger, *Toward a Field Theory of Behavior* (New York: McGraw-Hill, 1965).
[7] Yinger, p. 74.

what he does, politically and otherwise, will bear the imprint of his involvement in various positions in the social world of which he is a part.

But an individual is by no means a helpless pawn, pushed and pulled by cultural and social forces. Rather he is a distinct, autonomous person whose behavior, while influenced by the cultural and social situations in which he finds himself, will reflect the kind of individual he is. What he is, in part, is determined by his biological makeup. His physical powers and his intelligence will be limited by his natural endowments, that is, by his genetic inheritance. No parents, however doting and devoted to their child, can make a genius of a son or daughter whose IQ is near 80. A person's biological attributes, in short, impose limitations on the ways in which he may develop.

Within these limits, however, individual development may proceed along a nearly infinite variety of paths. As he matures, the individual discovers how to deal with the environment in which he lives; he comes to develop characteristic modes of responding, in thought and in action, to situations in which he finds himself. Recognizing this fact, implicitly at least, we refer to people who shy away from social contacts, preferring isolation to the company of others, as "introverted" or we label as "aggressive" those whose response to frustrating circumstances is to strike out violently at the source of their discomfort. What this means is that the individual brings something of himself to his behavior. Yinger refers to this as the individual's *character*— "what he brings into the behavioral situation"[8]—while other writers use the term "personality" to convey the same meaning.

What is important for present purposes is not the word used, but the fact that the field theoretical approach to individual behavior, like the SOR model discussed previously, explicitly recognizes that personality (or character) may be one of the factors which help us to understand why people act and believe as they do. This is not to say that personality is the only, or even the most important, factor in determining individual behavior. Rather, it should be made clear that other factors—cultural, sociological, and biological—must also be taken into account in any effort to comprehend human behavior in general and political behavior in particular.

Field theory is an effort to make all this clear. The field theorist attempts to assess behavior as a function of forces on all four levels. He recognizes that elements of all four factors are important, but

[8] Yinger, p. 141.

that the relative importance of each will vary with the situation under study.[9] In each situational context, the field theorist must ask himself a number of questions, all of which are important for an understanding of individual attitudes and actions. What are the cultural norms which are operative in a given context? How, if at all, do they influence behavior? What sociostructural (for example, group) forces impinge on an individual? How, if at all, does he respond to them? What personal characteristics does the individual bring to a situation as defined by cultural and societal forces? Under what conditions are they likely to influence behavior? All these questions need to be answered if we are to understand behavior. The only point in contention here is that, on logical grounds, there is no reason to omit those questions which relate to the personal attributes of the individual. On the face of it, such attributes seem as important as any other kind in accounting for differences in the way people behave politically.

EMPIRICAL GROUNDS

It is not necessary to stop with the simple assertion that personality factors are logically related to individual behavior. We can also adduce some empirical evidence to support the argument that personal characteristics need to be considered in an attempt to understand and explain political beliefs and activities. Research on a number of factors supports such a contention; the following discussion of two examples should make this position clear.

One personality characteristic which has received substantial attention from political scientists is authoritarianism. Following the pioneering work *The Authoritarian Personality* by T. W. Adorno and his collaborators,[10] a number of studies have shown that authoritarians (that is, those who make high scores on an attitude scale constructed to measure this factor) differ from nonauthoritarians (low scorers) in distinctive ways. The authoritarian individual is a person whose attitudes show, among other things, a willingness to submit to strong authority, a desire to dominate those seen as weaker, a tendency to view other people in terms of stereotypes, and a pervasive concern for power and toughness.[11]

---

[9] For an attempt to specify some of the sorts of situations in which personality will influence attitudes and behavior, see Selection 4.

[10] T. W. Adorno *et al., The Authoritarian Personality* (New York: Harper & Row, 1950).

[11] Adorno *et al.,* pp. 224–242 and *passim.*

To take one example, it seems clear that authoritarians possess a rather distinctive view of the proper content of American foreign policy. They seem to prefer an isolationist course of action (that is, they are reluctant to see the United States become entangled in world politics)[12]; they favor a more nationalistic (a more independent and uncommitted) policy posture.[13] A detailed analysis by Smith and Rosen showed that individuals who were isolationist in their policy orientations (or low in "worldmindedness") possessed many of the attributes of authoritarianism. Those who rejected cooperative participation in world affairs were more likely to think in stereotypes, to see threats arising from external sources, to prefer compliance to independence, to be pessimistic about the future, and to select as an ideal to be emulated a political-military type in preference to an artistic-humanistic model.[14] Finally, and more specifically, authoritarians have been found more likely than nonauthoritarians to oppose American trade with the Soviet Union and the establishment of classes on Russian society in American schools[15]; to expect war, presumably with the USSR, in the immediate future[16]; and to opt for extreme solutions to complex international problems.[17] This evidence provides substantial support for the proposition that "personal authoritarianism constitutes an important inner source (though by no means the only source) of the disposition toward nationalist and related ideologies."[18]

[12] Bernard Fensterwald, Jr., "The Anatomy of American 'Isolationism' and Expansionism. II," *Journal of Conflict Resolution* 2 (1958), pp. 280–309.

[13] Daniel J. Levinson, "Authoritarian Personality and Foreign Policy," *Journal of Conflict Resolution* 1 (1957), pp. 37–47; and Charles D. Farris, "Selected Attitudes on Foreign Affairs as Correlates of Authoritarianism and Political Anomie," *Journal of Politics* 22 (1960), pp. 50–67.

[14] Howard P. Smith and Ellen Weber Rosen, "Some Psychological Correlates of Worldmindedness and Authoritarianism," *Journal of Personality* 26 (1958), pp. 170–183.

[15] William J. MacKinnon and Richard Centers, "Authoritarianism and Internationalism," *Public Opinion Quarterly* 20 (1956), pp. 621–630.

[16] Farris, pp. 50–67.

[17] Robert E. Lane, "Political Personality and Electoral Choice," *American Political Science Review* 49 (1955), pp. 173–190.

[18] Levinson, p. 44. It must be confessed that not all researchers share Levinson's confidence in this proposition. Many point to methodological difficulties in the work of Adorno *et al.* and others who followed their lead which require caution in attributing meaning to authoritarianism. The best statement of the criticism is Richard Christie and Marie Jahoda (eds.), *Studies in the Scope and Method of "The Authoritarian Personality"* (New York: Free Press, 1954). For a convenient summary of the arguments, pro and con, see Roger Brown, *Social Psychology* (New York: Free Press, 1965), chap. 12, pp. 477–546.

A second personal characteristic which seems demonstrably related to political behavior is a feeling of alienation or estrangement. While there has been much confusion and controversy surrounding the use of the concept of alienation, it seems clear that at the core of the idea is the notion that an individual comes to feel detached from the world around him. He senses a lack of guidance from appropriate cultural values (normlessness); he believes himself to be incapable of influencing the world around him (powerlessness); and he feels cut off from that world (social isolation).[19] In short, because of his inability to see himself as a relevant member of society, the alienated individual cuts himself off from his environment, tending to be cynical about it and mistrustful of its members.

A number of studies show the alienated to behave in distinctive ways in the political arena. In general, they are less likely to care about politics, to discuss political affairs, or to be well informed about politics.[20] It follows from such findings that the alienated see less reason to participate actively in politics, for the fact of their cynicism, mistrust, and estrangement leads them to believe that their involvement would be pointless.[21] Specifically, the alienated citizen is likely to stay home on election day rather than go to the polls and cast his ballot.[22] Even when he does vote the quality of his action appears to have a highly negative character. He is likely to view the electoral contest as a choice between evils and, thus, to vote against the greater evil, not for a candidate in whom he has some confidence.[23] Similarly, the alienated voter tends to oppose local bond issue referendums,

[19] For attempts to sort out the various ideas central to the alienation concept, see Melvin Seeman, "On the Meaning of Alienation," *American Sociological Review* 24 (1959), pp. 783–791, and Dwight G. Dean, "Alienation: Its Meaning and Measurement," *American Sociological Review* 26 (1961), pp. 753–758.

[20] See, for instance, Angus Campbell *et al., The American Voter* (New York: Wiley, 1960) and Robert E. Agger *et al.,* "Political Cynicism: Measurement and Meaning," *Journal of Politics* 23 (1961), pp. 477–506.

[21] Lester W. Milbrath, *Political Participation* (Chicago: Rand McNally, 1965), pp. 78–81, summarizes the evidence on this point.

[22] Compare Kenneth Janda, "A Comparative Study of Political Alienation and Voting Behavior in Three Suburban Communities," in *Studies in History and the Social Sciences: Studies in Honor of John A. Kinneman* (Normal, Ill.: Illinois State University Press, 1965), pp. 53–68, and Milbrath, *Political Participation.*

[23] Murray Levin speculates that the upset victory of John F. Collins over the much more well-known John E. Powers in the 1959 mayoralty election in Boston was caused by a powerful reaction against Powers among the alienated voters. See his *The Alienated Voter* (New York: Holt, Rinehart and Winston, Inc., 1960).

apparently seeing no reason why the society at large should undertake such things as school and hospital construction or fluoridation of local water supplies.[24]

This evidence should be sufficient to buttress the contention that alienation, like authoritarianism, is related to the ways in which people think and act politically. Again, there are empirical as well as logical grounds for believing that personality factors need to be considered in any attempt to understand political behavior. Furthermore, it seems clear that these characteristics, and perhaps others, of the human organism operate independently of social and cultural factors. If one attempts to hold these latter factors constant,[25] that is, to examine the relationship between personality and behavior across different social classes, the relationships persist. In other words, if we find personality leading to a given attitude or activity among the upper, middle, and working classes, almost certainly it is the personality factor, not some contaminating third force such as social class, which is associated with the observed behavior. There is ample evidence to support the conclusion that personality is important in its own right.[26]

Finally, it should be repeated that although personal attributes do not provide a magic key with which to unlock the mysteries of political activity, we cannot afford to ignore personality characteristics in our efforts to fathom the sources of such behavior. To this point, the term "personality" has been used in a loose, unsystematic fashion. Now it is time to set forth more precisely what the term means.

PSYCHOLOGY, PERSONALITY, AND POLITICS

Broadly speaking, psychology is the scientific study of behavior. In dealing with human behavior, the subject matter is often called "per-

---

[24] John Horton and Wayne Thompson, "Powerlessness and Political Negativism: A Study of Defeated Local Referendums," *American Journal of Sociology* 68 (1962), pp. 485–493.

[25] Put more formally, we are controlling for extraneous variables. Interested readers may consult any of a number of useful volumes on the methodology of social research. For example, see Herbert Hyman, *Survey Design and Analysis* (New York: Free Press, 1955), esp. chaps. VI and VII.

[26] While authoritarianism and alienation have been studied more often than most personality factors, they are by no means the only ones whose relationship to political behavior has been noted. A number of others, which also seem independent of class and education levels, are included in Part IV of this book. See Greenstein (Selection 14) on party identification, Campbell *et al.* (Selection 16) on ego strength, and Milbrath (Selection 12) on esteem and sociability.

sonality." For the purposes of this book, the two are synonymous. There are enough definitions of personality to make originality unnecessary in this endeavor. The job is not to find a definition, but to choose an adequate one. What criteria should govern our choice? Without delving into the intricacies of the philosophy of science or semantics, it should be clear that the objects we label ought to be things worth talking about. For instance, personality may be defined as "a wet thumb and a warm blanket." But political scientists have no reason to study wet thumbs and warm blankets, so why bother giving them a special name?

Each definition of personality is inextricably bound up in the theory for which it was formulated. The authors of the definitions labeled those parts of the world which they found it important to discuss. It follows that the choice of a definition is also the choice of a theoretical orientation.

To reduce the dilemma of choice not one but three uses of the term "personality" are employed here. Each of the labels will cover a topic area, not a scientific concept to be directly employed in research. For the latter, the research problem at hand dictates the definition. Since the problems being studied here are political, we need not limit ourselves a priori to a particular psychological theory.[27]

Personality as Human Nature

People differ from each other in many ways, but there is some resemblance between the two most dissimilar people in the world. There must be, or they would not both be people. We may call this minimal resemblance the "universal component" of personality, or *human nature*.[28]

This universal component includes the biological commonalities

---

[27] For a similar viewpoint, see Heinz Eulau, *The Behavioral Persuasion in Politics* (New York: Random House, 1963), pp. 85–107.

[28] The remainder of this essay draws heavily on Clyde Kluckhohn and O. H. Mowrer, " 'Culture and Personality': A Conceptual Scheme," *American Anthropologist*, 46 (1944), 1–29. However, we depart from their usage in that we offer no single definition of personality. Rather, as stated above, we suggest topic areas which are rightfully included under the rubric of "personality." A more recent statement of this formulation is Clyde Kluckhohn and Henry A. Murray, "Personality Formation: The Determinants," in Clyde Kluckhohn and Henry A. Murray, *Personality in Nature, Society, and Culture* (New York: Knopf, 1948), pp. 35–48.

of *Homo sapiens* along with "those physical and behavioral traits which are accepted as normal and desirable in *all* human societies."[29] Such traits seem to include a need to know, understand, and manipulate the environment, a need for favorable evaluation by oneself and others, and a high capacity for learning and highly symbolic thinking. Generalizations about traits in this component of personality are assumed to apply to virtually all human organisms.

Political scientists of all eras have been concerned with human tendencies to manipulate the environment (needs for power) and with the learning of habitual ways to gratify these needs. The need for self-respect has motivated many a social movement, as it now sparks nationalism in the United States and abroad.[30] These are a few of the countless features of the human organism which spark the variety of political behavior.

Personality as Communal Character

People of the same social group are alike in certain ways which set them apart from nonmembers. "Group" is used here in the broadest sense, to refer to any collectivity of two or more people who interact for the achievement of common goals. Two men rolling a heavy stone fit this definition, as would a whole nation or society.

Their common purpose and experience impart similarities in thought and behavior to the members of the group. Enduring groups make extensive efforts to ensure conformity to the group's standards, by recruiting like-minded people and expelling deviants, by instilling common values into members, and by punishing nonconformists. Over time, group members grow more and more alike. Concepts like "national character" and "social character" come under the category of "communal character." They refer to the ways in which people, not specific groups, are alike.

Within the communal component of personality is a major subdivision, the *role* component. A role is a social position which imposes specified behavioral and attitudinal obligations. A soldier is thus different from a statesman, and both differ from a college professor. But two college professors from different nations may resemble each other more than a soldier and a professor from the same nation. For this

---

[29] Kluckhohn and Mowrer, p. 19.

[30] For an explanation of American black nationalism as the outgrowth of frustrated needs for self-respect see Part IV, Selection 20. Some other features of human nature in politics are treated in Selections 1–3, 13, and 19.

reason, Kluckhohn and Mowrer take "role" as a separate component of personality. In politics, it may tell us a great deal about Mr. X to know whether he is charged with administrative responsibility or with the enlightenment of the public. For the two types of jobs require different kinds of people; they will attract and retain some while they repel and evict others.

Bureaucratic organizations presumably foster predispositions to "overconform" to rules and to treat people impersonally, whereas the agitator thrives on personal, emotional responses from others.[31]

Personality as Individual Differences

Finally, no two people are identical. When the Presidency passed from John F. Kennedy to Lyndon B. Johnson, many national policies changed. Yet both men occupied the same role in the same nation as human beings.

Individuals may be distinguished by the degree to which they are high or low in a wide range of dispositions. Authoritarianism, sociability, dominance, ego strength, and a sense of political efficacy are some factors which, as the selections will show, give rise to variance in the political behavior of individuals.

In sum, the individual's organization of dispositions to behave has at least three main components: human nature, communal character, and individual differences. Although a person will act on the basis of all three—perhaps simultaneously—the selections in this volume illustrate the contention that "personality," as denoted by each of these components, affects the quality of man's political existence.

LIMITATIONS

As the foregoing makes clear, personality is important for an understanding of politics, but there are some limitations involved in the use of personality, as defined in the previous section. In the first place,

[31] On administrators see Robert K. Merton, "Bureaucratic Structure and Personality," in *Social Theory and Social Structure,* rev. and enlarged ed. (New York: Free Press, 1957), pp. 195–206. On agitators, see Guy E. Swanson, "Agitation in Face-to-Face Contacts: A Study of Personalities of Orators," *Public Opinion Quarterly,* 21 (1957–1958), pp. 288–294 and Guy E. Swanson, "Agitation through the Press: A Study of the Personalities of Publicists," *Public Opinion Quarterly,* 20 (1956), pp. 441–456. The original distinction between these role types is in Harold D. Lasswell, *Psychopathology and Politics* (New York: Viking, 1960), pp. 78–152.

there may be a tendency for the reader to confuse personality with pathology; to do so would be highly misleading. While some pathologies—neuroses, psychoses, and the like—may be expressed in political behavior,[32] these are probably infrequent cases. What is important to realize is that normal people, no less than abnormal people, have personalities. Each individual, whether normal or not, develops a way of looking at and dealing with the environment in which he lives. These modes of responding differ for different people. It should be kept in mind that differences among individuals in terms of personal makeup may be reflected in differences in political behavior.

Secondly, as Smith, Bruner, and White put it, "the motives for holding an opinion can throw no light whatever on its soundness. . . . In the pure sense, we write *ad hominem*, not *ad rem*."[33] Two people can hold the same opinion or commit the same act for different reasons. It is the personal reasons and not the opinions or acts themselves which this volume treats.

Thirdly, the entire controversy that rages over which is the most appropriate personality "theory" to employ has been ignored here. There exist many formulations which seek to explain how personality differences arise; among them are psychoanalytic, learning, and cognitive approaches.[34] The emphasis here is not why people differ—though this is a fascinating topic in its own right—but rather how these differences may influence political behavior. Thus the attempt has been made to avoid commitment to any school of personality theory.

In addition, since the study of personality is still in its infancy, especially as it relates to political and social life, it is necessary to admit that there is still much to be learned about how to identify and gauge various personality characteristics. The methodological issues of personality assessment are well beyond the scope of this book; here it need only be noted that as the scientific study of individual differences advances, some of the techniques currently employed will be found wanting and will be replaced by newer, more advanced methods.

---

[32] For examples where this is the case, see Selections 17 and 21.

[33] M. Brewster Smith, Jerome S. Bruner, and Robert W. White, *Opinions and Personality* (New York: Wiley, 1956), p. 6.

[34] For a useful presentation and evaluation of a number of personality theories, see Calvin S. Hall and Gardner Lindzey, *Theories of Personality* (New York: Wiley, 1957).

In sum, we believe that personality, in the various senses in which the concept is used, can contribute to the understanding of why and how people behave politically. While much remains to be done to specify the nature of the relationships between psychological factors and political thought and action, a beginning has already been made. The selections which follow illustrate the variety of contributions which the study of psychology has made, and can make in the future, to the increased comprehension of political phenomena.

I
The Relevance
of Personality
for Politics

Only a few words need to be said about this section of the book. The purpose of Part I is to pick up and weave together some threads of the argument advanced in the Introduction concerning the relevance of personality for political behavior and the need to specify the conditions under which that relevance is most likely to exist.

Central to theories of the formation, quality, and continuity or instability of political systems are assumptions about human capabilities. Plato's *Republic,* for instance, is built on a foundation of infinitely plastic human nature which can be molded (educated or socialized or both) as one pleases. As long as one is careful to teach children the "right" things (and nothing else) in the "right" way, argued Plato, even a highly authoritarian political system can be smoothly maintained.[1]

In the same tradition of understanding what political systems *might* be through a theory of what people can do is Aristotle's treatment of the "psychological" and "habit" foundations of virtue. For Aristotle, it is clear that an irrational component exists within the personality (which he calls the "soul"). This irrational element can, and must, be controlled by a rational one; where man cannot reason, as in the area of morals, he must be taught. Moral virtue is thus seen as learned; man is not naturally moral and he must learn the proper modes of belief and conduct. Hobbes, by contrast, sees man as moved by a different set of human needs. For him, man's nature is such that life is a war "of every man against every man" where nature has implanted in each individual a need to dominate others, a need to be powerful. If a society of such organisms is to persist, somehow a strong control must be imposed upon these aggrandizing impulses. Hobbes recommended an absolute ruler.

For Christian Bay, a political system is to be judged by the extent to which it fulfills human needs. Drawing upon Maslow's theory of the hierarchy of (organismic) needs, which he suggests might be supplemented with (socially learned) *wants,* he warns contemporary political theorists and politicians that economic abundance is not enough to cure the world's sociopolitical ills. If the good ("free") life is to be attained, then man's higher needs, as current research has sketched them and as future research should elaborate on them, must be met after comfort is achieved.[2]

The selections themselves develop the arguments fully. For the present it should be enough to repeat the point that philosophers, ancient and modern, in searching for the best of worlds, have felt constrained to examine human nature—the underlying character of

---

[1] Plato, *The Republic*, B. Jowett, trans. (New York: Modern Library, n.d.). The capacity of humans to learn is so important for politics that it receives an entire section in this reader. See Part II, Socialization: The Acquisition of Political Dispositions.

[2] The main roots, implications, and weaknesses of this theory are treated in George I. Balch, "On Self-Actualization: Clarification of a Political Goal," in James W. Dyson (ed.), *Attitude and Action in Politics* (Boston: Blaisdell, forthcoming).

man—and to base their formulations of the proper form for society on the results of this examination.

While the selections from Aristotle, Hobbes, and Bay are intended to make clear the relevance of personality for an understanding of political behavior, they should not cause us to forget the earlier remarks about the limited character of that relevance. The remaining articles in Part I elaborate on some of these restrictions.

Personality is more likely to influence behavior in some situations than in others. Robert E. Lane (Selection 4) suggests some of the conditions under which the impact of personality is likely to be high. In general, the more unstructured and ambiguous a situation is, the more likely it is that the response of an individual confronted by that situation will reflect his personality dispositions. These unstructured and ambiguous situations are likely to be new ones in which there is no familiar way of acting that the individual can fall back on, or they may be so complex that the individual is beset by conflicting pressures, which he resolves by relying on his attitudes, skills, motives, values, expectations, anxieties, beliefs, and habits, that is, on his personality. On the other hand, the existence of punishments or sanctions attached to possible courses of action, the existence of a firmly held set of attitudes dealing with a situation, or the existence of a widely held set of expectations about how a person in a given position should behave will so structure a situation and reduce its ambiguity that personality factors are much less likely to come into play.[3]

From the more individual-oriented psychoanalytic perspective, Harold D. Lasswell contributes further to specifying some conditions under which personality affects politics. In his classic formulation of the problem, Lasswell has explained extraordinarily strong political involvement as compensation for personal frustrations. As he puts it, private motives are displaced on public objects and rationalized in terms of public interest.[4]

An elaboration of this thesis is developed in Selection 5. The "political type," or power-hungry man, seeks to influence others in order to overcome his low self-image. When an individual feels *hope-*

---

[3] The foregoing remarks rely heavily on Fred I. Greenstein, "The Impact of Personality on Politics: An Attempt to Clear Away Underbrush," *American Political Science Review* 61 (1967), pp. 629–642, esp. pp. 635–639.

[4] See Harold D. Lasswell, *Psychopathology and Politics* (New York: Viking, 1960), and Harold D. Lasswell, *Power and Personality* (New York: Viking, 1962).

lessly weak or worthless, however, he is apt to avoid attempts to influence others. When the low self-image is offset by occasional glimpses of self-confidence, especially confidence based on political skills and past successes in interpersonal influence, we can expect the individual to plunge deeply into political life. He is then likely to rationalize his personal satisfaction at wielding power as a sense of pride in public duty.

Like all scientific generalizations, the Lasswellian formulation is limited in scope. It applies to some kinds of people, but not to others. Clearly, not all political participants are "political personalities," nor are all "political personalities" likely either to enter public life or, once there, to succeed in it.[5] Furthermore, some people who are plagued by personal disturbances or frustrations are drained of all energy by their anxieties and have little left for such peripheral activities as politics.[6] Yet, there are people whose disturbances seem quite amenable to displacement and projection onto external objects. We all know people who blame others for their own shortcomings, people who are always finding a scapegoat. Hitler immediately comes to mind. As Rutherford puts it, "The distinction of personality types for political participation should be, not between the mentally ill and the mentally well, but rather between internalizers and externalizers."[7] And given the externalizing orientation, a systematic exposure to politics as a means of obtaining rewards, along with the social position which makes this possible, are essential features mediating between the individual's frustrations and his recruitment into political life.[8]

One subject matter area which seems to be of the unstructured, ambiguous variety, or alternatively, one onto which personal motives may be displaced, is the issue of American foreign policy, that is, the question of the proper posture for the United States to assume toward the other nations of the world. William A. Scott (Selection 6) argues that Americans, on the whole, do not have the interest in, or knowledge about, foreign policy sufficient to permit them to

---

[5] See Milbrath's selection in Part III.
[6] Robert E. Lane, *Political Life* (New York: Free Press, 1959).
[7] Brent M. Rutherford, "Psychopathology, Decision-Making, and Political Involvement," *The Journal of Conflict Resolution*, X (December, 1966), p. 402. This article has an excellent treatment of the problem at hand, along with a highly original research study.
[8] Kenneth Prewitt, "Political Socialization and Leadership Selection," *The Annals of the American Academy of Political and Social Science*, 361 (September, 1965), pp. 96–111.

structure the subject. Thus, personality factors come into play when they are required to respond to events in the international political realm.[9] But, Scott makes clear, other forces of the cultural and sociological sort also are related to how foreign affairs are viewed. Personality and other elements, then, seem necessary for any adequate understanding of attitude formation and expression.

[9] For further elaboration of this point, see Scott's "Rationality and Nonrationality of International Attitudes," *Journal of Conflict Resolution* 2 (1958), pp. 8–16.

1 *The Psychological and Habitual Bases of Virtue*

ARISTOTLE

THE PSYCHOLOGICAL FOUNDATIONS OF THE VIRTUES

Since happiness is a certain activity of the soul in conformity with perfect virtue, we must now examine what virtue or excellence is. For such an inquiry will perhaps better enable us to discover the nature of happiness. Moreover, the man who is truly concerned about politics seems to devote special attention to excellence, since it is his aim to make the citizens good and law-abiding. We have an example of this in the lawgivers of Crete and Sparta and in other great legislators. If an examination of virtue is part of politics, this question clearly fits into the pattern of our original plan.

There can be no doubt that the virtue which we have to study is human virtue. For the good which we have been seeking is a human good and the happiness a human happiness. By human virtue we do not mean the excellence of the body, but that of the soul, and we define happiness as an activity of the soul. If this is true, the student of politics must obviously have some knowledge of the workings of the soul, just as the man who is to heal eyes must know something about the whole body. In fact, knowledge is all the more important for the former, inasmuch as politics is better and more valuable than medicine, and cultivated physicians devote much time and trouble to gain knowledge about the body. Thus, the student of politics must study the soul, but he must do so with his own aim in view, and only to the extent that the objects of his inquiry demand: to go into it in greater detail would perhaps be more laborious than his purposes require.

Some things that are said about the soul in our less technical discussions are adequate enough to be used here, for instance, that the soul consists of two elements, one irrational and one rational. Whether these two elements are separate, like the parts of the body or any other divisible thing, or whether they are only logically separable though in reality indivisible, as convex and concave are in the circumference of a circle, is irrelevant for our present purposes.

Of the irrational element, again, one part seems to be common to all living things and vegetative in nature: I mean that part which is responsible for nurture and growth. We must assume that some such capacity of the soul exists in everything that takes nourishment, in the embryonic stage as well as when the organism is fully developed; for this makes more sense than to assume the existence of some different capacity at the latter stage. The excellence of this part of the soul is, therefore, shown to be common to all living things and is not exclusively human. This very part and this capacity seem to be most active in sleep. For in sleep the difference between a good man and a bad is least apparent—whence the saying that for half their lives the happy are no better off than the wretched. This is just what we would expect, for sleep is an inactivity of the soul in that it ceases to do things which cause it to be called good or bad. However, to a small extent some bodily movements do penetrate to the soul in sleep, and in this sense the dreams of honest men are better than those of average people. But enough of this subject: we may pass by the nutritive part, since it has no natural share in human excellence or virtue.

In addition to this, there seems to be another integral element of the soul which, though irrational, still does partake of reason in some way. In morally strong and morally weak men we praise the reason that guides them and the rational element of the soul, because it exhorts them to follow the right path and to do what is best. Yet we see in them also another natural strain different from the rational, which fights and resists the guidance of reason. The soul behaves in precisely the same manner as do the paralyzed limbs of the body. When we intend to move the limbs to the right, they turn to the left, and similarly, the impulses of morally weak persons turn in the direction opposite to that in which reason leads them. However, while the aberration of the body is visible, that of the soul is not. But perhaps we must accept it as a fact, nevertheless, that there is something in the soul besides the rational element, which opposes and reacts against it. In what way the two are distinct need not concern us here. But, as we have stated, it too seems to partake of reason; at any rate, in a morally strong man it accepts the leadership of reason, and is perhaps more obedient still in a self-controlled and courageous man, since in him everything is in harmony with the voice of reason.

Thus we see that the irrational element of the soul has two parts: the one is vegetative and has no share in reason at all, the other is the seat of the appetites and of desire in general and partakes of reason insofar as it complies with reason and accepts its leadership; it possesses reason in the sense that we say it is "reasonable" to accept the advice of a father and of friends, not in the sense that we have a "rational" understanding of mathematical propositions. That the irrational element can be persuaded by the rational is shown by the fact that admonition and all manner of rebuke and exhortation are possible. If it is correct to say that the appetitive part, too, has reason, it follows that the rational element of the soul has two subdivisions: the one possesses reason in the strict sense, contained within itself, and the other possesses reason in the sense that it listens to reason as one would listen to a father.

Virtue, too, is differentiated in line with this division of the soul. We call some virtues "intellectual" and others "moral": theoretical wisdom, understanding, and practical wisdom are intellectual virtues, generosity and self-control moral virtues. In speaking of a man's character, we do not describe him as wise or understanding, but as gentle or self-controlled; but we praise the wise man, too, for his characteristic, and praiseworthy characteristics are what we call virtues.

MORAL VIRTUE AS THE RESULT OF HABITS

Virtue, as we have seen, consists of two kinds, intellectual virtue and moral virtue. Intellectual virtue or excellence owes its origin and development chiefly to teaching, and for that reason requires experience and time. Moral virtue, on the other hand, is formed by habit, *ethos*, and its name, *ēthikē*, is therefore derived, by a slight variation, from *ethos*. This shows, too, that none of the moral virtues is implanted in us by nature, for nothing which exists by nature can be changed by habit. For example, it is impossible for a stone, which has a natural downward movement, to become habituated to moving upward, even if one should try ten thousand times to inculcate the habit by throwing it in the air; nor can fire be made to move downward, nor can the direction of any nature-given tendency be changed by habituation. Thus, the virtues are implanted in us neither by nature nor contrary to nature: we are by nature equipped with the ability to receive them, and habit brings this ability to completion and fulfillment.

Furthermore, of all the qualities with which we are endowed by nature, we are provided with the capacity first, and display the activity afterward. That this is true is shown by the senses: it is not by frequent seeing or frequent hearing that we acquired our senses, but on the contrary we first possess and then use them; we do not acquire them by use. The virtues, on the other hand, we acquire by first having put them into action, and the same is also true of the arts. For the things which we have to learn before we can do them we learn by doing: men become builders by building houses, and harpists by playing the harp. Similarly, we become just by the practice of just actions, self-controlled by exercising self-control, and courageous by performing acts of courage.

This is corroborated by what happens in states. Lawgivers make the citizens good by inculcating (good) habits in them, and this is the aim of every lawgiver; if he does not succeed in doing that, his legislation is a failure. It is in this that a good constitution differs from a bad one.

Moreover, the same causes and the same means that produce any excellence or virtue can also destroy it, and this is also true of every art. It is by playing the harp that men become both good and bad harpists, and correspondingly with builders and all the other craftsmen: a man who builds well will be a good builder, one who builds badly a bad one. For if this were not so, there would be no need for an instructor, but everybody would be born as a good or a bad craftsman. The same holds true of the virtues: in our transactions with other men it is by action that some become just and others unjust, and it is by acting in the face of danger and by developing the habit of feeling fear or confidence that some become brave men and others cowards. The same applies to the appetites and feelings of anger: by reacting in one way or in another to given circumstances some people become self-controlled and gentle, and others self-indulgent and short-tempered. In a word, characteristics develop from corresponding activities. For that reason, we must see to it that our activities are of a certain kind, since any variations in them will be reflected in our characteristics. Hence it is no small matter whether one habit or another is inculcated in us from early childhood; on the contrary, it makes a considerable difference, or, rather, all the difference.

2 Of the Natural Condition of Mankind as Concerns Their Felicity and Misery

THOMAS HOBBES

MEN BY NATURE EQUAL

Nature has made men so equal in the faculties of the body and mind as that, though there be found one man sometimes manifestly stronger in body or of quicker mind than another, yet, when all is reckoned together, the difference between man and man is not so considerable as that one man can thereupon claim to himself any benefit to which another may not pretend as well as he. For as to the strength of body, the weakest has strength enough to kill the strongest, either by secret machination or by confederacy with others that are in the same danger with himself.

And as to the faculties of the mind, setting aside the arts grounded upon words, and especially that skill of proceeding upon general and infallible rules called science—which very few have and but in few things, as being not a native faculty born with us, nor attained, as prudence, while we look after somewhat else—I find yet a greater equality among men than that of strength. For prudence is but experience, which equal time equally bestows on all men in those things they equally apply themselves unto. That which may perhaps make such equality incredible is but a vain conceit of one's own wisdom, which almost all men think they have in a greater degree than the vulgar—that is, than all men but themselves and a few others whom, by fame or for concurring with themselves, they approve. For such is the nature of men that howsoever they may acknowledge many others to be more witty or more eloquent or more learned, yet they will hardly believe there be many so wise as themselves; for they see their own wit at hand and other men's at a distance. But this proves rather that men are in that point equal than unequal. For there is not ordinarily a greater sign of the equal distribution of anything than that every man is contented with his share.

FROM EQUALITY PROCEEDS DIFFIDENCE

From this equality of ability arises equality of hope in the attaining of our ends. And therefore if any two men desire the same thing, which nevertheless they cannot both enjoy, they become enemies; and in the way to their end, which is principally their own conservation, and sometimes their delectation only, endeavor to destroy or subdue one another. And from hence it comes to pass that where an invader has no more to fear than another man's single power, if one plant, sow, build, or possess a convenient seat, others may probably be expected to come prepared with forces united to dispossess and deprive him, not only of the fruit of his labor, but also of his life or liberty. And the invader again is in the like danger of another.

FROM DIFFIDENCE WAR

And from this diffidence of one another there is no way for any man to secure himself so reasonable as anticipation—that is, by force or wiles to master the persons of all men he can, so long till he see no other power great enough to endanger him; and this is no more than his own conservation requires, and is generally allowed. Also, because there be some that take pleasure in contemplating their own power in the acts of conquest, which they pursue farther than their security requires, if others that otherwise would be glad to be at ease within modest bounds should not by invasion increase their power, they would not be able, long time, by standing only on their defense, to subsist. And by consequence, such augmentation of dominion over men being necessary to a man's conservation, it ought to be allowed him.

Again, men have no pleasure, but on the contrary a great deal of grief, in keeping company where there is no power able to overawe them all. For every man looks that his companion should value him at the same rate he sets upon himself; and upon all signs of contempt or undervaluing naturally endeavors, as far as he dares (which among them that have no common power to keep them in quiet is far enough to make them destroy each other), to extort a greater value from his contemners by damage and from others by the example.

So that in the nature of man we find three principal causes of quarrel: first, competition; secondly, diffidence; thirdly, glory.

The first makes men invade for gain, the second for safety, and the third for reputation. The first use violence to make themselves masters of other men's persons, wives, children, and cattle; the second, to defend them; the third, for trifles, as a word, a smile, a different opinion, and any other sign of undervalue, either direct in their persons or by reflection in their kindred, their friends, their nation, their profession, or their name.

OUT OF CIVIL STATES THERE IS ALWAYS WAR OF EVERY ONE AGAINST EVERY ONE

Hereby it is manifest that, during the time men live without a common power to keep them all in awe, they are in that condition which is called war, and such a war as is of every man against every man. For WAR consists not in battle only, or the act of fighting, but in a tract of time wherein the will to contend by battle is sufficiently known; and therefore the notion of *time* is to be considered in the nature of war as it is in the nature of weather. For as the nature of foul weather lies not in a shower or two or rain but in an inclination thereto of many days together, so the nature of war consists not in actual fighting but in the known disposition thereto during all

the time there is no assurance to the contrary. All other time is
PEACE.

THE INCOMMODITIES OF SUCH A WAR

Whatsoever, therefore, is consequent to a time of war where every
man is enemy to every man, the same is consequent to the time
wherein men live without other security than what their own strength
and their own invention shall furnish them withal. In such condition
there is no place for industry, because the fruit thereof is uncertain:
and consequently no culture of the earth; no navigation nor use of
the commodities that may be imported by sea; no commodious building; no instruments of moving and removing such things as require
much force; no knowledge of the face of the earth; no account of
time; no arts; no letters; no society; and, in which is worst of all,
continual fear and danger of violent death; and the life of man soli-
tary, poor, nasty, brutish, and short.

It may seem strange to some man that has not well weighed
these things that nature should thus dissociate and render men apt
to invade and destroy one another; and he may therefore, not trusting
to this inference made from the passions, desire perhaps to have
the same confirmed by experience. Let him therefore consider with
himself—when taking a journey he arms himself and seeks to go
well accompanied, when going to sleep he locks his doors, when
even in his house he locks his chests, and this when he knows there
be laws and public officers, armed, to revenge all injuries shall be
done him—what opinion he has of his fellow subjects when he rides
armed, of his fellow citizens when he locks his doors, and of his
children and servants when he locks his chests. Does he not there
as much accuse mankind by his actions as I do by my words? But
neither of us accuse man's nature in it. The desires and other passions
of man are in themselves no sin. No more are the actions that proceed
from those passions till they know a law that forbids them, which,
till laws be made, they cannot know, nor can any law be made till
they have agreed upon the person that shall make it.

It may peradventure be thought there was never such a time
nor condition of war as this, and I believe it was never generally
so over all the world; but there are many places where they live
so now. For the savage people in many places of America, except
the government of small families, the concord whereof depends on
natural lust, have no government at all and live at this day in that

brutish manner as I said before. Howsoever, it may be perceived what manner of life there would be where there were no common power to fear by the manner of life which men that have formerly lived under a peaceful government use to degenerate into a civil war.

But though there had never been any time wherein particular men were in a condition of war one against another, yet in all times kings and persons of sovereign authority, because of their independency, are in continual jealousies and in the state and posture of gladiators, having their weapons pointing and their eyes fixed on one another—that is, their forts, garrisons, and guns upon the frontiers of their kingdoms, and continual spies upon their neighbors—which is a posture of war. But because they uphold thereby the industry of their subjects, there does not follow from it that misery which accompanies the liberty of particular men.

IN SUCH A WAR NOTHING IS UNJUST

To this war of every man against every man this also is consequent: that nothing can be unjust. The notions of right and wrong, justice and injustice have there no place. Where there is no common power, there is no law; where no law, no injustice. Force and fraud are in war the two cardinal virtues. Justice and injustice are none of the faculties neither of the body nor mind. If they were, they might be in a man that were alone in the world, as well as his senses and passions. They are qualities that relate to men in society, not in solitude. It is consequent also to the same condition that there be no propriety, no dominion, no *mine* and *thine* distinct; but only that to be every man's that he can get, and for so long as he can keep it. And thus much for the ill condition which man by mere nature is actually placed in, though with a possibility to come out of it consisting partly in the passions, partly in his reason.

THE PASSIONS THAT INCLINE MEN TO PEACE

The passions that incline men to peace are fear of death, desire of such things as are necessary to commodious living, and a hope by their industry to obtain them. And reason suggests convenient articles of peace, upon which men may be drawn to agreement. These articles are they which otherwise are called the Laws of Nature. . . .

3 *Politics and Pseudo-Politics*

CHRISTIAN BAY

In the study of political behavior, "analysis must start from somewhere, and the existing set of rules and institutions is the only place from which it is possible to start," according to Buchanan.[1] Students of comparative politics have nevertheless demonstrated the

From Christian Bay, "Politics and Pseudo-politics: A Critical Evaluation of Some Behavioral Literature," *American Political Science Review* 59 (1965), pp. 39–51. Reprinted with the permission of author and publisher.

[1] James M. Buchanan, "An Individualistic Theory of Political Process." Paper prepared for delivery at the 1963 Annual Meeting of the American Political Science Association in Commodore Hotel, New York City.

feasibility of analysing political developments in some countries in terms of valuable outcomes achieved in others.[2] It remains to be shown that political behavior and institutions can be analysed also in terms of normative assumptions to the effect that the purpose of politics is to meet human needs and facilitate human development.

Contrary to an apparently prevailing assumption among political behavioralists, psychological phenomena are just as *real* as economic and voting behavior phenomena, even though admittedly less accessible to observation and measurement. Some more of the same conceptual boldness displayed in the recent literature on comparative politics is required if political inquiry is to become related to important human wants and needs. For one thing, we need to distinguish more clearly between pseudo-political and more strictly political behavior,[3] if we want to learn how to encourage the latter at the expense of the former.[4]

A major conceptual and theoretical task is to develop a satisfactory theory of human needs and of the relationships between needs and *wants*—here referring to perceived or felt needs. Wants (or, synonymously, desires) and demands can be observed and measured by way of asking people or observing their behavior. Needs, on the other hand, can only be inferred from their hypothetical consequences for behavior or, more manifestly, from the actual consequences of their frustration. Whenever superficial wants are fulfilled but underlying needs remain frustrated, pathological behavior is likely to ensue.

Prior to the development of a viable theory of political development is at least a beginning toward a theory of individual human development. Such a beginning exists in psychological literature, but

---

[2] See especially Robert E. Ward and Dankwart A. Rustow, *The Political Modernization of Japan and Turkey* (Princeton University Press, 1964).

[3] I would define as *political* all activity aimed at improving or protecting conditions for the satisfaction of human needs and demands in a given society or community, according to some universalistic scheme of priorities (i.e., norms for guiding the choice among conflicting needs and demands), implicit or explicit. *Pseudo-political* in this paper refers to activity that resembles political activity but is exclusively concerned with either the alleviation of personal neuroses or with promoting private or private interest-group advantage, deterred by no articulate or disinterested conception of what would be just or fair to other groups.

[4] However, we should not assume without inquiry that *all* pseudo-political behavior is dysfunctional for all high-priority human wants and needs; not, of course, that all varieties of political behavior are to be preferred to pseudo-political self-seeking or neurotic striving.

it has so far been inadequately drawn on by students of political behavior. Let me very briefly suggest the direction of this theorizing, and some of its implications for the study of political behavior.

Basic human needs are characteristics of the human organism, and they are presumably less subject to change than the social or even the physical conditions under which men live. Wants are sometimes manifestations of real needs, but, as Plato and many other wise men since have insisted, we cannot always infer the existence of needs from wants. Wants are often artificially induced by outside manipulation, or they may be neurotically based desires whose satisfaction fails to satisfy needs, or both. Emphasis on a civic-culture type of democracy as the goal for political development may well perpetuate a state of affairs in which human needs as seen by the political-minded (in my strict sense of "political") will remain in the shadow of much-advertised human wants as promoted by pseudo-politicians and other enterprisers whose horizons do not extend beyond their own occupational or career interests and status anxieties.[5]

I say *may*, for I am raising a question rather than adopting a position. In order to investigate the relationship between needs and wants as they pertain to political functions we must start out with a tentative conception of priorities among human needs. The best available point of departure, in my opinion, is in A. H. Maslow's theory of a hierarchy of human needs; this theorizing ought to be drawn on until a more plausible and useful theory becomes available.

Maslow lists five categories of needs in the order of their assumed priority: (1) physical needs (air, water, food, etc.); (2) safety needs (assurance of survival and of continuing satisfaction of basic needs); (3) needs to love and be loved; (4) need for esteem (by self and others); and (5) need for self-actualization and growth. This list presents a hierarchy, according to Maslow, in the sense that the "less prepotent needs are minimized, even forgotten or denied. But when a need is fairly well satisfied, the next prepotent ("higher") need emerges, in turn to dominate the conscious life and to serve as the center of organization of behavior, since gratified needs are not active

---

[5] Joseph Tussman also stresses the danger of destroying the integrity of political communication when the modern bargaining approach to politics enters the "forum or tribunal" that a democratic electorate ought to constitute, according to classical theories of democracy. "We teach men to compete and bargain. Are we to be surprised, then, at the corruption of the tribunal into its marketplace parody?" *Obligation and the Body Politic* (New York, Oxford University Press, 1960), p. 109 and pp. 104–121.

motivators."[6] Note, however, that whenever in the course of a human life the "higher" needs have become activated, they are not necessarily extinguished as a result of later deprivation of "lower" or more basic needs. For example, some individuals, provided they have once known physical safety, will unhesitatingly sacrifice all of it for love, or for standards of right conduct tied in with their self-esteem, etc.

In a recent volume, James C. Davies has suggested the utility of Maslow's theory as a generator of propositions regarding political behavior, and he illustrates the plausibility (without demonstrating the validity) of such propositions with a wealth of historical and contemporary political behavior data. For example, according to Davies's theorizing it is impractical to suggest, with La Palombara, that it might be "possible to manipulate demands" in economically underdeveloped countries so that widespread loyalties to democratic institutions could emerge: "Long before there can be responsible or irresponsible popular government, long before the question of dictatorship or democracy can be taken up, the problem of survival must be solved so that a political community itself can develop, so that people can direct some of their attention to politics."[7] In another context he says, "Propaganda cannot paint a picture which conflicts with reality as it is seen by individuals in the light of their basic needs" (p. 134); the picture can be painted all right, but it will be a wasted effort. And Davies quotes Kwame Nkrumah, whose implicit rejoinder to La Palombara's argument is hard to improve on: "We cannot tell our peoples that material benefits in growth and modern progress are not for them. If we do, they will throw us out and seek other leaders who promise more . . . We have to modernize. Either we shall do so with the interest and support of the West or we shall be compelled to turn elsewhere. This is not a warning or a threat, but a straight statement of political reality" (p. 135).

One shortcoming in Davies's as well as Maslow's work, in my judgment, is that both authors seek to relate events and behavior directly to the elusive concept of "need," without the use of an intermediate and more manageable concept such as "want." Both concepts are badly needed, and their interrelations and their application in hypotheses must be developed if we want to move toward a more

---

[6] Abraham H. Maslow, "A Theory of Human Motivation," *Psychological Review*, Vol. 50 (1943), p. 394 and pp. 370–396. See also his *Motivation and Personality* (New York, 1954).
[7] *Human Nature in Politics* (New York, 1963), p. 28. Davies does not refer to La Palombara.

adequate knowledge of political behavior. It must be granted that manifest wants are important aspects of our political reality, especially in democracies; what matters is that we also keep remembering, unlike many behavioralists, that there also are genuine needs to worry about, elusive though they may be to the researcher's conventional tools. The volume of competing loudspeakers, if I may use a metaphor, is in a pluralist democracy perhaps more likely to depend on the power of the purse than on the urgency of the need. Even the most democratic governments are likely to come to a bad end—to say nothing of the individuals living under them—unless they learn to become at least as responsive to the basic needs of all their citizens as they are to the most insistent wants of the various articulate and influential interest groups and parties.

Most of Maslow's as well as Davies's discussion is highly speculative; only a beginning has been made. But their theory does lend itself to the production of testable hypotheses. For example, Almond's theory of political "input functions" (political socialization and recruitment; interest articulation; interest aggregation; political communication) and "output functions" (rule making; rule application; rule adjudication),[8] would seem to provide a fertile field for exploring what the participation in or other ego-involvement with each type of function can mean, in satisfying individual personality needs as well as wants. Moving in this direction we can perhaps get away from the customary *clichés* about the value of democracy, toward research-based knowledge on what (aspects of) democratic institutions have what kinds of value for human development.

I have argued elsewhere that the human goals of politics should be conceived in terms of maximizing individual freedom—psychological, social and potential.[9] Democracy and indeed every law and constitutional clause should be judged as a means to this end. A comprehensive treatment of norms of liberty with interrelationships and empirical consequences is necessary for this purpose, and so is a theory of human needs such as Maslow's, which in effect predicts that with increasing satisfaction of sustenance and security needs men's tendency will be to become less anti-social, more capable of respecting and eventually perhaps insisting on respect for the basic needs and liberties of others.

---

[8] *Cf.* his introduction to Gabriel A. Almond and James S. Coleman, eds., *The Politics of the Developing Areas* (Princeton, Princeton University Press, 1960).
[9] *The Structure of Freedom* (Stanford, Stanford University Press, 1958, and New York, 1965).

The normative research[10] to be recommended can be done with far more precision than was attempted or achieved in the work on freedom just referred to. Perhaps philosophers working with political scientists can be expected to be active on this research frontier in future years. One good example of normative research of this kind, even though its reference to empirical data is for purposes of normative interpretation only, is Naess's study of Gandhi's ethics of conflict resolution.[11]

The burden of this paper, then, is to plead for an expansion and a more systematic articulation of the psychological and the normative perspectives of political behavior research. I propose as a normative basis the proposition that politics exists for the purpose of progressively removing the most stultifying obstacles to a free human development, with priority for the worst obstacles, whether they hit many or few—in other words, with priority for those individuals who are most severely oppressed; as Harrington points out with respect to the poverty-stricken in the United States, they are also the least articulate, and the least likely to achieve redress by way of the ordinary democratic processes.[12] It is argued in this paper that the current preoccupation with pseudo-political behavior carries conservative and anti-political implications, and that the best hope for a more politically useful reorientation of behavioral research—in addition to and beyond the comparative politics perspective—is to study how the various functions of government bear, and could bear, on the satisfaction of basic needs as well as conscious wants.

Among the questions to ask are these: What kinds of enduring satisfactions tend to be associated, for example, with particular participant and subject roles established by alternate forms of centralized or decentralized decision processes? Under what socio-cultural and

---

[10] The term "normative research" may be puzzling to some, who think of research exclusively as systematically re(peated) search for empirical data, in the real world or in contrived experimental worlds. And "research" has been one of the empirical social scientist's proud banners in his uphill fight against the sometime supremacy of armchair speculators. In our time a less parochial use of "research" is called for, as a way of recognizing the close interplay between the empirical, normative and logical aspects of inquiry that, as the present paper argues, is necessary for the further development of our knowledge of political as of other human behavior.

[11] Arne Naess, "A systematization of Gandhian ethics of conflict resolution," *Journal of Conflict Resolution*, Vol. 2 (1958), pp. 140–155; and also Johan Galtung and Arne Naess, *Gandhis politiske etikk* (Oslo, Tanum, 1955).

[12] Michael Harrington, *The Other America: Poverty in the United States* (Baltimore, Penguin Books, 1963; New York, 1962).

socio-economic circumstances are majoritarian decision processes, of given types, likely to produce substantive satisfaction of the basic needs of, in Harrington's phrase, society's "rejects"?

As so often in our human condition, the dimensions of our ignorance appear to grow larger the closer we come to the most enduringly important issues of our social life. Much conceptual as well as basic psychological work remains to be done before our technical proficiency in the study of the relation of political forms to basic needs and to liberty can come to match the current work on analysis of voting patterns. But in this work political scientists should participate; our stakes in its progress are as high as anyone else's.

One particular type of research that should be pushed, as a much needed complement to the large supply of data on pseudo-political behavior, is work that would focus on just how some citizens "graduate" from the role of pseudo-political actor to that of political actor. Or, more accurately—for surely there are more pseudo-political actors in the older age groups, "hardened in the school of life"—how it is that some categories of individuals (or individuals in some categories of situations) manage to remain concerned with ideals and with politics, i.e., with the welfare of their fellow men, all their lives?

A theory of human development is implied in the research approaches here recommended. It asserts that man is likely to become increasingly capable of being rational, or intellectual,[13] to the extent that he no longer needs the services of his beliefs and attitudes for the purpose of keeping his various anxieties in check. Deep-seated neurotic anxieties about one's worth as a human being predispose to right-wing or occasionally left-wing extremism, with glorification of ingroups or individuals, living or dead, along with hatreds against outgroups and deviants. Neurotic status anxieties predispose to eager adherence to whatever views appear expected in one's reference groups. Realistic fears about employment or future career prospects predispose against maintaining the luxury of political opinions at all, unless they are "safe." Only for individuals whose main anxiety problems have been faced and in some way resolved is it generally possible to think of and care about problems of politics in terms of standards of justice or the public interest, independently of personal worries.

The development of strictly political incentives in the individual,

---

[13] *Cf.* my "A Social Theory of Intellectual Development," in Nevitt Sanford, ed., *The American College* (New York, 1961), pp. 972–1005, esp. pp. 978 and 1000–1005.

then, depends on a gradual process of liberation from a preoccupation with personal anxieties and worries. Stages in this process can be identified by research, although our concepts and instruments need some improvement before we can with confidence relate specific categories of political irrationality to (repressed or acknowledged) anxieties associated with specific levels in a hierarchy of human needs. Human nature being complex, so is the task of fully comprehending the dynamics of political behavior. My essential argument here is that we must face up to but not complacently accept, as the pseudo-political outlook does, the fact that most of our citizens live too harassed lives or lack the education or opportunities for reflection to permit them the real satisfactions and the full dignity of democratic citizenship. We must pose the empirical problem of how the more stultifying pressures on adults and pre-adults can be reduced. A premature ruling out of the classic democratic citizenship ideal, with its stress on reason as a crucial factor in politics, would seem particularly inappropriate in our age of rapid technological change; never was the need for politics in the strict sense greater.

It is conceivable that our prospects for developing much larger proportions of political-minded citizens will improve substantially if or when the "cybernetics revolution" does away with our omnipresent worries about making a living.[14] On the other hand, unless educational and cultural resources can be expanded as rapidly, so that more people may be enabled to base their sense of identity and self-esteem on their own attributes or ideals rather than on their occupational roles, status anxieties and despair about lack of purpose in life might remain at present levels, and become aggravated for some. But the over-all prospects surely would be brighter, to the extent that more

---

[14] W. H. Ferry and 25 associates have recently issued a statement that received front-page attention in the *New York Times* and other newspapers, under the title "The Triple Revolution: An Appraisal of the Major U.S. Crises and Proposals for Action" (Washington: Maurer, Fleischer, Zon and Associates, 1120 Connecticut Ave., 1964). Referring to the revolution in cybernetics, in weaponry, and in human rights, but particularly to the first of the three, Ferry *et al.* argue that there "is an urgent need for a fundamental change in the mechanisms employed to insure consumer rights" (p. 9), now that the problem of production has been solved and the problem of full employment has become impossible to solve with our present system. "We urge, therefore, that society, through its appropriate legal and governmental institutions, undertake an unqualified commitment to provide every individual and every family with an adequate income as a matter of right. This undertaking we consider to be essential to the emerging economic, social, and poltical order in this country" (p. 16).

of the principal *real* worries on which our current anxieties feed were removed.

In any event, let us not as political scientists rule out the possibility that a real *polity* may emerge eventually—a community of people capable of giving some of their energies to political as distinct from pseudo-political reflection and activity. A less utopian first step that may be hoped for is that many more political scientists will adopt a more political (or a less pseudo-political) perspective in their theorizing and research. As the horizons of behavior research expand to encompass latent need-behavior as well as manifest want-behavior, our political science will not only produce a new order of intellectual challenge; it may also become a potent instrument for promoting political development in the service of human development.

4 *Why Is the Study of Human Nature Important for the Study of Electoral Behavior?*

ROBERT E. LANE

       Political science has always had to came to terms with the nature of man, the political animal. Plato (*Republic*) dealt with the problem of instilling in youth the qualities of character necessary for effective citizenship; Aristotle (*Politics*) remarked on the necessity of fitting the constitution of a city state to the character of the people; Hobbes (*Leviathan*) dealt with the question of national character and personality, under the heading "the interiour beginnings of volun-

Reprinted with permission of the Macmillan Company from *Political Life* by Robert E. Lane. © The Free Press, A Corporation, 1959.

tary motions commonly called the passions; and the speeches by which they are expressed"; and John Stuart Mill wrote:

> . . . political machinery does not act of itself. As it is first made, so it has to be worked by men, and even by ordinary men. It needs not their single acquiescence, but their active participation; and must be adjusted to the capacities and qualities of such men as are available.[1]

These capacities and qualities are themselves articulated elements of a total personality system, the whole man. Allport puts it this way:

> The political nature of a man is indistinguishable from his personality as a whole, and . . . his personality as a whole is not the sum-total of his specific reactions, but rather a congruent system of attitudes, each element of which is intelligible only in the light of the total pattern. A man's political opinions reflect the characteristic modes of his adjustment to life.[2]

Today this is a common view: ". . . ideology regarding each social area must be regarded as a facet of the total person and an expression of more central ('subideological') psychological dispositions,"[3] and "look far enough into the origins of any opinion and one will find not just an opinion but a sample of how the holder of that opinion copes with his world."[4]

The answers to these questions about the nature of man color, perhaps even determine, a person's attitude toward alternative political systems. As we have seen, those who argue that man is educable, pacific, self-reliant, and rational are likely to be democrats; those who view man as instinct-ridden, belligerent, a creature of the mass-mind, and irrational, are likely to prefer some other political system. In one sense men's political behavior has demonstrated with rich variety that he is at different times everything that has been said about him on either side.

In a less global sense, the inquiry into the nature of man contributes to an understanding of political behavior within the demo-

---

[1] John Stuart Mill, "Representative Government," in *Utilitarianism, Liberty, and Representative Government* (New York: Dutton, 1910, Everyman ed.), p. 177.

[2] Gordon W. Allport, "The Composition of Political Attitudes," *American Journal of Sociology*, 35 (1929–1930), p. 238.

[3] T. W. Adorno and associates, *The Authoritarian Personality* (New York: Harper, 1950), p. 207.

[4] M. Brewster Smith, Jerome S. Bruner, and Robert W. White, *Opinions and Personality* (New York: Wiley, 1956), p. 40.

cratic framework. Explanations of political decisions which rely wholly upon analyses of the social environment, while they may have high predictive value, neglect a vital link: they never explain why an individual *responds* to the environment the way he does. Such purely external analysis tends to presume that two individuals behaving in the same way in a given situation are responding identically. But as seen from the inside out, from the point of view of the individuals, the forces to which they respond may be quite dissimilar. For example, our analysis shows that persons rated as authoritarians according to one attitude scale, vote in about the same proportions as those rated as equalitarians. But the equalitarians respond to a sense of civic duty, to conscience, while the authoritarians respond to the pressure of their social groups to act conventionally, and possibly also to a desire to exercise a small degree of political power.[5]

Without knowing the attitudes on which a decision is based, the observer may generalize in a wholly wrong direction. In 1948 when political scientists predicted a Dewey victory on the basis of early surveys on attitudes toward the *candidates,* they were wrong partly because underlying *party* loyalties were for many people more salient than candidate preferences.[6] The opposite mistake, the misinterpretation of party loyalties as conclusive when a dramatic candidate in fact was perceived as the more salient feature of the election, occurred in 1952.[7] In a deeper sense, the phenomena of Communist party membership in the 1929–1940 depression was misinterpreted as a function of economic deprivation, when, in fact, in the United States the party members, perhaps triggered by general economic failure, were dealing with the problem of acculturation, social adjustment, and the expression of a generalized hostility.[8]

If a purely social and external analysis has trouble "explaining" the behavior of those who do in fact behave in the expected direction, how much more difficult it is for such analysis to explain the deviants.

[5] Robert E. Lane, "Political Personality and Electoral Choice," *American Political Science Review, 49* (1955), pp. 173–190.
[6] For a discussion of this and related problems, see Frederick Mosteller and associates, *The Pre-Election Polls of 1948* (New York: Social Science Research Council, 1949); Bernard R. Berelson, Paul F. Lazarsfeld, and William N. McPhee, *Voting* (Chicago: University of Chicago Press, 1954), pp. 253–276.
[7] American Institute of Public Opinion, Release, Nov. 3, 1952. For confirming evidence see Angus Campbell, Gerald Gurin, and Warren E. Miller, *The Voter Decides* (Evanston, Ill.: Row, Peterson, 1954), pp. 165–177.
[8] See Gabriel Almond, *The Appeals of Communism* (Princeton: Princeton University Press, 1954).

If one finds that increased exposure to the media during election time is associated with higher rates of participation, one can, in a sense, explain the higher participation by the greater stimuli and the interest they arouse. But what shall the analyst do with those who were equally exposed and who failed to participate? A fruitful analysis must rely upon a psychologically informed interpretation of the meaning of exposure to different people.

The control over behavior given by a knowledge of the psychological processes at work in any situation is much greater than may be provided merely by a knowledge of the situation and the response. For example, while the study of the followers of nativist agitators through an analysis of the ideological themes presented and the membership of their various organizations gives a picture of what is happening in this area of politics, it gives very little idea of how it may be controlled. But if some insight is available into the psychic needs of the followers which are served by such agitation,[9] then an approach is possible through alternate means of satisfying those needs, or through reducing these needs by increasing other life satisfactions, or through giving self-insight to these audiences feeding on delusion, or in some other way.[10] Only when the intervening psychological variables are explored and brought into the analysis can many social problems (such as authoritarian politics, ethnic prejudice, or intolerant "Americanism") be brought under control.

In order not to overstate the case, let us be explicit on the limitations of psychological forces in political analysis. Some situations so clearly structure behavior; some roles leave so little room for personal choice; and some social norms are so unambiguous that personal differences have little effect upon behavior. On the other hand some situations afford considerable "scope" for personality to affect behavior. Among these are the following:

Situations where reference groups have politically conflicting points of view.

Situations at the focus of conflicting propaganda.

Current situations which for any individual are in conflict with experience.

[9] See Bruno Bettelheim and Morris Janowitz, "Reactions to Fascist Propaganda— a Pilot Study," *Public Opinion Quarterly*, 14 (1950), pp. 53–60.

[10] See T. W. Adorno, "Democratic Leadership and Mass Manipulation," in Alvin W. Gouldner, ed., *Studies in Leadership* (New York: Harper, 1950), pp. 418–438.

Situations where social roles are ambiguous, strange, and unfamiliar.

Some types of behavior are less likely to offer scope for the expression of personal differences. These would, by and large, include the more conventional items, such as voting, expressing patriotic opinions, and accepting election results as final, at least temporarily. On the other hand, those types of expression which are more likely to reveal the idiosyncratic features of personality include:

Selection of the grounds for rationalizing a political act.
Selecting topics for political discussion.
Selecting types of political behavior over and above voting.
Expression of the probable consequences of participation.
Holding particular images of other participants.
Styles of personal interaction in political groups.

5 *The Political Personality*

HAROLD D. LASSWELL

POWER AS COMPENSATION

Our key hypothesis about the power seeker is that he pursues power as a means of compensation against deprivation. *Power is expected to overcome low estimates of the self,* by changing either the traits of the self or the environment in which it functions.

The self typically includes more than the primary ego, which

Reprinted from *Power and Personality* by Harold Dwight Lasswell by permission of W. W. Norton & Company, Inc. Copyright 1948 by W. W. Norton & Company, Inc.

is the symbol used by a person to refer to his irreducible "I," "me."[1] The self takes in whatever is included with the primary ego as belonging with it. The boundaries of the self ordinarily include—besides the primary ego symbols—symbols that refer to parents, wife, children, friends, countrymen, coreligionists and other groups and individuals. These are the symbols of identification.

The personality includes demands made *by* the self *on* the primary ego and on each constituent part of the self. Everyone makes demands on every member of a group with which he is identified, including himself.

Besides identifications and demands, there are expectations about the self in relation to the world. The primary ego or the constituent elements are deprived to the extent that they do not enjoy the value position demanded, whether the value in question is well-being or any other in the list we have been using for descriptive purposes. Furthermore, the self is regarded as deprived when it is moving into a future in which loss of value position is held likely, or failure to overcome obstacles in the way of expanding values is foreseen. (Deprivations are endured or threatened losses, and endured or threatened obstructions to an improved value position.)

Our hypothesis about the power-accentuating type is that power is resorted to when it is expected to contribute more than any alternative value to overcoming or obviating deprivations of the self.[2] The deprivations may be appraised in terms of any value, and any component of the self-structure may be involved.

WHEN COMPENSATION OCCURS

Deprivations may be met not by compensatory strivings but by withdrawal from active participation in human relationships. What are the conditions favoring compensation rather than acquiescence?

---

[1] On the self, see especially George Herbert Mead, *Mind, Self and Society.* Recent social psychology has moved increasingly in this direction, as in Muzafer Sherif and Hadley Cantril, *The Psychology of Ego-Involvements.*

[2] This applies the basic postulate of response, the I:D ratio, which expresses the ratio of indulgence to deprivation and states the principle that response maximizes net indulgence over deprivation. Under the impact of behaviorism the older "pleasure-pain" postulate is often rephrased as "abolishing stimuli" in modern systems of psychology. Unconscious as well as conscious dimensions are included, and in this way equivalency is achieved with the Benthamite "calculus of felicity."

One set of conditions is related to the deprivation: *compensation is favored when the deprivation is not overwhelming.* For if the blows of fortune are too hard to bear, the individual and the group may withdraw from the arena of power. The individual may commit suicide, even when not threatened by retaliation; and the group may abandon its own institutions, either taking over the culture of another or physically disappearing.[3]

Deprivations are not regarded as overwhelming *when lost or denied indulgences are not demanded absolutely.* The man who kills himself when he is rejected at the polls has made an absolutely rigid demand upon himself; this *or else.*

Deprivations are not regarded as overwhelming *when they are not wholly attributed to the self.* If it is possible to absolve the self from responsibility by blaming superior forces at the disposal of an enemy, or immoral conduct on the part of the antagonist, the demand on the self is sufficiently flexible to permit life to go on.

It is also true that deprivations can be better borne when they are *accompanied by some indulgences.* The man who fights a good fight can sometimes save his self-respect when he loses power or wealth. Losses can sometimes be minimized, as when they are less than expected.

A second set of conditions is favorable to compensation; *compensation by the use of power is facilitated when it is expected to yield more net values than can be obtained by the use of other alternatives.*

Favorable expectations about power occur among those who have *successfully used power* in the past under similar circumstances, or who know of such use by others. Professional soldiers are often more calm in military disaster than civilians who imagine "all is lost." Seasoned party politicians are famous for the cold-bloodedness with which they can survive defeat.

INDOCTRINATION WITH A MISSION

The conception of political type that has just been outlined is put forward as a means of unifying the data of history, social science,

---

[3] See H. D. Lasswell, "Collective Autism as a Consequence of Culture Contact: Notes on Religious Training and the Peyote Cult at Taos," *Zeitschrift für Sozialforschung,* vol. 4 (1935), pp. 232–246; Clyde Kluckhohn, "Navaho Witchcraft," *Papers of the Peabody Museum of American Archeology and Ethnology,* Harvard University, vol. XXII, pp. 33–72, 145–149. Responses to deprivation may be predominantly *object orientations, adjustive thinking, autistic reactions* or *somatic reactions.* (They may involve one or more values and institutions.) See the forthcoming study of *Anomie* by Sebastian DeGrazia.

psychology and medicine. It appears to be confirmed by what we know of many of the outstanding figures in the history of political life, especially in the case of men who were indoctrinated from the earliest years with a political mission. In these instances all of our specifications are met. The individual was identified with the destiny of a group larger than his primary ego. The emphasis on mission rose from the discrepancy between the goals of the group and the present or prospective situation in which the group appeared to be. Group losses or obstructions, it was believed, could be removed by power (though not necessarily to the exclusion of other means). Moreover, power was glorified as a probable—if not inevitable—means of fulfilling the collective mission and hence of removing and preventing deprivation. The focus of attention of the developing youngster has been absorbed with symbols of reference to power and with rationalizations of power. Immediate indulgences have been granted to him as he acquired the skills deemed appropriate to the mission to be fulfilled. Such intense indoctrination usually occurs when a changing political situation is surcharged with conflict, or when checks and losses are fresh.

Recall the story of Hannibal, indoctrinated from childhood with burning hatred of Rome and loyalty to Carthage by his able father, the Carthaginian general Hamilcar Barcas. This occurred in the thick of the duel which ultimately led to the extinction of Carthage in the struggle for Mediterranean primacy between the two great super powers of the time.[4]

Gustavus Adolphus of Sweden was trained from the first by his austere parents (Charles IX and Christina) to be a champion of Protestantism. He learned Swedish and German as his mother tongues, and at twelve had mastered Latin, Italian and Dutch. Later he acquired a working knowledge of Spanish, Russian and Polish. The boy began to take a responsible place in public ceremonies during his ninth year. At thirteen he received petitions and conversed officially with foreign ministers. Two years later he administered a Duchy, and within a year was practically coregent. He was trained in martial and chivalric skills, and his subsequent record speaks for itself in the struggle against the Catholic powers.

The importance of ambitious and loving parents in shaping the ego ideal (the demands made on the self) is a commonplace of everyday wisdom and scientific observation. Although we know little of

[4] On the political pattern referred to, consult William T. R. Fox, *The Super-Powers.*

the details of the early life of Genghis Khan, everything points to the decisive influence of his mother in preparing him to restore the position of the family. It was a period in which the great clans were giving way to smaller social units, the family. Families with large herds of horses were able to support a large following of armed riders as well as slaves to do the menial work of the camp. Weaker families were compelled to get on as best they could outside the lands of the aristocrats. Temujin (later Genghis Khan) was born into a broken-down family of Mongols with memories of a heroic past but surrounded by present adversity. Temujin's father was poisoned by enemies before the boy went on his first hunt. Temujin and his brothers hunted marmots and mice, and they even caught fish in the streams, which no self-respecting Mongol was supposed to eat. The mother kept them alive and did what she could to inspire them with the pride and self-confidence that came from the heroic legends of past greatness. She tried to keep together the small band that had still clustered around her husband. In the rough and tumble of the steppes, Genghis formed his whole life in the struggle to survive, to overcome, to bend men to his will. As he once declared, "a man's highest job in life is to break his enemies, to drive them before him, to take from them all the things that have been theirs, to hear the weeping of those who cherished them, to take their horses between his knees, and to press in his arms the most desirable of their women."

This is typical of the burning ambition for restoration and revenge of those who have been deprived of the power to which they believed themselves entitled. And in fashioning the instrument of restoring the family fortunes, the role of the mother, as in the case of the great Khan, is often exemplified. A more humble instance is the life of Napoleon III, who was so profoundly shaped by his mother. Louis Bonaparte, his father, was a brother of Napoleon I and had been king of Holland. At one point in Louis's career, he had compelled his wife, by a "scandalous" legal action, to give up to him the elder of her two children. With Charles she wandered from Geneva to Aix, Carlsruhe to Augsburg, and supervised the son's education, whether he studied in a school or with tutors.

EXTREMES OF INDULGENCE AND DEPRIVATION

Our recent advances in studying personality development have given us greater understanding of the process by which extreme cravings for power, respect and related deference values come into existence and find outlet in positive forms of activity, rather than in total withdrawal. An essential factor is the balancing of deprivation by indulgence; and, more particularly, the tensions arising from extremes of both. Without a compensating flow of affection and admiration, deprivations may appear too overwhelming to justify the exertions necessary to acquire the skills essential to eventual success. And if the flow swings erratically from extreme to extreme, the tensions of uncertainty can be kept within bearable limits, so that energies are concentrated upon the task of mastering the environment.

We know that one of the tension-inducing environments is created when affection, respect and other values are (or are felt to be) contingent upon the acquisition and exercise of skills. To some degree, of course, this process is inseparable from the early contact of the infant and child with the standards imposed upon him by the carriers of the culture into which he is born. Unless some obedience is given, there is punishment in the form of bodily chastisement, withdrawal of affection and other deprivations. With conformity, on the other hand, rewards are forthcoming in the form of food, affection and other indulgences. It is a question, here, not of this process in general but of the special form given to it when the young person is exposed to a relatively elaborate set of requirements, which are rewarded or punished with special intensity. Almost all learning of set tasks gives rise to characteristic deprivations. One must practice grammar, for instance, at a set time whether one is in the mood or not. The inhibiting of impulses to run and play or to study something else often carries with it rage reactions, reactions which may never rise to full expression in what is said and done or even thought. But these answers to a command, whether emanating from outside or from the internalized commander (the conscience), characteristically arouse tendencies to get out of the situation, either by escape or by destruction. Such tendencies, if not deliberately recognized and rejected, may give rise to a recurring level of tension against which defensive measures are spontaneously taken. One of these measures is a blind urge to act with intensity and rigidity; in short, the dynamisms of compulsiveness. The primary ego, caught in the tug of conflicting impulses and requirements, can develop a very extreme set of expectations about the characteristics of the ego: on the one hand, the ego may appear to be loving and admired; on the other, the same ego can appear as unloved, shameful, guilty and weak. Pessimism may rest on the idea that one is loved only "conditionally";

that is, that love can only be received as part of a bargain or a battle.

Certain eminent historical figures were subjected to great extremes of indulgence and deprivation, and they responded to the tension by great, even though reluctant, concentration upon power. Frederick the Great is a conspicuous example. His father, Frederick William I of Prussia, was reacting against the "French" standards that he thought had too much influenced his own father. Hence Frederick William imposed a regime of Spartan rigor on his son, hoping to make him a model soldier and a man of "thrift and frugality" after his own pattern. But the young Frederick sought and found indulgence in other pursuits. Encouraged by his mother and his governess, Madame de Roucouille, and his first tutor, Duhan, a French refugee, Frederick acquired a taste for music and literature, secretly learned Latin, which had been forbidden by his father, scoffed at religion, refused to ride or shoot and affected the French language, dress and manners, while deriding German uncouthness. Revolting against the harsh treatment received from his father, Frederick planned to run away to the English. But the secret was betrayed, with well-known results. One of the conspirators, Frederick's friend Katte, was beheaded in his presence. Eventually the crown prince began to conform as a means of obtaining power.

The impact of exposure to extreme indulgence and deprivation during formative years is exemplified further in such a career as that of Peter the Great. He saw one of his uncles dragged from the palace and butchered by a mob in 1682. He witnessed his mother's mentor and own best friend torn from his grasp and hacked to pieces in his presence. Exposed to the contempt of the boyars, and knowing of the contempt in which Russia was held abroad, Peter groped toward a career devoted to the internal consolidation of the Crown and the laying of the foundation for Russian power and frame abroad.

An interesting test case is Alexander the Great. Although we cannot completely penetrate the cloud of glorification with which his career is veiled, several strong indications can be found. His father, Philip of Macedon, was a strong and successful king in the very process of enlarging and consolidating his domain, taking advantage of the shifting constellation of power throughout the known world. In the full stride of conflict, he did not underrate the importance of having a successor properly equipped to deal with his new and heavy responsibilities. Alexander was not only given distinguished tutors, like Aristotle, but from early times he was subjected to a busy and by no means "soft" life. Of decisive significance, perhaps, was the soaring ambition of Alexander's mother, who was well acquainted with Eastern mystery cults, if not indeed a priestess before her marriage to Philip. How seriously Alexander took the tales of his divinity and his mission in the world, we cannot say. (When he gave encouragement to the belief in his divine attributes, he may have been deliberately employing a myth to consolidate his empire.)

We know that the devaluation of power among those born to power has been most conspicuous among those whose power is unchallenged, leaving them comparatively free to pursue other values.

When we consider less glamorous careers among those born to or claiming great power, the result is in harmony with our hypothetical picture of the political type. We know that middle-class homes are hothouses of ambition, holding their children to high standards of achievement, thus providing the tension between indulgence and deprivation so congenial to the accentuation of power.[5]

We know, too, that a disproportionately large contribution is made to the public service by professional families, especially by clergymen and teachers. Many factors affect this result. One element is exposure to a stream of talk that typically contains many of the dominant rationalizations of public life. Facility in the use of words and familiarity with the history and traditions of public life are skills that expedite the shaping of an active career in politics. Contrast the articulateness of the clergyman or the teacher with the inarticulateness of the typical manual toiler. The symbols of reference to public targets and to plausible means of rationalizing power foster the displacement of private affects upon public objects. Middle-class professional families are the custodians of the dominant myths of the community; and more. They emphasize the public interest and glorify the professional standard of serving collective rather than purely private advantage. This means that business activity, for instance, is looked down upon, however much the economic advantages of wealth are openly or covertly desired. To be professional is to curb the business standard of "charging what the traffic will bear." The ideal is some form of direct public service, as in law, medicine, education; and law, in particular, leads to active participation in the power process.

Where crisis conditions prevail in modern society, the educated

[5] The literature on middle-class ambitiousness is large. A methodologically interesting application of contextual analysis is found in Bruce Lannes Smith, "The Political Communication Specialist of Our Times," in *Propaganda, Communication, and Public Opinion; a Comprehensive Reference Guide,* by B. L. Smith, H. D. Lasswell and R. D. Casey, pp. 31–73.

and professional middle class has contributed heavily to the leadership of political movements. Those who sacrifice for the acquisition of any skill undergo self-discipline; and they develop a moral claim on the world for reward. Moreover, they are equipped with the symbols most appropriate to the making of these claims plausible to themselves and their fellows. When deprivations fall upon them, they tend to respond with moral indignation. Not only do they see that they are worse off; they believe it is unjust that they should be subject to deprivation. Hence it is easy for articulate professional families to rationalize their assertiveness in terms of the public good.

Furthermore, young people who have been reared in such an environment, even when they are unable or unwilling to acquire a long education, continue to apply strenuous standards to themselves. Whether they admit it or not, they feel acutely inferior when they fail to follow the accepted path. And their modes of compensation frequently take the form of what they conceive to be short cuts to the seizure of power and the regaining of a sense of total worth.

It is not to be forgotten that the tension between demands on the ego for both independence and dependence is intensified by a disciplinary-indulgent environment. This increases the likelihood of those vigorous compensations against dependency that enable many persons to impress upon others their seeming courage, intensity of conviction and strength of will. The child of our middle classes, for instance, is somewhat baffled by the intricate code that is forced upon him. On the one hand he is supposed to "be a nice boy" and not fight or engage in perversity, but on the other he is supposed to "stand up for himself" in altercations with other boys. And the niceties of the conduct appropriate to these commands are as intricate as the code of what is phrased as "selfishness" or "service." We laud business, yet deplore selfishness in the sense of outspoken pursuit of personal advantage. And our double standards create problems of adjustment that not infrequently are resolved by ruthless determination to escape from quandaries into action, and to use action as a means of silencing doubts by the fact and the fame of power.

"Mobility upward" along the power ladder is fostered by a home in which one member of the family, usually the mother, feels that she has married "beneath" her social (respect) class. These women are sensitive to the blight in their careers and obstinately determined to vindicate themselves by the vicarious triumphs of their children. Whether or not such ambitions are explicitly connected with the power myths and operations of society, they frequently create that taut internal state (that bifurcation of the ego into the secure and the insecure part) that favors the use of power as a way of relief.

A variant of the same compensatory response is the drive of the "provincial" or the "small-town boy" or the "country boy" to succeed against the stigma of rusticity.[6] One advantage of a marginal position in terms both of class structure and territory is that new power opportunities may be perceived and utilized free of older commitments. But the advantage from the side of motivation is the overcoming of a low-respect position through the use of power and other available means. Commentators have not failed to recognize that Napoleon came from the periphery of French power, Corsica, and that his family had long opposed the inclusion of the island in France. More recently the rise of Hitler and Rosenberg has emphasized certain advantages of a peripheral starting point.

That blighted careers make politicians is another observation in accord with our basic idea of the dynamic factors in leadership. A career is blighted when expectations are thwarted and when the responsibility can readily be projected from the self upon society. When power is the frustrator, restitution and retaliation in terms of power are plausible possibilities. The failure of the established order to put Doctor of Philosophy Marx in a Prussian university post was of no small consequence in launching him on his career. And this is not untypical of the response to be expected of men who have sacrificed to acquire a skill for which society provides no suitable scope. Hence the dynamic role so often noted of students and unemployed intellectuals in movements of political protest.[7]

The person who has not passed the preliminary qualifications expected for a recognized place in society is another potential recruit in the power struggle. Sometimes disturbed times or economic adversity has prevented the completion of a regular education. Or the person is rebellious against the exactions of a teacher and falls by the wayside on the way to a degree. As Bismarck contemptuously

---

[6] See part 5, section A, of the volume cited in footnote 14. In general, on social mobility and power consult: P. A. Sorokin, *Social Mobility;* Jules Kornis, *L'Homme d'état: Analyse de l'esprit politique.*

[7] For example: John G. Heinberg, "The Personnel Structure of French Cabinets," *American Political Science Review,* vol. 33 (1939), pp. 267–278; "State Legislators," in *Annals of the American Academy of Political and Social Science,* vol. 195 (1938), pp. 1–252; Leo C. Rosten, *The Washington Correspondents;* Sigmund Neumann, "The Political Lieutenant," in *Permanent Revolution; the Total State in a World at War,* pp. 73–95.

remarked, such a one may join the profession of the untrained—journalism; political journalism continues to be an avenue to power in modern societies.

There are famous cases in which a severe deprivation relatively late in life had led to furious concentration upon power. Joseph II of Austria, "the revolutionary emperor," as Saul K. Padover has called him, was transformed into the grim figure of his later days not only by the untimely death of his beloved wife but also by the shattering humiliation of the discovery that his wife had not loved him.[8] A turning point in the hitherto somewhat unfocused career of John Bright was the critical experience of losing his first wife. Three days after her death Richard Cobden after offering words of condolence said: "There are thousands of homes in England at this moment where the wives, mothers and children are dying of hunger. Now, when the first paroxysm of your grief is spent, I would advise you to come with me, and we will never rest until the Corn Laws are repealed." And he did.

The same principle of using power for compensatory purposes is exemplified in the undeniably important role of real or fancied physical limitations.[9] We remember the "withered arm" of William II of Germany, attributed to a fall when he slipped out of the hands of an English governess. And there was the short stature of Napoleon. We think, too, of the rapacious ambition of the palace eunuchs in the history of both China and the Near East. The fact or the fear of sexual inadequacy has been a bitter spur to the accentuation of power. Queen Elizabeth was plagued by persisting doubts as to her attractiveness and capacity as a woman. The smallpox that scarred Mirabeau turned him into an object of distaste to his father. The ugliness of the famous political orators, Lord Brougham and John Randolph of Roanoke, was undoubtedly a factor in their political

[8] Specific studies are: Werner Sombart, *Der Proletarische Sozialismus* (vol. 2); Hans Gerth, "The Nazi Party: Its Leadership and Composition," *American Journal of Sociology*, 45 (1940), pp. 517–541; Max Nomad, *Rebels and Renegades;* Julien Benda, *The Treason of the Intellectuals;* Hendrik de Man, *Die Intellektuellen und der Sozialismus;* G. P. Gooch, *History and the Historians in the Nineteenth Century.*

[9] Alfred Adler's *Individual Psychology* put heavy stress on compensations against organic inferiority as a major dynamism of personality. Eduard C. Lindeman phrased the hypothesis with his customary skill in *The Meaning of Adult Education:* "We are slowly coming to see that all 'power-grabbers' and dictators who reach out for unusual power are in reality compensating for inner deficiencies of their personalities."

intensity. The infantile paralysis that Franklin D. Roosevelt overcame left him a better disciplined and more power-centered personality
than when it struck him down. Like many men who escape death,
he achieved the inner self-confidence and perspective of one who
lives "on borrowed time."

An early illness or enforced period of inactivity has sometimes
played a more important role in the development of personality than
even the determination to overcome handicaps. Delicate children have
gained knowledge from reading that aided in the consolidation of
political aims. Mazzini, for instance, and William Pitt, Jr., appear to
have made productive use of early invalidism.

The intensive study of infancy and childhood, conducted by
modern methods of careful record taking, has underlined the decisive
importance of the early years in shaping the structure of personality.
These data have prodigiously documented and refined ancient maxims
about the crucial significance of the early years. The data go in the
direction toward which we have been pointing. The accentuation
of power is to be understood as a compensatory reaction against
low estimates of the self (especially when coexisting with high self-
estimates); and the reaction occurs when opportunities exist both
for the displacement of ungratified cravings from the primary circle
to public targets and for the rationalization of these displacements
in the public interest; and, finally, when skills are acquired appropriate to the effective operation of the power-balancing process.[10]

The factors that accentuate power in the person likewise operate
in molding the response of the group. In general, according to our
theory of power, we expect that power will be accented by groups
when they expect it to protect them against deprivation or to restore
and expand their influence. At the same time adverse estimates of
the self must not be overwhelming, or the resort to power will be
blocked by sentiments of utter hopelessness, such as have demoralized
certain folk cultures after exposure to the deprivations inflicted by
the carriers of modern industrial civilization. Expectations favorable
to the use of power in the future are strengthened by the recollection
of successful applications of power in the past under similar circumstances. The paradigm case is Prussia in particular and Germany
in general. To Prussians it was power in the disciplined form of mili-

[10] For a compendious review of research, see Marian E. Breckenridge and E. Lee
Vincent, *Child Development; Physical and Psychological Growth through the
School Years;* Gardner Murphy, *Personality.*

tary violence and, to a lesser extent, diplomacy that brought the group from the sandy barrens of the North Prussian plain to the startling eminence of a middle-sized and then a great power. Was Germany crushed by the Entente in 1918? Prussia had revived after being crushed to the earth by Napoleon and the French; and in the more distant past by the trauma of the Thirty Years' War and the depopulation and partition of the German people. The self of the representative German incorporated the symbol "German" and with it the entire myth of German history, character and destiny. The extremes of self-admiration and self-debasement present in this mythology provided a potent determiner for the accentuation of power in the name of the collective self throughout the group, and for the service of the central myth by the power-seeking personality.[11]

In reviewing the theory of political personality outlined in this chapter it may be useful to match it with the *homo politicus* of much popular and scientific tradition.[12] The image I refer to is that of the power-hungry man, the person wholly absorbed in getting and holding power, utterly ruthless in his insatiable lust to impose his will upon all men everywhere. Suppose that we refine this traditional conception into a speculative model of the political man comparable with the economic man of the older economic science.

The following postulates can be laid down (the numbering is arbitrary):

1. He demands power and seeks other values only as a basis for power.
2. He is insatiable in his demand for power.
3. He demands power for himself only, conceived as an ego separate from others.
4. His expectations are focused upon the past history and future possibilities affecting power.

[11] The detailed study of comparative politics has barely begun. Beginnings are made in Ruth Benedict, *Chrysanthemum and the Sword;* P. Kecskemeti and N. Leites. "Some Psychological Hypotheses on Nazi Germany," *The Library of Congress, Washington, D.C., Experimental Division for the Study of War Time Communications,* Document No. 60 (1945), 104 pp.; Geoffrey Gorer, "Themes in Japanese Culture," *Transactions of the New York Academy of Sciences,* vol. 5 (1943), pp. 106–124; Weston LaBarre, "Some Observations on Character Structure in the Orient. I. The Japanese," *Psychiatry,* vol. 8 (1945), pp. 319–342; "II. The Chinese," *ibid.,* vol. 9 (1946), pp. 215–237; Geoffrey Gorer, *The American People; A Study in National Character.*

[12] George E. G. Catlin undertook to formulate a general theory in *The Science and Method of Politics.*

5. He is sufficiently capable to acquire and supply the skills appropriate to his demands.

It is evident that the model, thus constructed, can only be completely satisfied by a world ruler, since the fifth postulate includes the idea of success. Since there have been no world rulers, this model can be used to investigate no known cases. (However, there have been universal states, if we take the expression to mean that the "known world" was under the domination of a single power of overwhelming strength.) Therefore, we can profitably begin to revise the postulates for the purpose of fitting the model to illuminate a broader range of concrete circumstances.

We can, for example, withdraw the success postulate, which makes the political man omnipotent, and simply make him omniscient, in the sense that he always foresees correctly the power consequences of the moves open to him in any given situation. This makes it possible for the political man to remain less than a world ruler, if he is counter-balanced by other power operators who similarly exploit to the full their power potential on the basis of correct calculation. But to postulate omniscience excludes the very features of reality that most require investigation if we are to build up a body of knowledge related to human behavior. One of the most rewarding questions to raise about decision making is this: on what expectations are wars declared, treaties signed, diplomatic intercourse resumed, international organizations launched or other measures used? Unless we can understand the interaction of expectations upon demand (and identification) we are not far along in comprehending anything worth knowing about the decision process. The examination of such perspectives calls for knowledge about how they interact not only in the person but also in the group; and how a given set of expectations or demands or identifications is affected by other perspectives and by other factors in the sociopolitical process.

The third postulate prescribes a wholly egocentric personality, since all demands are made solely for the expected enhancement of the primary ego. Hence the *homo politicus* is not permitted to have a self (by which is meant a symbol structure included with the primary ego and given equal treatment). According to our speculative model, the perfect power type is wholly absorbed with advancing the value position of the "sacred me" (not "us"). Hence he sacrifices anyone and everyone at convenience for his power, and does not conceive of power as a means of advancing the value position of family, neighborhood, nation or any other group. If we allow unconscious as well as conscious demands to be included in our model, the psychiatrist at least is likely to say that this *homo politicus* is never found in nature, and is most closely approximated by a few paranoid psychotics or psychopaths. It must be admitted, however, that these are met in history in positions of power, as in the notable instance of "mad King Ludwig" of Bavaria who liked a bit of human blood in his hunting bag.[13]

Let us conclude by saying that while everyone is compelled to agree that this model of the political man of tradition does, in fact, perform a certain scientific purpose by highlighting some historical and contemporary figures, such as the "mad Caesars," the model is unsuitable for the most comprehensive inquiries into the decision-making process. The conception is far out of line with many known cultures, social structures and even crisis facts. The emendations and elaborations called for in relation to such circumstances are almost literally "too numerous to mention."

There is the danger, often exemplified in economic analysis, of choosing a speculative model, which applies to a few extreme instances, and becoming absorbed with the refined restatement of the postulates, rather than with exploring the varied phenomena of society. As one economist wrote when criticizing a book on economic theory by a colleague,[14] "On pp. 76–77 his marionettes start as 'normal human beings . . . familiar in a modern Western nation . . . acting with ordinary human motives . . . knowing what they want and seeking it intelligently.' But by p. 268 they have become 'mechanical automata.'" "Institutional economists" have attempted to absorb themselves in the context of concrete cultures and specific circumstances. But they have been rather slow in spinning a web of useful theory between the classical models of the perfect market and the many-colored tapestries of everyday life. In more recent times there are signs of a deliberate quest for speculative models of sufficient richness to further the interests of science and policy.[15]

Warned by this example, we use a theory of the political type

[13] A guide to "pathographies" is provided by Wilhelm Lange-Eichbaum, *Genie, Irrsinn und Ruhm.*

[14] T. W. Hutchinson, *The Significance and Basic Postulates of Economic Theory*, footnote, page 124, referring to Frank H. Knight, *Risk, Uncertainty, and Profit.*

[15] A clear instance: Milton Friedman, "Lange on Price Flexibility and Employment: A Methodological Criticism," *American Economic Review*, vol. 36 (1946), pp. 613–631.

that can be directly implemented with data of observation stemming from any concrete situation. Our political man:

1. accentuates power
2. demands power (and other values) for the self (the primary ego plus incorporated symbols of other egos)
3. accentuates expectations concerning power
4. acquires at least a minimum proficiency in the skills of power

The man who accentuates power is doing so *relative* to others, and therefore power personalities can be detected, by comparing them with standard expectancies for a culture, a social layer, a crisis or some other specified frame of reference. Besides accentuating power, it is recognized that the political type is not fully described until we know whether he is accentuating power in relation to one part of the self or all. We know that some identifications with the nation, for instance, guide and indeed swallow up the energies of the person. So far as the acquiring and exercise of skills is concerned, we provide only for some minimum degree of mastery which permits some measure of survival in the arena of power.

Our central picture of the political man, therefore, reduces the wolf man, the *homo lupus*, to a special pigeon hole. He is but one of the entire process by which primary motives are displaced onto public targets and rationalized in the name of public good.

6 Correlates
of International
Attitudes

WILLIAM A. SCOTT

The rate of development of theretical and applied science in a given area is likely to depend, in part, on the social utility of understanding the phenomena with which it deals. The beneficiary of this utility is perhaps most frequently not the total society but a potent sub-group within it. In social psychology, impetus for the development of methods of predicting elections and studying employee morale came from powerful, interested, and wealthy segments

From William A. Scott, "Correlates of International Attitudes," *Public Opinion Quarterly* 22 (1958–1959), pp. 464–472. Reprinted with the permission of author and publisher.

of the society. These methodological advances have been accompanied by elaborations of theories about determinants of the relevant behavior, and the cumulative result has undoubtedly been an advancement of understanding.

It is conceivable that increasing public influence on foreign policy will cause powerful, interested, and wealthy circles to provide the impetus for better understanding of the determinants of public opinion about international events. Such attention to the area as exists among policy makers at present appears to be focused more on the "what" than the "why" of attitudes. But the more apparent the complexity of the phenomena becomes, the greater is the likelihood that concern with their determinants will emerge. It is to a consideration of determinants that this study is addressed.

Several public opinion research agencies have made available the results of over a hundred surveys concerning the United Nations, conducted during the first ten years of that organization's history. A review of these findings has recently been published.[1] The aim of this paper is to select certain of them as a springboard for speculation concerning somewhat broader relationships that might be established through imaginatively designed research.

The schema proposed here is a modest one. It merely delineates certain classes of variable which might be conceived as determiners of attitudes toward foreign affairs. Very rarely can the precise nature of the relationships be specified at this stage. The classes of variable to be considered are (1) international events, (2) cognitive characteristics of the person, (3) unconscious personality factors, and (4) characteristics of the person's social milieu. For each of these classes, some of the United Nations data will be adduced as evidence of their relevance, and then certain directions will be suggested for future research to help clarify the nature of the relationships.

INTERNATIONAL EVENTS

When comparable questions are asked repeatedly over an extended period of time, it is sometimes possible to attribute variations in the over-all distribution of attitudes to the occurrence of certain well-known relevant events. Before analyzing the UN data the authors searched the *New York Times* annual listings of significant world

---

[1] W. A. Scott and S. B. Withey, *The United States and the United Nations: The Public View*, New York, Manhattan Publishing Company, 1958.

events and selected the major events that were most immediately related to the United Nations—the Palestine cease-fire, the Berlin blockade, the Indonesian peace agreement, the outbreak of hostilities in Korea, the Inchon landing, and so forth. Trends in public opinion concerning some aspects of the UN were then compared to this calendar of UN-related events.

Such a trend analysis proved *useless* in connection with attitudes toward United States participation in the United Nations, measured by such questions as "Do you think our government should continue to belong to the United Nations or should we pull out of it now?" Over the five-year interval during which this question was asked, the proportion of people who said the United States should "pull out now" never exceeded 13 per cent, and the average was around 10 per cent. Thus fluctuations in this figure were so slight that they could not be meaningfully associated with world events of the period.

Another trend which could be studied from comparable questions was satisfaction with UN performance. Satisfaction was repeatedly assessed by questions like: "In general, are you satisfied or dissatisfied with the progress that the United Nations has made so far?" The proportion of satisfied respondents has fluctuated widely throughout the organization's history, ranging from low points of around 20 per cent to high points of around 60 per cent. It appeared that there was a relation between over-all public satisfaction and the UN-related events which had been independently selected. In general, when the UN was unsuccessfully involved in events which appeared to threaten the interests of the United States, satisfaction was low. When UN activities favorably affected the United States, satisfaction tended to be high. When there was no particular world crisis involving the UN, satisfaction tended to be high, probably simply for lack of any focus for discontent.

Such time-sequence data as these suggest that relating international attitudes to contemporary world events does represent a fruitful subject of analysis. But more refined study is demanded. Eventually one would like to be able to predict *what* sorts of world event will have *what* effects on *what* kinds of attitude. This obviously demands, first of all, an appropriate system for classifying world events—which is clearly not available at present. One possibility is a classification of world events according to the major public values which they are likely to engage. White, Dodd, and the writer, among others, have attempted preliminary listings of dominant values in United

States culture.[2] What is needed is an abbreviated list of those major values which are commonly applied by various segments of the general public in assessing world events. This could be compiled through interview surveys with probability samples of the entire nation.

Next, one would want to determine how various current international developments—such as the United Nations, the disarmament talks, the cold war, and South African Apartheid—are seen in relation to these major values; that is, what values are seen as either enhanced or threatened by them. Given these data, for the entire population and for various sub-groups, one might be able to predict either public reactions to a new event or the effect of a new event on reactions to an old event. This could be done crudely by making a judgment classification of the new event along each of the major value dimensions, and then forecasting the probable reactions to it of various segments of the population, depending on which values they held predominantly and how these were related to past world events. Applied to the realm of UN attitudes, for example, such a procedure would probably lead one to the conclusion that the UN is seen by the great bulk of the population almost exclusively in the context of war prevention, rather than in the light of its less spectacular activities in such fields as public health and technological development. One would therefore expect that events which increased or decreased the threat of war would be most likely to affect attitudes toward the UN, and that other sorts of world events, be they economic or political, would be unlikely to have much impact.

This method would, of course, provide only gross estimates of popular reactions, but it would be relatively quick at the time of the critical event, and often even such crude guesses at public opinion are adequate for purposes of foreign policy construction.

COGNITIVE CHARACTERISTICS

It is not unusual for public opinion surveys to include, along with measures of the principal attitudes under study, questions which deal with related issues, or which tap other aspects of the respondents'

[2] R. K. White, *Value Analysis—the Nature and Use of the Method,* Ann Arbor, Mich., Society for the Psychological Study of the Social Issues, 1951; S. C. Dodd, "How to Measure Values," *Research Studies of the State College of Washington,* Vol. 18, 1950, pp. 163–168; and Scott and Withey, *The United States and the United Nations.*

cognitive structures. Thus, in the UN data one frequently finds attitudes toward the UN related to more general cognitive attributes, such as interest in foreign affairs or isolationism and internationalism.

It is typically found that persons who express greater interest in foreign affairs, or are better informed about them, are likely to be more favorably disposed toward the UN than the less interested or ill-informed. An appealing interpretation of such findings is that the familiar and well understood is likely to pose less threat than the strange and unknown. To the extent that international affairs are outside the realm of familiar experience to the man-on-the-street, one might expect him to advocate caution in foreign involvements for this country—especially foreign involvements which cannot be readily justified in terms of national defense.

This interpretation is difficult to test by correlational or time-trend analysis of survey data, since these procedures do not provide adequate control over many other variables, ideological and socio-economic, which are correlated with both information about foreign affairs and attitudes toward the UN. Perhaps experimental manipulation of the level of information about foreign affairs would provide one appropriate test of the hypothesis that increased information induces more favorable attitudes toward international involvement. But the Cincinnati UN campaign several years ago showed that increase of information level in a large natural population was difficult to accomplish—largely, perhaps, because people are exceedingly resistant to the casual absorption of information which is antithetical to their pre-existing attitudes or irrelevant to their immediate daily concerns.[3]

Another finding which appears repeatedly in the studies reviewed is that attitudes toward the United Nations are related to more basic orientations concerning the preferred role of the United States in world affairs. General isolationist sentiments are associated with anti-UN attitudes, but whether or not activist sentiments are associated with pro-UN attitudes depends on the kind of activism advocated. It was found that favorable attitudes toward economic aid or cooperative military activities, such as NATO, are positively related to approval of the UN, but advocation of unilateral military action by this country—such as "bomb Russia now"—is negatively related.

[3] *Cincinnati Looks at the United Nations,* Chicago, National Opinion Research Center, 1947.

Thus there is some tendency toward consistency among these specific attitudes.

This raises the question of whether the many diverse attitudes toward international affairs can be reduced to, or correlated with, a smaller number of basic values or general orientations toward foreign policy. One might expect, for example, that international attitudes stem, in part, from rationally maintained values that the individual applies in his daily interpersonal relations. Smith showed, some years ago, that not all personal values are equally generalized to the realm of international affairs.[4] One might suggest that the degree to which a value is generalized is a function of the degree to which the goal involved in it can be simultaneously shared by a number of actors. Applying Morton Deutsch's terminology, it appears likely that values with promotively interdependent goals will be more widely generalized than values involving contriently interdependent goals.[5] This hypothesis could be readily tested in a public opinion survey by first classifying values according to the kind of interdependence of their goals, then assessing respondents' values as they are applied to a progressively wider range of events, from the intimate to the unfamiliar.

It is by no means necessary, however, that international attitudes be rationally interrelated for the bulk of the populace. As Fisher and Belknap have pointed out:

> Attitudes which most people have toward foreign affairs are, in a sense, peripheral rather than psychologically central. . . . Not only are foreign affairs questions ordinarily less immediately consequential for the individual than such questions as employment, recreation, and family life, but they are also less real. . . . This situation makes the usual role of the ordinary citizen more one of a customer than a process participant. He can "buy" a point of view, or several of them; and if these viewpoints are logically in conflict, he need only avoid using them simultaneously. . . . Because it is not functionally necessary for most people to develop a complete and consistent philosophy of foreign affairs (since they are not part of the immediate environment which the individual must organize or adjust to), the

[4] M. B. Smith, "Personal Values as Determinants of a Political Attitude," *Journal of Psychology,* Vol. 28, 1949, pp. 477–486.
[5] M. Deutsch, "A Theory of Cooperation and Competition," *Human Relations,* Vol. 2, 1949, pp. 129–152.

gross pictures offered the citizen can be accepted piecemeal, and we should not be surprised to find them sometimes contradictory.[6]

Some research recently performed by the writer with a sample of college students indicates that for the average subject, attitudes and values relevant to universal military training do not form a consistent cognitive structure,[7] and it is likely that such inconsistency is the rule as far as international attitudes are concerned. However, one can distinguish respondents according to the *degree* to which they manifest cognitive consistency in a given area. As a measure of cognitive consistency one may use a modification of a procedure reported by Rosenberg.[8] Results of this recent work suggest that subjects whose attitudes and values relating to a particular issue *do* form a consistent structure are more resistant to pressures toward attitude change than are subjects with initially inconsistent cognitive structures. One is led to predict that such findings might hold for the total national population in regard to international attitudes. When the attitudes are coherently structured, one would expect them to be more stable in the face of propaganda, group pressures, or even changing world events than when they are loosely or inconsistently organized. Such a prediction could be tested either by experimental investigation of small groups or by panel studies on probability samples of large populations.

UNCONSCIOUS PERSONALITY FACTORS

Besides the realm of cognitive factors of which the respondent is aware, there is a whole host of unconscious personality processes which might conceivably be related to his international attitudes. In this area speculation is more prevalent than empirical fact, but a few sets of possibly relevant data may be cited. In the UN study it was found that antagonism toward the UN tended to be associated with what one might call a threat orientation toward the international environment. Anti-UN respondents were more likely to feel that world war was imminent and less likely to feel that various major world

[6] B. R. Fisher and G. Belknap, *America's Role in World Affairs,* Ann Arbor, Mich., Survey Research Center, 1952.
[7] W. A. Scott, "Personal Values and Group Interaction," in *Report of U.S.A.F. Behavioral Science Conference, 1957,* Albuquerque, University of New Mexico. (Dittoed.)
[8] M. J. Rosenberg, "Cognitive Structure and Attitudinal Affect," *Journal of Abnormal and Social Psychology,* Vol. 53, 1956, pp. 367–372.

powers could be trusted. It is possible that both these orientations—the anti-UN attitudes and the expectation of threat from the international arena—derive, in part, from a more basic sense of insecurity within the unconscious personality.

Douvan and Walker have shown that feelings of effectiveness in regard to public affairs are related to feelings of competence in handling one's own interpersonal environment.[9] Levinson has indicated that unfavorable attitudes toward international cooperation measures are associated with the basic personality syndrome of authoritarianism.[10] The interpretation suggested by such a combination of findings is that feelings of personal insecurity are reflected in a threat orientation toward the international environment. In an attempt to counteract this feeling of threat the individual might identify with power figures both in his personal environment and in the world arena. Such an identification would be accompanied by concern over loss of status, either for himself or for the relevant authority figures. This would engender a reluctance to see the United States engage in any form of cooperative international activity which threatens to submerge its national power and identity.

A somewhat different set of unconscious personality processes could be tapped by means of an approach proposed by Robert Weiss (personal communication), and this might provide some interesting insights into correlates of international attitudes. It is possible that one's feelings about nation-actors in the international arena represent, in part, a projection onto them of more primitive cathexes relating to figures in one's family of orientation. This suggests the research technique of requiring a person to construct an extended family, composed of personifications of various nations, and then attempting to infer the emotional attachments that are likely to be involved in these personifications. Evidently this approach has not yet been applied to the exploration of determinants of international attitudes, but it is certainly a feasible one for sample interview surveys to employ.

SOCIAL FACTORS

The final class of variables to be considered here relates to the individual's social environment. From a socio-psychological point of view,

[9] Elizabeth Douvan and A. M. Walker, "The Sense of Effectiveness in Public Affairs," *Psychological Monographs*, Vol. 70, No. 22, 1956.
[10] D. J. Levinson, "Authoritarian Personality and Foreign Policy," *Conflict Resolution*, Vol. 1, 1957, pp. 37–47.

a person's attitudes toward events in his life space are conditioned by the norms of his associates and of his positive reference groups. Data from sample interview surveys on international attitudes do not usually provide evidence directly relevant to this general hypothesis, for three reasons: First, the number of persons from any particular interacting group who fall into the sample is generally too small to permit adequate assessment of the group's norms. Second, there are few groups for which the area of foreign affairs is sufficiently salient to encourage the development of norms. Finally, it is difficult to disentangle a respondent's perception of a reference group norm from his tendency to project his own attitudes onto persons he likes. For these reasons, sample interview surveys are probably not the most appropriate device for the study of social influences from the standpoint of reference group theory. Preferable approaches are provided by experimental manipulation of artificial groups or long-term study of complete natural groups.

Some of the data from the UN surveys can be interpreted from the standpoint of reference group theory. In 1949 a considerably larger proportion of Catholics favored admitting Spain to the UN than did Protestants or Jews. And in 1948 many more Jews than non-Jews favored United States participation in a UN police force to keep order in Palestine. These two issues, more than any others presented in the available polls, were appropriate for distinguishing members of different demographic categories, since the problems were clearly relevant to the several religious organizations, and they were likely to elicit certain amounts of normative pressure within the interested groups.

Besides the reference group formulation of the effects of social factors on attitudes, it is possible to make a strictly sociological assumption that attitudes derive directly from one's position in the social structure, without any mediation by normative pressures related to specific international issues. An individual in a certain role tends to internalize attitudes and behavior patterns suited to that role. When he is confronted with a new event for which no patterned reactions are available, he may generalize his internalized reaction pattern in responding to that event.

Some data from the UN studies are relevant to this interpretation. It has been repeatedly noted that persons of lower socio-economic status are less likely than middle class persons to advocate measures for international conciliation and cooperation, such as the UN, and more likely to advocate either violence or withdrawal in response to world frustrations. Withdrawal and overt aggression are said to be preferred modes of reaction to interpersonal frustration in the lower class, while reaction formation, verbalization, and displacement—all ingredients of peaceful diplomacy—are said to represent preferred modes of interpersonal adjustment in the middle class. Miller and Swanson have suggested that socialization procedures within the various social classes provide different opportunities for learning favored defense mechanisms.[11] If these mechanisms for interpersonal adjustment are generalized and cognitively applied to new realms of experience, one might expect people to advocate, on the international scene, relationships and behavior patterns analogous to those they find in their immediate social environments.

CONCLUSION

This study has discussed some classes of determinants of international attitudes which have been suggested in public opinion studies concerning the United Nations. It has also indicated in some cases the sorts of data or research procedures that might shed light on the nature of the relationships which such factors bear to international attitudes. It is apparent that interview surveys do not, in all cases, provide the most appropriate research technique for exploring these relationships. There are certain limitations inherent in the method itself. It is difficult to subject a non-volunteer respondent to the lengthy assessment procedures required to gain information about unconscious personality processes. And it is rarely possible to inject relevant experimental manipulation into the interview survey.

Other limitations are not inherent in the method but stem from the failure of some researchers to exploit its full potentialities in ferreting out explanatory relationships. It is distressing to note the great frequency with which certain questions about the UN have been asked over the years, in contrast with the very few times when these questions have been accompanied by others which might have shed light on cognitive or personality or social factors behind the UN attitudes.

It would seem that astute use of interview surveys, combined with small-group experiments and intensive assessment of individuals and natural groups, could yield much more information about the

---

[11] D. R. Miller and G. E. Swanson, "A Proposed Study of the Learning of Techniques for Resolving Conflicts of Impulses," in *Interrelations between the Social Environment and Psychiatric Disorders*, New York, Milbank Memorial Fund, 1953.

determinants of international attitudes than is available at present. Sample interview surveys of the national population represent a necessary component of this research battery, since it is only through them that one can test the generality of findings from more restricted populations. Beyond this, they provide an opportunity to examine the usefulness of psychological and sociological explanations in accounting for attitudes which might be of critical concern to the architects of United States foreign policy.

II

Socialization: The Acquisition of Political Dispositions

Perhaps the most important feature of human nature is that people learn from each other. Thus, they can hand down through the generations their language, tools, and ideas rather than start from scratch each time. Part II presents a chronological approach to the most immediate problem. If the characteristics of the individual affect politics, then so do the ways in which individuals acquire them.

In her general essay on political socialization, Roberta Sigel explains that socialization is successful when the individual accepts the new ideas or actions as *his*, that is, when rewards, punishments, and models for imitation are unnecessary for the person to think and act in the new ways; he does it because he *wants* to. Thus, conflict and tension are reduced where socialization is adequate; people learn to accept the existing regime as a legitimate source of authority and its rules as proper.

Because it is usually not deliberate or formal, the learning of political values is mostly indirect and uncritical. As Easton and Dennis put it, the child "learns to like the government before he really knows what it is."[1] The same can be said for many other "lessons," especially partisan identification.[2] These early dispositions, moreover, are the hardest to alter; they form a screen through which later political information is filtered in order to eliminate thoughts inconsistent with prior opinions.[3]

Sigel goes on to note that learned political dispositions may be high in overt political content, like party identification and the sense of political efficacy, or totally nonpolitical in content, like authoritarianism and sociability.[4] What counts are the political consequences of the traits, not their content. Nonpolitical incidental learning, which is nothing like formal citizenship training, seems the more common and critical determinant of political behavior.

Political socialization works not only to minimize conflict and thereby stabilize the system, but to maintain existing divisions. Class and sex differences in political attitudes and orientations are apparent in early childhood.[5] It is important to remember that "not all segments of society share all the values of the larger society."

Systems vary in the degree to which they prepare their citizens to accept or initiate change, thereby affecting "the strain or ease with which change takes place." In general, though, children are taught the political tastes and patterns of their parents.

Political learning starts before school and may go on throughout life. Easton and Hess suggest that national identity is first learned by generalization from closer, more diffuse objects than the nation

---

[1] David Easton and Jack Dennis, "The Child's Image of Government," *The Annals of the American Academy of Political and Social Science*, 361 (1965), p. 56.

[2] Cf. Fred I. Greenstein, "The Importance of Party Identification," in Part III.

[3] Fred I. Greenstein, *Children and Politics* (New Haven: Yale University Press, 1965), pp. 78–84.

[4] See Part III for the significance of these attributes in politics.

[5] Herbert H. Hyman, *Political Socialization* (New York: Free Press, 1959), pp. 25–50; Greenstein, *Children and Politics*, pp. 85–127; David Easton and Jack Dennis, "The Child's Acquisition of Regime Norms: Political Efficacy," *American Political Science Review*, 61 (1967), pp. 25–38.

itself. A home, a family, and friends *are* the nation which earns the child's earliest loyalty. Only as a teen-ager is pride in being American related to specifically political things. Moreover, young children find it hard to separate loyalty to country from loyalty to God—because the daily pledge of allegiance to the flag so strongly resembles prayer in solemnity and content (both mention God).

Similarly, they report that attitudes toward political authority, as embodied in the first focus of awareness, the President, are generalized from attitudes toward parental authority. Such authority, moreover, appears to be idealized: ". . . children tend to view all significant and approved authority, political or otherwise, as similar to an ideal parental model." Presumably, this idealization allays the anxieties of the helpless child; he conjures up an image of someone strong enough to protect him who, at the same time, would never hurt him. Also, this idealization may partially result from the alleged tendency of American parents to hide the flaws of the system from their children.

Despite the fact that many American children identify with one of the two major parties, they nonetheless have internalized the norm of bipartisan support for the winner, making orderly political succession possible. Yet the child is not the mirror image of his parents, nor is one generation ever identical to its predecessor in political dispositions. After examining several factors which promote political change through voting in national elections, Herbert H. Hyman summarizes evidence that parental influence decreases as the child grows up and as peers, media, and other agencies exert competing influences on the individual's voting and ideological preferences.

Middleton and Putney find that defection from the party of one's parents is especially likely among children who claim extremely indulgent or permissive upbringing from parents who are highly involved in politics. It would make little sense for the child to express opposition to his parents on a matter which hardly concerns them. It is important to note here that most children—the overwhelming majority—keep their parents' partisan orientation and, further, that the "rebels" of adolescence merely switch to the opposite party; they rarely (if ever) become revolutionaries.

In their study of state legislators, Eulau, Buchanan, Ferguson, and Wahlke illustrate the point that diversity in background may nonetheless result in similar political roles. There is no strict one-to-one correspondence between one's political experience from the cradle to the grave on the one hand, and the holding of legislative office—

except for winning at least one election. The major sources of political interest among state legislators are varied and may occur at almost any age.

In a later study, using almost the same data, Prewitt, Eulau, and Zisk[6] made two major findings regarding whether the legislator (or city councilman) acquired his initial interest in politics as an adult or beforehand. Those who acquired an interest as adults came from a less intensely involved and politically rich environment, whereas those whose interest arose earlier had less specific and pragmatic attachments to their office. But the time of initial political interest was not related to differences in public decision-making orientations. From these findings, the authors inferred that "intervening between initial political socialization and incumbent behavior are political experiences that condition subsequent behavior irrespective of factors associated with initial socialization."[7]

Almond and Verba[8] found that in each of five nations a feeling of competence on the job was more closely related to a feeling of competence in politics than was a feeling of (recalled) competence in childhood or in school. Taken together, these two studies remind us that much political socialization may occur after childhood.

[6] Kenneth Prewitt, Heinz Eulau, and Betty H. Zisk, "Political Socialization and Political Roles," *Public Opinion Quarterly*, 30 (1966–1967), pp. 569–582.
[7] Prewitt, Eulau, and Zisk, p. 582.
[8] Gabriel A. Almond and Sidney Verba, *The Civic Culture* (Princeton, N.J.: Princeton University Press, 1963), pp. 370–373.

7 *Assumptions about the Learning of Political Values*

ROBERTA SIGEL

Every society that wishes to maintain itself has as one of its functions the socialization of the young so that they will carry on willingly the values, traditions, norms, and duties of their society. The newborn child is not born socialized. Socialization is a learning process. Such learning, however, is not limited to the acquisition of the appropriate knowledge about a society's norms but requires that the individual so makes these norms his own—internalizes them—

From Roberta Sigel, "Assumptions About the Learning of Political Values," *Annals of the American Academy of Political and Social Science* 361 (1965), pp. 1–9. Reprinted with the permission of author and publisher.

that to him they appear to be right, just, and moral. Having once internalized the society's norms, it will presumably not be difficult for the individual to act in congruence with them. A politically organized society has the same maintenance needs and consequently has an additional function: the political socialization of the young. Political socialization is the gradual learning of the norms, attitudes, and behavior accepted and practiced by the ongoing political system. For example, members of a stable democratic system are expected to learn to effect change through elections, through the application of group practice, rather than through street riots or revolutions.

> Viewed this way political socialization would encompass *all* political learning, formal and informal, deliberate and unplanned, at every stage of the life cycle, including not only explicitly political learning but also normally nonpolitical learning which affects political behavior, such as the learning of politically relevant social attitudes and the acquisition of politically relevant personality characteristics.[1]

The goal of political socialization is to so train or develop individuals that they become well-functioning members of the political society. While the definition of a well-functioning member will vary with the political system—from obedient passive subject in one system to active participating citizen in another—a well-functioning citizen is one who accepts (internalizes) societ's political norms and who will then transmit them to future generations. For without a body politic so in harmony with the ongoing political values the political system would have trouble functioning smoothly and perpetuating itself safely. And survival, after all, is a prime goal of the political organism just as it is of the individual organism.

At no time in history has the importance of successful political socialization been demonstrated more dramatically than today. Old and new nations today are faced with the problem of rapid political change. This change has brought about disruption of old familial social patterns, ideological orientations, and economic conditions, to name but a few. Such change—like change in general—is always fraught with tension, discomfort, and disequilibrium. If it proceeds with a minimum of these, all is well for the political system. But the danger always exists that the tensions are more than the system can endure. Chances are that one of the factors which contribute to relatively tension-free change—and hence to system stability—is

---

[1] Fred I. Greenstein, "Political Socialization," article prepared for *International Encyclopedia of the Social Sciences* (in preparation), offprint p. 1.

the successful political socialization of its members. One of the many difficulties besetting the newly developed nations is precisely this one: how to quickly train or socialize young and old alike so that they will internalize the norms of the new nation and thus assure its survival. And even for the older, stabler nations this is an important task, for they are confronted with the problem of how to insure the loyalty and engagement of their members in the face of rapid political, technological, and social changes and in the presence of governments ever growing in complexity, geographical distance, and general impersonality. To the extent, for example, that in a modern industrialized nation the citizen finds political decisions to have become increasingly complex, technical, and difficult to understand, the danger exists that the citizen will lose his touch with the political system, that he will become disengaged, apathetic, or even alienated. An apathetic citizen in times of crisis, even in times of hardship and political or economic setbacks, forms a very shaky foundation for any political system. The system cannot count on his active support or loyalty. An alienated citizen is an even greater threat to the system, since he can become its active foe. Tanks and bayonets can and do keep disloyal citizens subdued but they can at best maintain an uneasy peace. It is perhaps no exaggeration to say that a nation's stability and survival depends in large measure on the engagement of its members.

No wonder that both philosopher and practicing politician as long ago as Plato—and probably long before that—have devoted thought and effort to the question of how to bring about such engagement. Such practitioners and philosophers, however, did not call the training process political socialization; rather they called it civic education, lessons in patriotism, training for citizenship, or character-training. Every one of these terms indicates that political values and attitudes are acquired, not inborn—that they are the result of a learning process. The reason we today prefer to call this learning process political socialization rather than civic education is that the latter has too deliberate a connotation. It presumes that system-appropriate political values are acquired as a result of deliberate indoctrination, textbook learning, conscious and rational weighing of political alternatives, and the like. It seems to assume that there is a definite point in time—a certain grade in school—when such learning can profitably start and a certain point when it is completed. This view is far too naive and narrow; it completely ignores what we know about the way in which people go about "learning" society's norms. For instance, it ignores the fact that much of this norm-internalization goes on casually and imperceptibly—most of the time in fact without our ever being aware that it is going on. It proceeds so smoothly precisely because we are unaware of it. We take the norms for granted, and it does not occur to us to question them. What Cantril has to say about the learning of religious norms would probably apply with equal force to the learning of political norms.

> The relative uniformity of a culture from one generation to another, the usual slow rate of change, is clear indication that many norms of the culture are uncritically accepted by a large majority of the people. . . . For the norms of society are by no means always merely neutral stimuli from which the individual may pick and choose as he pleases, which he may regard as good or bad, as right or wrong when the spirit moves him. Most of them have already been judged by society, by the individual's predecessors, when he first experiences them. When people learn about a specific religion they generally learn at the same time that it is the "best" or that it is the "true" religion.[2]

Easton and Dennis graphically describe the uncritical way in which norms are accepted:

> In many ways a child born into a system is like an immigrant into it. But where he differs is in the fact that he has never been socialized to any other kind of system. . . . He learns to like the government before he really knows what it is.[3]

No doubt this is the reason why for young boys in an American summer camp a word like *freedom* was not a natural stimulus but one evoking positive feelings while the word *power* brought mixed reactions.[4] American society had prejudged for them and told them that freedom is a good thing. It had told them that when they had been much younger than they were then, when they had had no basis—or desire—to question the accuracy of such information.

And if such learning takes place at "every life cycle," then obviously we cannot be content with studying adults only, but we must look at adolescents and even children to see what values and norms

[2] Hadley Cantril, *The Psychology of Social Movements* (New York: John Wiley & Sons, 1963), p. 6.
[3] David Easton and Jack Dennis, "The Child's Image of Government," *The Annals of the American Academy of Political and Social Science,* 361 (1965), pp. 57, 56.
[4] These observations are drawn from lengthy, unstructured interviews conducted at a Young Men's Christian Organization camp by Eugene B. Johnson and Roberta S. Sigel (Report to be published later).

they acquire which may have a bearing on later adult political behavior. . . .

In fact, . . . political socialization is a learning process which begins very early and is most influenced by the same agents or forces which influence all social behavior: first and foremost, the family; then socially relevant groups or institutions, such as school, church, and social class; and finally—last but not least—society at large and the political culture it fosters. . . . [M]uch of this learning is incidental to other experiences: it is acquired in a subtle, nondeliberate way, often in a context which seems totally void of political stimuli yet is often rife with political consequences.

Because the consequences are political, political scientists recently have begun to ask questions such as: How and when is such learning acquired? Who most influences the young? What is the content of political socialization across cultures and subcultures? What are the consequences for the political system of different socialization processes and contents? Probably the least researched of all these questions is the one concerning the acquisition of learning. Unfortunately, political socialization studies are not yet sufficiently plentiful—nor sufficiently learning-oriented—to chart for us a detailed, empirically derived map which illustrates just how the above agents and institutions go about "socializing" the young. In the absence of such a map it seems safe to proceed from the assumption that political learning, like other social learning, falls into two broad categories: learning which is the result of deliberate conscious teaching and learning which is acquired incidentally and almost unbeknown to the learner himself (or even unbeknown to the teacher). Deliberate teaching may be further subdivided into formalized and informal teaching. Civic education in public schools would be an example of formal teaching while a father's talk to his son about the merits or demerits of trade unions would be an example of informal deliberate teaching.

Important though deliberate indoctrination is, it is probable that incidental learning—precisely because it is incidental—has a more lasting effect on the acquisition of political values and behavior. Incidental learning can perhaps also be further subdivided into the learning of politically relevant "lessons" and into the learning of social values which in and of themselves are not political but which carry in themselves the potentials for later political orientation. Incidental political learning can be acquired in a variety of ways. At times it may be the by-product of observation—watching a public official accept a bribe affords a youngster a certain view of the rectitude of government officials. Observations such as these can lead to political cynicism which in turn seems to be closely tied to political apathy, alienation, and the like. Incidental learning can also be acquired in the course of overhearing adult conversations. Wylie observed that French children in the Vaucluse constantly hear

> adults referring to government as a source of evil and to the men who run it as instruments of evil. There is nothing personal in this belief. It does not concern one particular government . . . it concerns government everywhere and at all times.[5]

Little wonder that Pinner found that French (as well as Belgian) youths had rather cynical attitudes toward politics and public officials. He attributes these attitudes, among other things, to parental child-rearing practices and makes a persuasive case demonstrating this.[6] Perhaps another explanation for children adopting parental political views can be found in the nature of the parent-child relationship. The child trusts his parents' judgments. As a rule, the young child who hears his parents voice political opinions has no personal information from which to judge the wisdom of parental opinions. In the South, for instance, he may never have asked a Negro if, indeed, he is as happy with segregation as his parents claim him to be. But the child sees no reason to doubt his parents' claim. He has accepted their standards on all other matters, why not on politics as well? Another important incidental way in which young people become politically socialized is, of course, life itself and the experience it brings to bear on youths. No Negro youth needs social studies classes to tell him that discrimination is condoned in wide sectors of American life. If, in addition, some close friends or relatives had in vain tried to fight such discrimination and perhaps had lost their livelihood or even lives in the process, it is quite possible that the political lesson learned from life experience for such a youngster will be that the safest way to get along is to be politically nonengaged, passive, and indifferent.

The second type of incidental political learning to which we referred involves social values, notions of morality, and the like, which are not per se political but which may well influence how political stimuli are perceived and internalized. For example, a child is taught to save part of his allowance for a weekly donation to the foreign

[5] Lawrence Wylie, *Village in the Vaucluse* (Cambridge, Mass.: Harvard University Press, 1951), p. 208.
[6] Frank A. Pinner, "Parental Overprotection and Political Distrust," *The Annals of the American Academy of Political and Social Science*, 361 (1965), pp. 58–70.

missions of his church. If he is told it is his Christian duty to help those less fortunate than himself and that their misfortune is not of their own making, he has received some deliberate indoctrination into the norms governing charity. On the surface, such deliberate indoctrination on the part of his family has no political implications. But it is not hard to see how such attitudes can later on predispose a person to develop attitudes with respect to governmental welfare measures, social security, and taxation. Similarly, what a family teaches its young about the evil of or the justification for violence and aggression carries in it the seeds for later views on capital punishment, war and peace, and a host of other political issues.

Nor must we overlook that the *manner* in which a child becomes socialized is as important as the content itself. Adorno *et al.*[7] found that American college youth with pronounced Fascist tendencies almost invariably came from homes where they had been treated harshly and with little respect, where they had been given little opportunity to express themselves, to make their own decisions, and the like. The homes did not espouse fascism; they merely failed to provide the youth with the atmosphere and opportunity to develop democratic, cooperative skills. Thus *the how as well as the what* of the familial socialization process contributes to political socialization in that it may or may not teach the child the skills which will facilitate adult political effectiveness. Lucian Pye in his study of Burma illustrates the all-pervasive political consequences of political socialization. Referring to general methods of socializing, he relates that the very young Burmese child is treated most indulgently. The school-age child is treated inconsistently but is expected to be totally submissive, passive, and yielding.

> He is not, however, given a clear set of standards of performance, the achievement of which might yield predictable rewards. The parents make few demands for achievement; indeed, there appears to be very little in the Burmese that would produce . . . a high sense of the need for achievement. . . . He learns only that he should avoid as best he can becoming in any sense a nuisance. He thus tends to expect security from being subservient and yielding to all who are his superiors.[8]

[7] T. W. Adorno, Else Frenkel-Brunswik, D. J. Levinson, and R. N. Sanford, *The Authoritarian Personality* (New York: Harper, 1950).
[8] Lucian W. Pye, *Politics, Personality, and Nation-Building* (New Haven: Yale University Press, 1962), pp. 182–183.

In a childhood setting like the Burmese the child never learns to express his own ideas, to participate in decision-making. Nor does he gain any confidence in himself. Yet self-confidence and some such skills as experience in participation, discussion, or decision-making are skills which are essential for people who wish to become actively involved in politics.[9]

The general *Weltanschauung* which the Burmese child learns during childhood further adds to his liabilities when it comes to the task of nation-building. For example, he is taught that only members of the family can be trusted and to have "unrestrained suspicion of strangers."[10] Consequently, he finds it difficult to work together with others and "to perform effectively in any organizational context."[11] Pye, in fact, bases many of his gloomy prognoses for Burma's chance for nation-building on the political effects of the nonpolitical aspects of childhood socialization. The Almond-Verba five-nations study[12] . . . has offered clear evidence that home atmosphere and adult political competence are closely interwoven. By and large, those people in the five nations became active, participating citizens who at home had been given the opportunity to express their opinion, make their own decisions, and the like. Litt comments on the fact that immigrant children and lower-class children are often given fewer opportunities in school to learn political skills, such as debating and running student governments, than are upper-class children in more exclusive schools.[13] This may, in part, explain why members of the working class are significantly less active in United States adult political life than are those of the upper middle class.

In summary, then, we can say that the child learns from adults the philosophical, social, and political values (not to mention outright political opinions) and the social and political skills with which to act upon these values. He acquires most of these without being aware that he is learning or that there may be other lessons with other

[9] Angus Campbell, Philip Converse, Warren E. Miller and Donald Stokes, *The American Voter* (New York: John Wiley & Sons, 1960), pp. 326–328, have shown that a sense of efficacy correlates highly with political participation.
[10] Pye, *op. cit.*, p. 205.
[11] *Ibid.*, p. 186.
[12] Gabriel Almond and Sidney Verba, *The Civic Culture* (Princeton, N.J.: Princeton University Press, 1963), chap. xi.
[13] Edgar Litt, "Educational and Political Enlightenment in America," *Annals of the American Academy of Political and Social Science*, 361 (1965), pp. 32–39, and see also his "Civic Education, Community Norms, and Political Indoctrination," *American Sociological Review* 28 (1963), pp. 69–75.

morals to be learned. More of the learning probably proceeds in a casual, nonpolitically charged setting than does in a deliberately political one.

There is, however, also an *essentially personal basis* for political behavior. This basis is furnished by personality. The authors of *The Authoritarian Personality* found that Americans with marked Fascist and ethnocentric political views have certain personality characteristics in common which are not as commonly found among people of more democratic persuasions. The origin for personality development is no doubt to be found in the socialization experience, but, once developed, personality does make a contribution all of its own to the articulation of political attitudes and behaviors. Historians have frequently commented on the extent to which Woodrow Wilson's stern idealism and uncompromising internationalism were rooted in his personality problems.[14] . . . Robert Lane clearly documents how political liberalism is for some college students a way of solving personal problems.[15] The authors of *The American Voter* pointed out that people who are well adjusted and feel effective tend to differ significantly in political orientation from people who are not so adjusted.[16] Studying the views of ten men on the subject of Soviet Russia leads Smith, Bruner, and White to conclude:

> The Russias to which our ten men were reacting were different objects, differently composed. That these objects of opinion shared common features reflecting world events and constancies in the information environment is evident. But the first and most striking impression . . . was that the Russia to which each referred was a conception selectively fashioned, a reflection of individuality.[17]

In short, people with different personality structures simply perceive the political world differently; their perceptions (opinions) are to some extent a reflection or extension of their personality. Thus, although political values are learned by the child at a very early age and tend to be in harmony with his important reference groups (notably the family), personality accounts for some of the variation in

[14] This interpretation is most fully developed by Alexander L. and Juliette L. George, *Woodrow Wilson and Colonel House: A Personality Study* (New York: Dover, 1956).

[15] Robert E. Lane, "The Need To Be Liked and the Anxious College Liberal," *Annals of the American Academy of Political and Social Science*, 361 (1965), pp. 71–80.

[16] Campbell *et al.*, *op. cit.*, pp. 326–328.

[17] M. Brewster Smith, Jerome S. Bruner, and Robert W. White, *Opinions and Personality* (New York: John Wiley and Sons, 1964), p. 244.

political beliefs. However, in a stable political system—personality differences notwithstanding—great numbers of people seem to be in consensual agreement on political norms, and these norms tend to be designed to perpetuate existing arrangements. Political socialization, in other words, is essentially a conservative process facilitating the maintenance of the *status quo* by making people love the system under which they are born.

The above discussion concentrated on the influence of adult institutions or adults over youth. It is, of course, patently clear that adults in turn are not independent agents who choose and pick what values they wish to transmit to the young; rather, adults have themselves been influenced—if not actually molded—by the political system and what it rewards and supports; or, as Greenstein points out . . . : "The political and social systems . . . provide the socializing environment."[18]

The essentially conservative effect of political socialization should not lead one, however, to equate it with complete or nearly complete changelessness. In none but the most static systems is the political value system transmitted completely intact from generation to generation. As generational and group needs change, values, too, do change. It must always be borne in mind that the political world of one generation differs from that of the next. The external and technological changes of modern society, for example, bring with them gradual or sudden changes in political values which then get transmitted as part of the socialization process. During the war many mothers went to work in defense plants. Today the acute need for women workers has passed, but working mothers have become part of the American scene. Consequently, young people are beginning to accept women as part of the working force to an extent their fathers never did—so much so that in 1964 a woman unsuccessfully competed for the Presidential candidacy without many protests that politics was strictly man's business. The gradual abandonment (or dilution) of the American ideal of rugged individualism seems to have come about in response to the Great Depression and the altered economy of the twentieth century. Values thus respond to changes in the environment.

Not only are there differences in the political worlds of different generations; there are also differences within the same generation. Different social, ethnic, and religious groups perceive the political

[18] Fred I. Greenstein, "Personality and Political Socialization: The Theories of Authoritarian and Democratic Character," *Annals of the American Academy of Political and Social Science*, 361 (1965), p. 81–95.

world differently. Lipset has demonstrated that members of the working class seem less attached to values centering around individual liberty and civil rights than do members of the middle class.[19] In the 1920s Merriam and Gosnell pointed out that immigrants did not condone active political participation (such as voting) on the part of their women while immigrant men often exceeded natives in such participation.[20] The immigrants' view of appropriate political behavior was thus at variance with that of the rest of the nation (or at least with wide segments thereof). Conflict is apt to occur when the value variance between generations or between groups is large. Conflict is also apt to crop up when different agents try to socialize the same person toward different, mutually exclusive norms. Such conflict at times can amount to individual or group trauma. Witness, for example, the agony experienced by some Southern Roman Catholics when the diocese decreed the integration of the parochial schools while public schools remained segregated. Wishing to be faithful to region and religion, some Catholics found themselves in the predicament of having to choose between excommunication and social ostracism. Another type of conflict situation occurs when political reality clearly contradicts political norms taught. The child who experiences police brutality, sees school doors closed to him because of race, or observes his father pay protection money to the police (and grow prosperous) cannot easily internalize the norms taught by society at large but rather will experience culture conflict or will develop attitudes learned from his personal experience. Marvick illustrates this for the case of the Negro who is taught to believe in the American norms but not to practice them.[21] Conflict is an all too frequent experience during the socialization process. The political socialization literature, in its heavy emphasis on culture learning and consensus, so far has paid far too scant attention to the role of conflict and tension. Yet conflict and tension play crucial roles in the political socialization process—at times creative ones and at times disruptive ones. In the future we would do well to try to establish both their empirical and their conceptual linkage. For when we speak of socialization as a process by which political values are transmitted from generation to genera-

[19] Seymour Martin Lipset, *Political Man* (Garden City, N.Y.: Doubleday, 1959), pp. 231–232.
[20] Charles E. Merriam and Harold F. Gosnell, *Non-Voting: Causes and Methods of Control* (Chicago: University of Chicago Press, 1924), pp. 110–122.
[21] Dwaine Marvick, "The Political Socialization of the American Negro," *Annals of the American Academy of Political and Social Science,* 361 (1965), pp. 112–127.

tion, we must always be mindful of the fact that some values change in the process of transmission and that not all segments of society share all the values of the larger society. Conflict engenders tension among generations and among political groups and such tension in turn can lead to change. The nature of the political system (police state or democracy) and the power or strategic position of the groups in conflict will determine what forms such conflict is apt to take; whether it will lead to withdrawal from public life or to attempts to effect change. It seems reasonable to assume that for a political society to flourish in the twentieth century, political socialization must teach the young to accept conflict as a natural ingredient of the political process and to consider change as inevitable. In other words, the socialization process must be congenial to change and not just to continuity. . . . Suffice it here to say that different systems vary in the ways in which they prepare their citizens for the acceptance of political change; some resist it more and others less. It is possible to speculate that a culture based on notions such as progress and the perfectibility of life by human efforts could accept change much more readily. This would be so most particularly where the process of political socialization also equips people with the tools by which to assert themselves in demands for change. Almond and Verba elaborate on this point when they talk about the multidirectional flow of influence in socializing experiences. They contend that, due to the practice of political democracy in the United States, citizens subsequently demand the practice of democracy in school, shop, and church. Since the demand is often met, school children, workers, and others acquire practice in articulation, debate, and decision-making. These experiences in turn help them towards developing the skills with which to participate[22] in political life and either to help bring about or to accept political change. Thus the socialization process contributes not only to a society's political stability but also to change and to the strain or ease with which change takes place.

Nonetheless, the net over-all effect of political socialization is in the direction of supporting the *status quo,* or at least the major aspects of the existing political regime. "Political socialization in both stable and unstable societies is likely to maintain existing patterns."[23] And therein lies its significance for political-system survival and stability.

---

[22] Almond and Verba, *op. cit.,* chap. xi.
[23] Greenstein, *op. cit.,* p. 8.

8 *The Child's Political World*

DAVID EASTON
ROBERT D. HESS

FRAMEWORK OF ANALYSIS

Most research with regard to adult perceptions of and attitudes towards political reality has been directed to factors operating on adults as such. The underlying assumption is that what adults see and the way in which they feel and behave in politics are outcomes of variables that act upon them as full-fledged members of a political system. This paper adopts what, but for Freud, we might identify as a Platonic

Reprinted from "The Child's Political World," *Midwest Journal of Political Science* 6 (1962), by David Easton and Robert D. Hess. Copyright 1962 by Wayne State University Press.

or Rousseauan point of view. It assumes that the range of alternative behaviors open to the adult is also intimately related to his experiences as a child and that the kind of political reality the adult perceives and his attitudes about it are restricted by what he has learned during his early years.

Not that these early influences on behavior are absolute in character; under appropriate circumstances the adult is able to escape, transcend or modify his early political inheritance. In politics as in other areas of experience, so-called reality testing continues throughout life. The significance of early impressions is that those values and attitudes acquired in childhood are likely to change much more slowly than those developed through later experience, especially in maturity. If this is so, unless we know something about the values and attitudes with which a person is armed in childhood, we cannot fully understand the matrix within which he interprets and responds to the ongoing stream of political events in adulthood.

The content that is transmitted from older to younger generations in the area of politics we shall call political orientations. They consist of political knowledge, attitudes, and standards of evaluation. The processes through which a young person acquires his basic political orientations from others in his environment we shall call political socialization. Our problem is: With regard to what subjects and through what processes of socialization are basic political orientations transmitted from generation to generation in the American political system?

In response to this question we might take a scatter-shot approach, unguided by serious conceptual considerations of a political kind. We could say that we are interested in any and all types of political orientations, choose them at random, and trust to our intuitions to steer us to the most significant ones. A recent inventory of political socialization demonstrates that little research has been done in this area and that what little there is, leaves the impression of being constructed through hit or miss tactics.[1] Criteria of theoretical significance are thoroughly implicit and probably reflect a choice of problems based either on policy rather than theoretical constraints, or upon criteria extraneous to political research.

Existing inquiry in political socialization touches on two major areas. The first relates to the nature of political involvement, probing into such matters as the way in which young people acquire their

[1] H. Hyman, *Political Socialization* (Glencoe, Illinois: Free Press, 1959).

party identification, their interest in party politics, their political information, and their attitudes towards political participation. The second area deals with the direction of political involvement, that is, the acquisition of political ideologies, usually measured along right-left politico-economic scales.

It is not likely that these subjects of investigation have been selected purely by accident. From the point of view of the practical problems raised in American society today, it makes a lot of sense to be concerned with these matters. But what this would indicate is that the limited research about political socialization currently available has emerged largely out of an interest in matters posed by immediate practical considerations. How can we make better citizens out of those coming of age? How can we educate our children so that they will become better informed in politics and more highly motivated to take an interest in public affairs and to participate more actively? How can we secure them more tightly to a set of democratic beliefs?

Without pausing to debate whether a direct concern with immediate matters such as these is the best way to solve them, it is possible to adopt a quite different approach, one that would stimulate new patterns and strategies of basic research. By basic research we simply mean an effort to illuminate and nurture theory. In politics this involves an understanding and explanation of those factors that contribute to the stability of different types of political systems, their change over time, and the direction of their change, whatever the nature of these systems,—whether they are democratic or dictatorial, modern or traditional, industrial or agricultural. In this context, the study of political socialization has critical theoretical relevance.[2]

What is the role of socialization in any political system regardless for the moment of the system's particular structure or mode of operation? Socialization joins a multiplicity of other factors that contribute to the stability or change of political systems. A political system may establish itself in many ways, as through agreement or force, fission or fusion. But having done so, every system is confronted with the task of coping with the stresses imposed upon it from internal factors, from its social environment such as the economy, culture, or social

[2] For a fuller statement of this theoretical relevance see: D. Easton, "An Approach to the Analysis of Political Systems," *World Politics*, 9 (April, 1957), 383–400; and D. Easton and R. D. Hess, "Youth and the Political System," in S. M. Lipset and Leo Lowenthal (eds.), *Culture and Social Character* (Glencoe, Illinois: Free Press, 1961), pp. 226–251.

structure, or from other political systems. To maintain its integrity as a system, even while it is in process of change, it must be able to mobilize support on its own behalf continuously, or at the very least keep the members of the system in a state of indifference. Typical procedures for stimulating support include coercion, perceived satisfaction of the needs and demands of the members, generation of positive motivation and identification through manipulation of symbols, verbal and otherwise, regulation of communications, and the like.

But regardless of the specific devices any system utilizes to perpetuate itself, no system is able to function, much less maintain itself for any length of time, without educating its young politically in the broadest sense of the meaning of these terms. Either intuitively or consciously it must undertake to transmit some of its political heritage to the maturing members of the society or to construct a new heritage for them so that a system that is undergoing serious transformations may anticipate future support. The vital significance of intergenerational influence on creating support is particularly apparent, for example, in the case of newly emerging political systems. In many instances a major need is to re-shape the attitudes and values of rising generations if they are to overcome their divided or tribal loyalties and arrive at some type of national identity. Today's developed nations faced similar types of problems as they sought to establish and perpetuate themselves in the past. But the particularly peculiar character about socialization is that for all systems it is a continuous matter. Each new generation emerges upon the political scene as a *tabula rasa,* politically speaking, upon which a political system must seek to imprint its image, however varying its measure of success, if it is to persist in some form.

It is obvious that in some political systems, the degree of consensus or uniformity with regard to the basic political orientations that are transmitted across generations may be very high. This is especially likely to be the case in societies that are relatively homogeneous, as where socio-economic, ethnic, religious, and geographical divisions are minimal. It is equally apparent that some political systems are able to withstand greater cleavages in the orientations of their members than others without experiencing distress. Not all types of differences among the members of a system need constitute a threat to a system's integrity or identity.

For example, it requires no profound analysis to reveal that many systems manage to persist even in the face of far-reaching and intensive conflicts. Deep cleavages with regard to party identification, candidate choice, and issue preferences may well indicate that the members of the system have sharply opposed cognitive images of their political antagonists, use divergent criteria for evaluating parties, persons, and issues, and feel strongly but differently towards the same political leaders and parties. But such disagreement alone is not sufficient to threaten the stability or survival of a system: it may indeed be one of the conditions of self-maintenance. Whether or not cleavage leads in the direction of change will depend, rather, upon the *subject-matter or objects* with respect to which the disagreements occur. This is entirely aside from any question about the intensity and duration of differences or their organization within the system; that is, we assume these to be held constant.

From the point of view of factors contributing to the maintenance or change of a system, there are three major objects with respect to which the extent of consensus or cleavage may prove to be significant. We shall call these the government, the regime, and the political community.[3] *Government* refers to the occupants of those roles through which the day-to-day formulation and administration of binding decisions for a society are undertaken. *Regime* is used to identify the slower changing formal and informal structures through which these decisions are taken and administered, together with the rules of the game or codes of behavior that legitimate the actions of political authorities and specify what is expected of citizens or subjects. The *political community* represents the members of a society looked upon as a group of persons who seek to solve their problems in common through shared political structures.

These objects or subject-matters towards which political orientations may be directed constitute three different analytic levels of a political system with respect to which consensus or cleavage may occur. Given the type of political system, it makes a profound difference whether consensus prevails with respect to any or each of the levels. In a democratic system, dispute concerning the occupants of governmental roles and their policies is common and expected; only under very special circumstances will such differences undermine the system as a whole. In a totalitarian system, however, governmental differences typically threaten the regime, although they may have little effect on the political community. But in numerous political systems, such as those characterized by segmentary lineage structures,

---

[3] *Ibid.* for an elaboration of these concepts.

Table 1:   Types of Political Orientations

Levels of a Political System	BASIC POLITICAL ORIENTATIONS		
	Knowledge	Values	Attitudes
Community Regime Government			

it is common for sharp cleavage over governmental authorities to leave the regime undisturbed but to lead to the fission of the community and the hiving off of one or more of the antagonists to form independent political systems.[4]

The identification of these analytically separate levels of a political system together with the three types of political orientations provides a way of conceptualizing research with regard to political socialization. We are freed from the dictates of fugitive policy imperatives or the impulse to explore a random variety of political attitudes, ideas, and values as they are acquired by maturing members of the system.

When presented in tabular form, this classification offers us a set of nine cells each of which represents a type of orientation acquired by each succeeding generation in a political system. Consensus and cleavage in the area of each cell is postulated as significant for the maintenance and change of a political system, depending upon the specific kind of system being examined and the circumstances under which we find it.[5]

---

[4] This unusual and unnoticed characteristic of some primitive political systems is discussed in D. Easton, "Political Anthropology," in B. J. Siegel (ed.), *Biennial Review of Anthropology* (Stanford: Stanford University Press, 1959).

[5] A final point about our theoretical underpinnings. "Maintenance of a system" as used here is not a static concept. We view political life as an ultrastable system of behavior. Unlike conventional interpretations suggested by equilibrium analysis, political systems normally do not respond supinely to the factors operating on them by tending to return to old or move to new positions of equilibrium. Rather, a political system is here interpreted as capable of purposively and selectively acting upon its internal and external social environment, thereby modifying itself, its environment or both in an effort to achieve its goals. Hence we can describe its behavior as ultrastable. It has built-in ways of changing its course of action and may even go so far as to transform its characteristic modes of behavior. In this positive and creative way it may be able to maintain its continuity at one or another of the three levels.

In this theoretical context, the current overemphasis in socialization research on attitudes and behavior related to party position, political ideology, and voting choices tends to freeze inquiry at the governmental level. It thereby serves to distract attention from other important aspects of socialization, if it does not conceal them entirely. In favor of problems at the governmental level, we are prone to neglect the need to understand the varying kinds of basic orientations members of a system acquire with regard to the regime and political community.

For example, one vital determinant affecting the probability of a system persisting over time consists of the kinds of attachments or sentiments (attitudes) towards the regime and community induced in young people through the processes of socialization. We have little understanding of the nature of this attachment, its variations, and its developmental pattern as the child matures. Although this is only one among a multitude of new perspectives suggested by this theoretical formulation, it is critical in the functioning of a political system. We shall now turn to an examination of the light that some empirical research we have under way can shed on the nature of these attachments and the underlying socializing processes.

THE FORMATIVE YEARS IN POLITICS

The following analysis is based on extensive pre-testing data collected over the last five years and most recently in connection with a national study of over twelve thousand elementary school children in selected areas of political socialization. The results of the pre-testing reported here involve certain limitations. For example, they do not take into account important variations due to ethnicity, religion, region, educational systems, family political background, and the like, characteristics that will receive considerable attention in our final study. But our preliminary data do yield some important impressions worth opening up for discussion at this early stage in our research, especially with regard to trends and possible relationships among significant variables.

Existing research on young people has put its main emphasis on the adolescent during his high school years (ages 14–17), perhaps on the assumptions that it is only the older child who displays the first glimmerings of an interest in politics and that this is where political development is likely to occur. Our preliminary investigations bear out neither of these premises. Every piece of evidence indicates that the child's political world begins to take shape well before he even enters elementary school and that it undergoes the most rapid change during these years.

A little-recognized fact is that political learning gets a good start in the family during the pre-school period. When the child first asks his parents a question typical in our society: "Daddy, who pays the policeman?" or "Why can't you park your car there?" and when the father replies: "The city or mayor pays him," or "It is against the law to park there," the child has here received from a trusted source an early and important introduction to politics broadly conceived. In effect he is being gently exposed to the notions that in the given regime there is a difference between public and private sectors of life, that there is a need to obey rules and regulations regardless of individual whim or desire, and that there exists some higher authority outside the family to which even all-powerful parents are subject. Through indirect and casual ways like these, the child at a tender age begins to build up his conception of political life. This is so even though, according to our preliminary data, the words *politics* and *politician* usually do not become part of his vocabulary until he is 11 or 12 years old and even though politics has a relatively low salience compared to school, sports, and other play activities and interests.

Our pre-testing also suggests that by the time the child has completed elementary school, many basic political attitudes and values have become firmly established. What is even more important, and dramatically contrary to expectations and implications of existing literature, it appears that by the time the child enters high school at the age of 14, his basic political orientations to regime and community have become quite firmly entrenched so that at least during the four years of high school little substantive change is visible. In that period his own interest in politics may be stimulated—although our data indicate that the high-point in reported political interest may occur in 7th and 8th grades—and, as we would expect, he learns much more about the structure and practices of government and politics. Formal education bolstered by the mass media is likely to be the source of such knowledge. But for most young people, there is little evidence that fundamental attitudes and values with respect to the regime and political community are any different when they leave high school than they were upon entrance.

The truly formative years of the maturing member of a political system would seem to be the years between the ages of three and thirteen. It is this period when rapid growth and development in political orientations take place, as in many areas of non-political socialization.

ATTACHMENT TO THE POLITICAL COMMUNITY

By the time children have reached second grade (age 7) most of them have become firmly attached to their political community. Imperceptibly they have learned that they are Americans and that, in a way they find difficult to define and articulate, they are different from members of other systems. As we find in most other aspects of the child's political world, and as we would expect, the responses are highly colored with emotion and occur long before rational understanding or even the capacity to rationalize political orientations are evident.

Thus the sentiments of most children with respect to their political community are uniformly warm and positive throughout all grades, with scarcely a hint of criticism or note of dissatisfaction. When interviewed about where they would like to live for one week, a year or the rest of their lives, some children favor travel for a shorter or longer time. But in most cases it is beyond their capacity to imagine themselves living anywhere other than the United States for the rest of their lives. And a high proportion would not even like to take permanent leave of the immediate places where they happen to live.

One of the processes contributing to this outcome we could easily have anticipated. The feelings initially aroused by immediate but diffuse social objects are extended to include specifically political ones. It would appear that national sentiment, loyalty, patriotism or love of country—all ingredients of attachment to political community—may rest on such unpretentious foundations as these.

In the development of this attachment, the child early learns to admire and cherish those things and persons that are local and close, that form part of his personal experience and are therefore meaningful to him, and that in most cases represent undifferentiated social objects. Thus when the political context of the question is not concealed from the child, and he is asked to list the three best things about America, children in the lower grades (ages 7–9) consistently speak about such general social objects as their schools, the beauty of their country, its animals and flowers, and the goodness and cleanliness of its people. Very few politically differentiated items appear. Those that do, convey pride in the President, the policeman, the flag, and freedom.[6] The President and policeman are two authority figures with which the child is quite familiar and, at the early grades, just about the only two for most children. Only one impersonal abstract symbol, that of freedom, regularly appears at this age level. The meaning attributed to it is quite non-political and diffuse, however. A person is conceived to be free when he can do whatever he wishes, an appealing thought to the adult dominated child.

Only as the child grows older do the warm feelings already generated with respect to these things of personal significance spread to impersonal political symbols, to differentiated political objects, and to the broader and more inclusive aspects of the political community. Thus although in the higher grades (ages 12–13) children continue to mention schools, the moral worth of people in the United States, and the like, by that time reference to items such as these declines sharply. The majority of responses to the same question now include such specifically political items of an abstract or impersonal character as democracy, government, voting, and elaborations of freedom to mean freedom of speech, press, religion, and choice of occupation. The same pride and positive feelings that were displayed more diffusely at an earlier age are now also invested in a distinctively political direction. The feelings stimulated by the concrete, personally experienced part of the child's immediate world seem to be transferred, as the child grows older, to abstract political symbols. "America" itself as a symbol of the political community now becomes laden with specifically political content, and an early non-political attachment to general social aspects of the community is transformed into a highly political one.

A second process joining forces with fondness for the immediate concrete environment quite unexpectedly proved to be religious in nature. In a secular society that adults have frequently described as essentially materialistic and where adults have sought to maintain a clear separation between church and state, there was little reason for suspecting that in the early grades religious sentiments would be instrumental in generating support for the political community. As it turns out, however, not only do many children associate the sanctity and awe of religion with the political community, but to ages 9 or 10 they sometimes have considerable difficulty in disentangling God and country.

[6] Even though children in grade 2 are already able to associate themselves with the label Republican or Democrat, this touches on the regime rather than the community level and will be discussed later.

In many schools it is customary to pledge allegiance to the flag each morning as classes begin or at other regular intervals.[7] The pledge is brief but it is said in a formal, solemn atmosphere. Levity brings down sanctions from the school authorities and sincerity is approved. The exact procedures associated with the pledge may vary. In some cases the flag is saluted; in others, the right hand is held over the heart. But the repetition of the pledge assumes the character of a ritual.

When the children in grades two and three were interviewed around the question, "To whom do you take the pledge of allegiance?" the answers were distributed among flag, country, and for the single largest minority, God. Not only do we find the explicit statement that God is the object of the pledge, but when probed with regard to its functions, many children interpreted the pledge as a prayer. They saw it as a request either to God or to some unidentified but infinite power for aid and protection. At times it is even understood as an expression of gratitude, again to some unspecified being, for the benefits already received. Only when we reach the fourth or fifth grade in our pre-test interviews, and more rapidly thereafter, do we find a tendency for children to stress the pledge as an expression of loyalty to country, solidarity with one's fellows, and an assertion of the need to perform one's duties as a citizen. The religious theme does not disappear entirely, but over the sample it becomes subordinate to the political.

Although our limited data do not permit full interpretation of the processes at work here in linking the child to the political community and its symbols such as the flag, in all likelihood there is an association in the child's mind of the form and feeling tone of religious ritual with the political ceremony of pledging allegiance. Specific invocation of God in the pledge itself would clinch the point for the child.

Religious affect, it appears, is being displaced upon political object, less by design than by the natural assimilation of political with religious piety and ritual. We might infer that the depth and peculiar strength of religious sentiments, if only because of their early introduction to the child and numerous social sanctions enlisted in their aid, become subtly transferred to the bond with the political community. The fact that as the child grows older he may be able to sort

---

[7] "I pledge allegiance to the flag of the United States of America and to the Republic for which it stands, one nation under God, indivisible, with liberty and justice for all."

out the religious from the political setting much more clearly and restrict the pledge to a political meaning, need not thereby weaken this bond. The initial and early intermingling of potent religious sentiment with political community has by that time probably created a tie difficult to dissolve.[8]

ATTACHMENT TO THE STRUCTURE
AND NORMS OF THE REGIME

As we have seen, when we refer to the maintenance or change of a political system, it is imperative to specify the level with respect to which we are speaking. Adequate provision may be made for the persistence of the political community, but it is not at all clear that attachment at this level must necessarily include positive affect towards other levels such as the regime. As a case in point, the French metropolitan political community has remained relatively intact for an historically lengthy period even though it has witnessed the rise and fall of numerous regimes.

Undoubtedly the degree and extent of support directed to the community or to the regime will each affect the other in important ways. But if we are to understand the early sources of support for either level, it is necessary to begin by viewing them separately and independently. We therefore turn now to an examination of some of the concrete ways in which members of a political system form attachments to the structure and norms of the regime in the United States.

Our pre-testing suggests that, as with regard to the political community, in a relatively stable system such as the United States firm bonds are welded to the structure of the regime quite early in childhood. By the time children reach the 7th and 8th grades, most of them have developed highly favorable opinions about such aspects of the political structure as the Presidency, Congress, or "our government" in general. The Constitution has become something of the order of a taboo that ought not be tampered with in its basic prescriptions. Yet children know very little about the formal aspects of the regime and much less, if anything, about its informal components. How then

[8] For such political systems as we find in the USSR where religious sentiment is discouraged or in many African societies where religion is not so clearly associated with newly developing political systems, it would be interesting to search for substitute mechanisms that come into play in the early years of the child to mold his sentiments with respect to the political community.

do they acquire and develop ties to the structure of a regime about which they have negligible and blurred information and equally little understanding?

Our data indicate several things. First, what is most apparent to most children in the realm of politics is the existence of an authority outside the family and school. Second, initially and continuously through the elementary school years, this external authority is specifically represented in the Presidency and the policeman, a local appointed official. Although as the child grows older he becomes increasingly aware of other institutions of authority, such as the courts, Congress, and local elected officials, the President and the policeman remain extremely visible. And third, emotional rather than rational processes are at work on these cognitions. They enable children to develop favorable feelings for the presidential form of authority in the United States long before they know very much of a concrete nature about it.

Interviews and questionnaires reveal that the first point of contact children are likely to have with the overall structure of authority is through their awareness of the President.[9] When children at a young age are asked in separate items about who makes the laws, runs the country, helps the country most, best represents the government, or, in a political context, who helps you most, the responses consistently favor the President. Authority figures at the lower reaches of the regime, such as the policeman or mayor, will be very familiar to most younger children. On occasion the Senate, Congress or the courts will cross their cognitive horizon. But in general, between the polar extremes of the policeman and the President, it is the rare child in the early grades who sees anything but a truly blooming, buzzing political confusion. For most children at this stage the President *is* the political structure. Even where the child knows about the Vice-President, he is frequently seen as an aid to the President; and the Senate and House of Representatives as well are considered to be subordinate and subject to the orders of the President.

In the acquisition of attachments to the regime as a whole, it turns out to be critical that there is this well defined point in the political structure that is highly visible and important for the children, whether young or old. Without it or some comparable institution

---

[9] For similar findings in an important contribution to research on political socialization see F. I. Greenstein, "The Benevolent Leader: Children's Images of Political Authority," *American Political Science Review*, 54 (December, 1960), 934–943.

we might have difficulty in understanding how the child would be able to formulate some introductory, if crude conception of political authority and some early feelings with regard to its worth. It provides the child with a means for "seeing" the structure in a clear and simple way and possibly identifying with it. Although in the United States the Presidency may be the vehicle for these purposes, in other systems of course we might suspect it to be a king, a chief or a great leader.

In an earlier paper[10] we have shown that it is likely that the child's attachment to the structure of the regime is mediated through the attitudes he acquires towards this focal point, the Presidency. From grade 2, the earliest grade it was feasible to test, most children in a group of approximately 350 reported highly positive feelings about the President. When children through grade 8 were asked to compare the President to most men with regard to such personal and moral characteristics as honesty, friendliness, overall goodness, and liking for others, and such performance qualities as his knowledge and application to work, the vast preponderance see him as measuring up to most men or surpassing them. And even when father was compared to the President with regard to these characteristics, few rate father higher, and in some role performance qualities they rank him even lower. In subsequent tests of other children, they uniformly see the President possessed of all the virtues: benign, wise, helpful, concerned for the welfare of others, protective, powerful, good, and honest.

It is not surprising to find that a high percentage of children hold as strongly positive feelings about their father as they do about the President. What is unexpected is that even though the President is subject to intense partisan dispute, children should have at least as high an opinion of the President, and an even higher one with regard to some qualities. As we have shown,[11] part of this can be explained by the increasing capacity of the child, as he grows older, to differentiate the role of President from that of father. But part is probably a function of other socializing processes at work.

These varied processes concern what we have found to be typical ways in which children may respond to all figures of authority. In the first place, children display a strong tendency to generalize attitudes developed in connection with authority in their immediate experience to perceived authority beyond their knowledge and direct

---

[10] R. D. Hess and D. Easton, "The Child's Changing Image of the President," *Public Opinion Quarterly*, 24 (Winter, 1960), 632–644.

[11] *Ibid.*

contact. The authority figures with which they have earliest and most intimate contact are of course their parents, and it is this image of authority that they subsequently seem to transfer to political figures that cross their vision. The child not only learns to respect and admire political authorities, but with regard to many characteristics sees them as parents writ large.

But more than that is involved. As noted already, maturing children develop the capacity to discriminate between qualities that are appropriate to the role of the President, and they see the latter as quite different from father in these respects. But with regard to those qualities of moral and personal worth already mentioned, even though there is a linear decline for children in successively higher grades, the absolute level of response remains quite high—at or above 50%.

These data suggest that in attributing so much personal and moral worth to both parental and political authority the child is responding not to what the authority figures are, but in terms of what he would expect them to be. Parents and President together are reported less in the image of any real parent than of one strongly reflecting the ideal expectations of our culture. Indeed additional testing that had the child compare teacher, father, President, and policeman bears out the broader hypothesis that children tend to view all significant and approved authority, political or otherwise, as similar to an ideal parental model.

The probable consequences of this idealization are apparent. In the first place, it should contribute to the ease with which maturing members of the American political system develop a strong attachment to the structure of the regime. The part that is initially visible and salient for the child represents everything that is good, beneficial, and worth cherishing. In the second place, in so far as feelings generated with respect to the Presidency as a focal point are subsequently extended to include other parts of the political structure—an area that still needs to be investigated—this may well be the path through which members of the system come to value the whole structure. If so, it would be a vital determinant contributing to the stability of the regime.

What still needs to be explained, however, is the origin of this impetus towards idealization. Here our preliminary data permit us to speculate broadly about the nature of the socializing processes.

In part, the high idealization of approved authority may reflect important psychological needs of the child. Confronted with the pervasive and inescapable authority of adults, and realistically aware of his own helplessness and vulnerability, the child must seek some congenial form of accommodation. For a small minority, rebellion, aggression, and mistrust may be the chosen avenues. But for most, adaptation is more likely to take the form of imputing to authority qualities that would permit the child to construe the authority in a most favorable light. By idealizing authority and by actually seeing it as benign, solicitous, and wise, the child is able to allay the fears and anxieties awakened by his own dependent state. A potentially threatening figure is conveniently transformed into a protector. Hence in spite of what he may learn about authority figures, about their foibles and shortcomings, he has a strong incentive to continue to idealize. As our data show, even though as they grow older fewer children hold the same high opinion of the President, the absolute level remains high. The security needs of the child in this way become an important ingredient in the socializing process.

In addition, however, the impetus to idealize authority also has its origin in the learning process itself, that is, in the attitudes children learn from adults. However little it may have been recognized, adults in the United States show a strong tendency to shelter young children from the realities of political life. In many ways it is comparable perhaps to the prudery of a Victorian era that sought to protect the child from what were thought to be the sordid facts of sex and parental conflict. In our society politics remains at the Victorian stage as far as children are concerned. Some adults—and there is reason to believe they are numerous—feel it is inappropriate to let the child know about what is often felt to be the seamy and contentious side of politics. He is too young, he will not understand, it will disillusion him too soon, awareness of conflict among adults will be disturbing, are some of the arguments raised against telling the whole truth. The child has to learn as best he can that in politics the stakes are high, passions are strong, motivations may be less than pure and altruistic, conflict is endemic, and men have the capacity to place self, party or occupation above country. Adults tend to paint politics for the child in rosier hues. And the younger the child the more pronounced is this protective tendency.

What this means is that in addition to learning political ideals from adults the child may also learn to idealize or romanticize politics. For example, some testing at the high school level (ages 14–17) indicates that romantic notions about politics are not fully or largely dissipated even by that stage. The child's inner need to create a benevolent image of authority coincides with and is thereby strongly reinforced by the partial, idealized, and idealizing view of political life communicated to him by protective adults.

But in spite of these forces working in the direction of idealization, our data do suggest that, contradictory as it may seem, at least in some areas the child is quite capable of facing up to the passions and conflict in political life and that he is equally capable of tolerating such stress without succumbing either to cynicism or to disenchantment with political authority. The area of conflict to which the child is particularly exposed at the youngest age is the presidential electoral campaign. In an age of television, it is an area which cannot be concealed from him. He is aware of the acrimony of debate over the merits of alternative candidates, and more important, he easily learns that people align themselves on different sides and that it is proper for people so to commit themselves. The child even goes further. Simultaneous with the emergence of high positive affect with regard to the President, it is quite revealing to discover that young as they are, children in the early grades learn to tolerate partisan commitment on their own part and to accept alternative partisanship on the part of others as one of the rules of the game. Partisan differences—and at times even conflict—so generated are not interpreted as hampering the acceptance of the outcome of electoral campaigns, esteem for the victor, or the legitimacy of the authority so established. This constitutes the beginning of what later in life becomes a rather complex set of attitudes and represents an introduction to a major norm of democratic society.

Most children do not become familiar with the term political party until the fourth and fifth grade at the earliest. But before this, as early as the second grade, large numbers are nevertheless able to assert a party identification. In a pre-test sample of about 700 children, a strong majority in each grade from two through eight state that if they could vote they would align themselves with either of the two major parties in the United States. Interviews around responses such as these indicate that in the early grades—the point at which party preference becomes well established—the children may be adopting party identification in much the same way that they appropriate the family's religious beliefs, family name, neighborhood location or other basic characteristics of life.

Nor do most children display partisan feelings in a purely formal way. They seem to be aware of the implications of party preferences as an expression of explicit commitment to a point of view, however superficial their understanding of this point of view may be. Thus of a pre-test sample of over 300 children, a large majority reported that they participated in a partisan spirit in the last presidential campaign by wearing candidate buttons. Most of these children who were in grades 4 through 8 responded that they did so as a way of taking sides or for purposes of helping their candidate win. A minority were less sensitive to the expression of partisan commitment involved, but said they took sides because they thought it was fun to do so, or because they were simply imitating their friends or parents. But they did feel the pressure to adopt a partisan posture, however apolitical its meaning was for them.

But partisanship does not seem to interfere with what we may interpret as the early origins of a belief in the legitimacy of political authority. When some 200 pre-test children were asked whether the candidate who loses an election should ask his followers to help the winner, an overwhelming majority beginning in the early grades and increasing with age responded in the affirmative. The dissenting minority here is of course interesting and needs to be explored.

Thus even though the child idealizes political authority as the result of the socializing processes to which he is exposed, at the same time he acquires regime norms that make it possible for him to tolerate comfortably the campaign conflict surrounding the choice of these authorities. As a result, the attachment to authority achieved through the mechanism of idealization is not disturbed or displaced by electoral passions and cleavage. The importance of this type of socialization for the stability of a democratic regime needs no elaboration.

CONCLUSION

We have touched on only a few selected topics of socialization of knowledge and attitudes with respect to two major objects, the political community and the regime. We have reported only from tentative and limited preliminary data. But what this theoretically determined approach does reveal is that processes of attachment to the political community and the regime begin at a considerably earlier age than one would expect. The political content that is socialized shows signs of being buttressed by powerful sentiments linked to religion, family, and internal needs of the dependent child. If what is learned early in life is hard to displace in later years, we have here an important increment to our understanding of the sources of stability in the American political system. Comparative research in systems experiencing considerable change and in those developing nations moving toward a unified entity for the first time should help us in better understanding the contribution of socialization to political instability and change.

9 *Political Stability or Change and the Role of Non-Family Agencies of Socialization*

HERBERT HYMAN

For the area political orientation and the specific aspect, party affiliation, we have demonstrated the *great* influence of the family on the child's behavior.[1] Moreover, some of the studies cited earlier dealt with adult voters or young voters, who were children only in the special sense of their status relative to their own parents. This, while a limitation for our earlier discussion on pre-adult socialization processes, is an especially telling advantage for our present

[1] H. Hyman, *Political Socialization* (Glencoe: The Free Press, 1959), pp. 69–84.

discussion. These studies must imply that the influence while a *non-adult* has persisted and influenced the child on into his adult life. Given the great and persistent influence, it appears that political life would move in an unchanging course—children mirroring parents, their children mirroring them, and so on into the endless future. There even seems to be other incidental data cited in these same studies which enhance this image.

> Thus, *The People's Choice* remarks that "the political homogeneity of the family may extend over several generations. Our panel members were asked, 'Do you consider that your family (parents, grandparents) have always been predominantly Democratic or predominantly Republican?' Fully three-fourths of the respondents with vote intentions in September followed the political lead of their families."[2]

> In the Michigan study, wherein it was demonstrated that the parents' party affiliation produced a corresponding party tie in the child, the elaboration of the offspring's voting history was obtained. From the retrospective report of the individual's *first* vote for the president, it is noted that "three-fourths of the people who report their first vote as going to one or the other of the *two major parties* still associated themselves to some degree with the same party." Other evidence is presented on the constancy of party attachment by asking the individual if he had *ever* thought of himself as having the contrary party tie. The inconstancy over the individual's history ranged for groups varying in strength of party identification from a minimum of zero to a maximum of 30%.[3] For the inconstant group, it is established that this was merely a temporary instability on the part of those Republicans who "strayed into the Roosevelt camp in 1932 and 1936." Individuals were also asked if they had *always* voted for the same party, and it is found that such constancy is true for about two-thirds of the voters.[4]

On the surface, the Erie County Study suggests a kind of never ending belt of parental transmission and consequent unchanging pattern of politics. Similarly, the Michigan study seems to argue the stability of adult politics starting from roots in family life. But, certainly there is something paradoxical involved, for there has been *political change* as a consequence of voting behavior. We have traced

[2] P. F. Lazarsfeld, B. Berelson, and H. Gaudet, *The People's Choice* (New York: Columbia Press, 1948), p. 142.
[3] A. Campbell, G. Gurin, and W. Miller, *The Voter Decides* (Evanston: Row Peterson, 1954), pp. 102, 103.
[4] *Ibid.*, p. 104.

the roots of stability, but where are the sources of instability and change?

First it should be noted that usually we have been examining the growth within given individuals of such political sentiments as *party affiliation and ideology.* This level of description is not the same as the level of description which deals with the *aggregate voting behavior* of the electorate in *particular* elections. There are many points of play within this larger system of national voting whereby these stable psychological phenomena could nevertheless lead to political change. These points of play within the larger system and the distinction between the two levels of description go far to resolve the paradox.

1. Lubell has suggested one such factor. Granted that children mirror their families' politics, change could come about through *differential birth* rates occurring within given classes of the population at given points in time and thereby altering the social composition of the electorate at given moments in history. Thus, without denying the psychological stability of the child's politics, Lubell argues that in the period beginning about 1900, there was a greatly expanded group of potential voters from families of immigrants, urban dwellers, and lower socio-economic groups.[5] For example, a measure of differential birth rates for political groups is available in the Michigan 1952 election study. In a special analysis of these data for the sample in Western States, De Grazia reports the number of children in school among parents of given political preferences.[6] Thus, among "strong Democrats," 34% had school age children, whereas among "strong Republicans" only 20% had school age children. Our concern is not with the specific content of Lubell's assertion, which is readily amenable to empirical treatment, but rather with the exemplification of the general argument about the distinction between psychological processes and net results in the political arena.

2. In some of the studies presented earlier, for example, *The People's Choice*, we are dealing with *current interaction* within the family in the course of a political campaign. Under such conditions, the family's

---

[5] S. Lubell, *The Future of American Politics* (New York: Harper, 1951), pp. 28–33. By extension, change could come about through differential *death* rates occurring within given classes at given points in time.

[6] A. De Grazia, *The Western Public, 1952 and Beyond* (Stanford: Stanford University Press, 1954), p. 24. The measure is, of course, not ideal since it only includes children of school age. Moreover, Lubell's theory could also demand such data for several points in time to see whether differential patterns are static or changing the political scene.

sway over the actual preference for a given *candidate* or its influence on the actual casting of a vote may be considerable. However, the phenomenon that would be of more general significance for our discussion would be the influence on the individual of socialization by a family *no longer present.* This is, after all, the essence of socialization —the *internalization* within the individual of another's views. For such phenomena, the family at best can transmit a *generalized* orientation towards a given party or a given ideology. But, the concrete voting situation involves the interplay of such ideological or party variables and specific reactions to the candidate or to the transient issues of the campaign. Consequently, the parental influences may be as previously described, but yet the emergence of especially strong issue or candidate considerations may attenuate family influence on the vote. While this would not occur frequently, it obviously can and has happened.[7]

3. Apart from the orientation toward a party or a candidate in a specific election, the parental influence is essentially to make a child have a certain *preference,* but whether these preferences are translated into the overt activity of voting may be a function of many other considerations. Consequently, political change may come about through differential patterns of turn-out in particular elections.[8]

4. Where parental patterns of preference are well established, we have documented the transmission to children. But, this is to ignore the frequency of instances where *no clear directives* come from the parents. Then, the child is so-to-speak uncommitted or perhaps committed to be uncommitted. Influences of a variety of other sorts, including transient ones, operating on this group can be a force for change. We have already alluded to instances where there are differentiated views among husband and wife with a consequent mixed effect on the child.[9] However, . . . the Michigan data . . . shows that there was a sizeable number of families who provided no partisan socialization into politics; these include families where neither parent voted or where the intensity was so minimal that the child cannot recall the politics of parents. These groups plus the families with

[7] Thus, the Michigan study which documents familial genesis of party identification also documents shifting in the Roosevelt era and in the 1952 Eisenhower election, presumably a reflection of the potency of the candidate variable. *Op. Cit.,* Chap. VII. For another demonstration of the influence of a dramatic candidate in upsetting traditional ties, see H. Hyman and P. B. Sheatsley, "The Political Appeal of President Eisenhower," *Pub. Opin. Quart.,* 17, 1953–1954, pp. 443–460.
[8] See Campbell, *et al., Op. Cit.,* for a demonstration that the act of voting in the 1952 election had little to do with party identification. *Ibid.,* Chap. VII, Table 7.11, p. 108.
[9] Hyman, *Op. Cit.,* pp. 76–84.

mixed political sentiments comprised over one-quarter of the national sample—a sizeable bloc in the determination of an election.[10]

A related phenomenon is presented in the Maccoby study. Detailed data establish that there is a small minority of families who transmit the clear directive, that they are *not* partisans, but "independents." In the Cambridge sample, this group was less than 10% in magnitude, but it is shown that their children are considerably more likely to become "independents," than children from partisan parents. However, it is also shown that such children are in part drained into the camps of the two parties. (This is, their tendency to be "independents" is not as great as the tendency of Republican or Democratic parents to produce Republican or Democratic children.) Thus, these children are more influenced by other considerations.[11]

5. We documented earlier a phenomenon which may be relevant to the problem of political change. We had observed that parental influence seems to be stronger in the transmission of party loyalty than in the transmission of the logically congruent area of ideology.[12] . . . We might suggest—without any present basis in fact—that such a disparity creates some ground for instability in voting or political behavior. If party choice were firmly rooted in an ideological context, it would presumably be better sustained. The fact that an ideology, discrepant from the *actual* and explicit goals of a party which an individual had inherited early in life, is open to other lines of development later in life may ultimately produce a conflict for him and a breakdown of his loyalty to that party.[13]

[10] Campbell, *et al., Op. Cit.,* Table 7.5, p. 99. The Table is reproduced with minor omissions as Table 17 in *ibid.,* p. 77.

[11] E. Maccoby, R. Matthews, and A. Morton, "Youth and Political Change," *Public Opinion Quarterly,* 18, 1954, Table 1, p. 27.

[12] Hyman, *Op. Cit.,* pp. 73–75.

[13] We find little evidence in the literature on this particular hypothesis. However, Maccoby does present some very interesting findings on differential changes in ideology and party preference among young voters who for other reasons are shifting away from parental party traditions. She suggests possible consequences for political instability. *Op. Cit.,* especially pp. 30–31 and p. 36. Fay and Middleton provide some suggestive evidence by comparing the scores on 5 attitude scales of college students contrasted in their father's political party. None of the differences was significant, suggesting that ideology may be inconsistent with the party loyalty transmitted. [P. Fay and W. Middleton, "Certain Factors Related to Liberal and Conservative Attitudes of College Students: II. Father's Political Preference; Presidential Candidates Favored in the 1932 and 1936 Elections," *J. Soc. Psychol.,* 11, 1940, pp. 107–119.] However, in a parallel analysis, Stagner compares scores on "Fascist Attitudes" for subjects contrasted in parents' political party affiliation and finds significant differences. R. Stagner, "Fascist Attitudes: Their Determining Conditions," *J. Soc. Psychol.,* 7, 1963, pp. 447–448.

6. Finally it should be noted that the studies presented earlier all show that a small proportion of children deviate from the views of their parents. This group provides some force for political change, and in close elections could well be crucial. The earlier findings were expressed in percentage or correlational terms and do not convey the *numbers* involved, which is the appropriate calculation in relation to elections. Maccoby conveys this latter logic nicely in the course of her analysis. She observes that the defections from the parental party allegiance are smaller in *proportion* for Democratic families, but she remarks: "In a Democratic stronghold like Cambridge, there are so many more sets of Democratic than Republican parents, that the small proportion of young people switching from Democratic to Republican party allegiance more than offsets numerically the larger proportion of young people switching from the Republican allegiance of their parents into the Democratic party."[14]

The individuals who depart from the patterns of their parents presumably are influenced by other agencies of socialization which operate in some systematic way at some points in the child's life. In addition, there may be a host of experiences . . . which intrude. Consequently, we turn to such forces and agencies.

As one model for the complex process, we might generally expect parental influence to wane somewhat as the individual grows up. He is widening his experiences and may well confront other groups presenting different norms for political conduct. Of course, these new experiences and agencies may also support the views of parents, but the patterning of life is not that uniform. Interference with the original parental guidance is bound to crop up.[15]

We turn first to the detailed examination of the studies involving intra-family correlations[16] in attitude where certain subtle findings are suggestive of the interaction of parents and other agencies of

---

[14] *Op. Cit.*, p. 27.

[15] For empirical evidence on such a developmental process in the formation of tastes and opinions about mass media, see E. Freidson, "A Prerequisite for Participation in the Public Opinion Process," *Publ. Opin. Quart.*, 19, 1955, pp. 105–111.

[16] *Correlation* is a measure of the degree to which two or more variables are associated. The greater the absolute value of the correlation coefficient (up to a maximum of $+1$ or -1 for most kinds of correlation), the closer the association. A positive coefficient means that the variables increase and decrease together. A negative coefficient means that as one variable increases, the other decreases. A zero correlation means that the variables go up and down independent of each other. In this example, the variables are *attitudes*. For the derivation, computation, and application of some measures of association, see Hubert M. Blalock, *Social Statistics* (New York: McGraw-Hill, 1960), pp. 212–358.—Eds.

socialization. Here we should expect the correlations to decline somewhat with age as other groups intrude.

In two of the studies, data are available on the intra-family agreement for children in *different age groups*. We should expect the older
children to show less agreement with their parents, because of the
wider array of influences they experience with age and independence.

> Remmers and Weltman report that the intra-family correlation for
> children in grades 9–10 is .90 whereas for children in Grades 11–12
> it is .79.[17]

> Newcomb and Svehla present data for three age groups. These groups
> all tend to be somewhat on the old side thus minimizing a real gradient
> of change; the youngest group being 19 or under, the oldest being
> 24 and over. For the two areas that have political relevance, "war"
> and "communism," the correlation between parent and child attitude
> declines slightly with age.[18]

Going back to the early work in child development, one finds
evidence from other types of studies in support of the waning influence of parents as other agencies emerge.

> Hall reports on an early study which confirms this general picture.
> About 2000 children were asked what they would do in the instance
> of a conflict between teachers and parents. Among young children,
> parental authority was preferred. A marked decline in parental au-
> thority began about age eleven and reached its maximum decline
> about age fifteen. Correspondingly there was an increase in the prefer-
> ence for teacher's authority.[19]

> Hill in his study of identification with adult figures, reports that boys,
> with age, show a declining identification with parents. However, girls
> continue to show a considerable idealization of parents.[20]

> Havighurst and Taba, using several modern variants on these tech-
> niques, report on children's ego-ideals for children living in a small
> mid-Western city.[21] Comparable data were obtained for a group of
> ten-year olds and a group of sixteen-year olds. The older group name

[17] H. H. Remmers and N. Weltman, "Attitude Inter-relationships of Youth, Their
Parents, and Teachers," *J. Soc. Psychol.*, 26, 1947, pp. 61–68.

[18] T. Newcomb and G. Svehla, "Intra-Family Relationships in Attitude," *Sociom.*,
1, 1937, pp. 180–205.

[19] G. Stanley Hall, *Adolescence* (New York: Appleton, 1914), Vol. II, p. 386.

[20] D. S. Hill, "Personification of Ideals by Urban Children," *J. Soc. Psychol.*, 1,
1930, pp. 379–392.

[21] R. Havighurst and H. Taba, *Adolescent Character and Personality* (New York:
Wiley, 1949), p. 72, 240.

fewer family figures as ego-ideals. Using different techniques, these investigators also establish the waning influence with age of familiar environment on character development. A test of the relations within the family was devised and scores were correlated with ratings of the child's moral traits. Among ten-year olds, the correlations for the different traits ranged from .5 to .8; for thirteen-year olds, from .2 to .4; for sixteen-year olds, from .2 to .3.

Using media behavior or communication as indicative of the processes, we find considerable evidence in support of the general model.

Meine reports on the tendency of children to discuss news events with family members, peers, and in school. The family remains a high source of discussion throughout all age or grade levels. However, while this agency for discussion of news remains stable, he demonstrates that the *school* and the *peers* become an increasing source of discussion of news with age.[22] Thus, the *relative* importance of parental influence is less.

Burton's early study of the growth of political knowledge provides some evidence on the problem. 255 of the Cincinnati school children were interviewed on their "civic information," and probing of their answers generally revealed the source of their knowledge. These sources were coded under various headings which for our purposes may be dichotomized into home influences vs. other influences, e.g., school, reading, etc. Moving from Grade 5 to Grade 8, the relative influence of the home as a source declines as the influence of the school increases.[23]

These early data on communication about news or political events are confirmed in the course of the large scale investigations of communication processes among youth now being conducted at Rutgers University.[24]

In the course of a large scale panel study among youth in eight schools in New Jersey the tendency of the child to discuss politics with particular other individuals, father, mother, or peers, was determined. The data presented in Table 1 were obtained from children

[22] F. J. Meine, "Radio and the Press among Young People," in P. F. Lazarsfeld and F. Stanton, eds., *Radio Research—1941* (New York: Duell, Sloan and Pearce, 1941), pp. 189–224.

[23] W. H. Burton, *Children's Civic Information 1924–1935* ("Southern California Education Monograph #7," [Los Angeles: University of Southern California Press, 1936]), pp. 275–284.

[24] The writer is indebted to Dr. and Mrs. John W. Riley for making certain unpublished materials available to him.

Table 1: The Increase with Age in Communication about Politics
to Peers as Revealed in the Rutgers Panel Study

Among Those Who Discuss	BOYS		GIRLS	
Politics, Discuss It With	1952	1954	1952	1954
Mother	34%	44%	44%	47%
Father	68	68	63	65
Friend in the grade	23	43	23	41
Friend outside the grade	15	26	13	24
$N =$	(1281)	(1127)	(1397)	(1300)

in the 9th and 10th grades in 1952, and again from these same children
two years later when they were in the 11th and 12th grades. They
show that political discussion *as such* increases with age, but the direction of such discussion increasingly goes to peers rather than to parents.
While discussion with parents does not decline in *absolute* terms, its
magnitude *relative* to other sources does decline. Other data in these
studies show that this is part of a general tendency for communication
on all topics to flow to peers with age, and politics is simply carried
along with the general trend.

Additional evidence in support of this model is available from
the Elmira study.

The agreement between father's political preference and child's vote
in 1948 is presented separately for various age groups of voters. By
contrast with the data presented thus far, all these individuals are
adult and subject to a greater flux of experience than the age groups
just described. However, in another perspective, it is clear that the
young voters, 21–25, have had less possibility of diverse experiences
than the voters in older age groups, e.g., 35–44 or 45 and over.
The data show a *progressive and continuous reduction* in parent-child
agreement for each successive age group.[25]

Newcomb's Bennington study provides a similar demonstration. . . .
The student reported on her own preference in the 1936 Presidential
election and on the parents' preferences. Comparisons were made
of the distributions of parent and daughter preferences for freshman
vs. sophomore vs. junior and senior years to determine the influence
of the relatively homogeneous Bennington environment which inter-
vened during these years. The findings demonstrate that the distribution of student preferences, almost identical with parent preferences

---

[25] *Op. Cit.*, Chart XXXVII, p. 89.

during the first year of college, diverges considerably from parent preferences by the sophomore year and becomes markedly different by the senior year.[26]

The studies of intra-family agreement in attitude provide one other type of evidence which inferentially supports our notion of the attenuation of parental influence as the child comes into contact with new groups through age and independence.

> In these studies, the agreement in views between siblings is sometimes determined. If parental political environment were the sole source, one would expect siblings to show a high resenblance. Newcomb in summarizing such data indicates that the agreements are only moderate and in some instances rather low. He notes the factors of age or sex of the two siblings do not seem important, and concludes that the differential absorption of views must therefore be due in part to "personality differences, including child-parent and sibling relationships" and to "those complicated chains of events which result in different circles of acquaintances and different spheres of influence among members of the same family."[27]

. . . Siblings, sharing the same familiar influences, nevertheless, diverge presumably because other sources of influence are not shared in common by them.

In line with our general model, we might also expect certain sex differences in these growth processes. Age presumably brings freedom and independence with consequent opportunity to orient oneself to others besides parents. We shall assume that the male sex role permits greater independence and conceivably the attenuation of the parental influence on politics should be greater.

> In the study of a national sample of college graduates, it was demonstrated that a small proportion of the graduates deviated from the politics of their parents. In examining these defections, which came mainly from Democratic families, it is established that sons defected much more frequently than daughters.[28]

[26] T. M. Newcomb, *Personality and Social Change* (New York: Dryden Press, 1943), p. 28.

[27] G. Murphy, L. Murphy, and T. M. Newcomb, *Experimental Social Psychology* (New York: Harpers, 1937), p. 1003.

[28] P. Salter West, "The College Graduate in American Society," (Unpublished Ph.D. dissertation, Columbia University, 1951), p. 150. With respect to politics, the greater dependency of the female may not merely be a matter of the lesser freedom permitted but also a reflection of a more basic value. Thus, Allport and Gillespie remark that the girls in their sample place greater emphasis on family values. *Op. Cit.*, p. 32ff.

In the studies of intra-family agreement in attitude, the findings, while not conclusive in all studies, show a consistent pattern. Fisher and Newcomb and Svehla report that daughters resemble parents attitudinally more than sons do.[29]

In *The People's Choice,* respondents were asked where they obtained most of the information or impressions that were responsible for the formation of their vote. Impersonal sources such as media were studied, but among human agents of influence, three types were analyzed, "relatives," "business contacts," and "friends or neighbors." When the relative influence of these three agencies was examined, it is very clear that men are essentially influenced by business contacts whereas women report influence predominantly from relatives. While these data refer to adult voters participating in the election, we may legitimately regard this adult pattern as expressive of a more general process, consistent with our other data, in which women would be more exclusively subject to the socialization influence of family.[30]

Comparative data from England are available for a panel study conducted during the General Election of 1950 on a sample of the electorate of Greenwich.[31] Women discussed politics with family members much more often than with friends or co-workers. Men by contrast direct discussion mainly to co-workers and thereafter equally to friends or family members.

In Elmira similar sex differences are obtained. Respondents were asked with whom they had discussed politics and to whom they would go to discuss a political question. Married women were more prone to mention a family member than were married men.[32]

Reexamination of the findings of the Rileys for sex differences (see Table 1, p. 115) gives some small confirmation of the point we are making about sex differences. The changes in direction of communication were presented separately for boys and girls, and it was to be noted that the magnitude of change in the direction of *peers* is about the same for both sexes. It is to be noted, however, that boys at the *younger* age level do not direct their political communications to mothers as much as girls do.

From these many different strands, we see that the *relative* influence of parental norms declines as peers and other agencies exert

[29] S. C. Fisher, *Relationships in Attitudes, Opinions, and Values among Family Members,* Univ. of Calif. Publ. Culture and Society, Vol. 2, #2, 1948, p. 89.
[30] *Op. Cit.,* Appendix, p. 171.
[31] M. Benney, A. Gray and R. Pear, *How People Vote* (London: Routledge, 1956), p. 108.
[32] *Op. Cit.,* Chart XLVI, p. 103.

their influence on the growing individual. The consequences of this process in a summary form may be seen in other data collected by Maccoby.

> She obtained agreement in political party affiliation between the *young voter* and three other non-parent groups, friends, fellow-workers, and spouse. "Seventy-seven per cent of the married young voters had the same party preferences as their spouses; 64% had the same party preference as the majority of their friends, and 46% of those who worked agreed in party choice with the majority of their fellow-workers."[33] As is pointed out, these figures probably reflect two processes, the choice of like-minded individuals by the respondent and their actual influence on his views. It is clear, however, from the juxtaposition of these findings with her findings on parent-child agreement that the parental source is still the most powerful at this stage of life.

The Elmira data provide several findings parallel to the Maccoby findings.

> First, if we examine the young age group, 21–25, for the agreement between the respondent's vote and the vote of the three close friends, agreement is obtained in 53% of the cases. Elmira documents the fact that such friend-respondent mutual agreement *increases with age.* Whether this represents the opportunity with time for the individual to iron out the inconsistencies in his social life and to form stable associations with like-minded individuals, or the concurrent operation of the fact (previously documented) that the younger individual is relatively more bound to parents than to other groupings or both processes is hard to say.[34]

> While the Elmira data support the Cambridge data on the lesser significance of friends, the findings on spouses' influence differ. An analysis is presented of the voting preferences of respondents from given parental political traditions, now married to individuals of given political views. Thus it is possible to determine whether the parental family pattern overrides the contemporary (conjugal) family's influence. "Voting is adjusted in the contemporary group at the expense of parents."[35]

Again, the difference between the two sets of findings may well be a function of the age levels studied. It seems thoroughly plausible

[33] *Op. Cit.,* pp. 31–32.
[34] *Op. Cit.,* Chart XLII, p. 97.
[35] *Ibid.,* Chart LXVII, p. 135.

Table 2: *Resemblances in Moral Knowledge between Children*
and Various Agents of Socialization as Obtained
by the Character Education Inquiry

Agent of Socialization	Correlation	N
Parents	.55	416
Friends	.35	1020
Club leaders	.14	204
Public-school teachers	.06	695
Sunday School teachers	.002	205

among older individuals, *married for long periods of time,* that the contemporary family would assert itself over a long gone parental influence. By contrast, the Cambridge study must have dealt with a relatively newly married group perhaps still dominated by parental ties.

An equivalent demonstration of the relative influence of parents vs. others is available for the realm of ideology from one study using intra-family correlations.

In the Remmers and Weltman study, the correlation in ideology for the parent-child pair was .86. The parallel correlation was computed for the teacher-child pair and the value obtained was .65.[36]

Another demonstration in the ideological realm is provided by the classic studies in The Character Education Inquiry. While the specific dimension is that of moral values, the data are included because of their almost unique features.

In 1925 over one thousand children in the fifth through ninth grades in a number of small suburban towns and one small city were given a test of "moral knowledge." The same test was administered independently to a variety of other individuals regarded as the sources of the child's values, parents, public-school teachers, Sunday School teachers, etc. On the basis of a sociometric type of question on friendship, the best friends (already administered the test) could be examined as another source of influence. The correlations between children's values and the values of these other possible sources of influence, presented in Table 2 express the hierarchy of influence.[37] It can be

[36] *Op. Cit.*
[37] Adapted from H. Hartshorne, M. May and F. Shuttleworth, *Studies in the Nature of Character* ("Studies in the Organization of Character," III [New York: Macmillan, 1930]), p. 98, Table I.

Table 3:   Increased Resemblance in Moral Values between Child and Peers with Age[39]

Grade	Correlation	N
9	.25	181
8	.21	237
7	.23	328
6	.05	157
5	.15	168

seen that for these *young* children the parents far outweigh other parties as agents of socialization.

. . . Hartshorne and May analyze the resemblance of child to mother vs. father, when the other parent's influence is excluded. The partial "r"[38] for mother-child resemblances is much higher than for father.

While the influence of peers is small for the group in the aggregate, Hartshorne and May show that peer influence, following our model, increases with age. The data are presented in Table 3.

[38] Partial "r" is a correlation between two variables while controlling for the effects of one or more additional variables. In this example, it is a measure of agreement between the attitudes of a child and the attitudes of *one* of his parents, which agreement is not common to the child and his *other* parent. See Hubert M. Blalock, *Social Statistics* (New York: McGraw-Hill, 1960), pp. 326–336.—Eds.

[39] *Op. Cit.,* p. 100, Table III.

10 *Political Expression of Adolescent Rebellion*

RUSSELL MIDDLETON
SNELL PUTNEY

In his pioneer psychoanalytic study of political attitudes Lasswell pointed out that, although political beliefs may be expressed in a highly rational form, they are often developed in highly irrational ways. "When they are seen against the developmental history of the person, they take on meanings which are quite different than the phrases in which they are put."[1] Using a series of case studies, he

Reprinted from "Political Expression of Adolescent Rebellion," *American Journal of Sociology* 68 (1963), pp. 527–535, by Russell Middleton and Snell Putney by permission of the University of Chicago Press. Copyright 1963 by the University of Chicago.

[1] Harold D. Lasswell, *Psychopathology and Politics* (Chicago: University of Chicago Press, 1930), p. 153.

attempted to demonstrate that family relationships were one of the non-rational determinants of whether or not an individual became an anarchist, a socialist, a highly conservative Republican, or a political assassin.

Political beliefs can be influenced by family relationships through rebellion; a youth may, for example, express rebellion against his parents by rejecting their political beliefs and adopting a divergent set. The probability of such political rebellion is enhanced by the fact that adolescence, which most authors regard as a period of generalized rebellion in American society,[2] is also the age at which most individuals seem to crystallize their political viewpoints.[3]

Clearly, adolescent rebellion cannot be attributed solely to the biological maturation process, for adolescence is not a period of storm and stress in every society.[4] Rather, there appear to be structural features in American society conducive to youthful rebellion. Parsons, for example, argues that, since there is a sharp limitation of "objects of cathexis" in the isolated conjugal family typical of American society, children tend to be highly dependent emotionally on their parents,

[2] Kingsley Davis, "The Sociology of Parent-Youth Conflict," *American Sociological Review,* V (August, 1940), 523–535; Kingsley Davis, "Adolescence and Social Structure," *Annals of the American Academy of Political and Social Science,* CCXXXVI (November, 1944), 8–15; Ernest A. Smith, *American Youth Culture* (Glencoe, Ill.: Free Press, 1962); Florence Kluckhohn and John P. Spiegel, *Integration and Conflict in Family Behavior* (Group for the Advancement of Psychiatry, Report No. 27 [Topeka, August, 1954]); P. Blos, *The Adolescent Personality* (New York: Appleton-Century-Crofts, Inc., 1941); Ruth Benedict, "Continuities and Discontinuities in Cultural Conditioning," in Clyde Kluckhohn and H. A. Murray (eds.), *Personality in Nature, Society and Culture* (New York: Alfred A. Knopf, Inc., 1955), pp. 522–531. For a variant view, however, see Frederick Elkin and W. A. Westley, "Myth of Adolescent Culture," *American Sociological Review,* XX (December, 1955), 680–684, and William A. Westley and Frederick Elkin, "The Protective Environment and Adolescent Socialization," *Social Forces,* XXXV (March, 1957), 243–249.

[3] See Herbert H. Hyman, *Political Socialization* (Glencoe, Ill.: Free Press, 1959), pp. 51–68, and Robert E. Lane, *Political Life: Why People Get Involved in Politics* (Glencoe, Ill.: Free Press, 1959), p. 217.

[4] Margaret Mead, *Coming of Age in Samoa* (New York: William Morrow & Co., 1928); Margaret Mead, "Adolescence in Primitive and in Modern Society," in Eleanor E. Maccoby, T. M. Newcomb, and E. L. Hartley (eds.), *Readings in Social Psychology* (3d ed.; New York: Henry Holt & Co., 1958), pp. 341–349; and Yehudi A. Cohen, " 'Adolescent Conflict' in a Jamaican Community," in *Social Structure and Personality* (New York: Holt, Rinehart & Winston, 1961), pp. 167–182.

especially on the mother.[5] As the individual nears adulthood, however, he is expected to break this dependency and choose his occupation and sexual partner with little adult support. In adolescence, therefore, a reaction formation may be generated against the dependency needs and may find expression in a rebellious youth culture, compulsively independent and defiant of parental norms and authority, and, at the same time, compulsively conformist to the peer group that satisfies individual dependency needs. Parsons maintains that the rebellion is especially strong among adolescent boys because of an additional reaction formation of compulsive masculinity against an original iden-tification with the mother.

The question remains, however, whether the adolescent is likely to use political beliefs as an instrument of rebellion. Hyman believes that he is not: "The almost complete absence of negative correlations [between the political attitudes of parents and children] provides considerable evidence *against* the theory that political attitudes are formed *generally* in terms of rebellion and opposition to parents."[6] The absence of negative correlations between the political beliefs of adolescents and their parents, however, does not demonstrate that rebellion tends to be non-political. It might simply indicate a relative lack of rebellion, even though such rebellion as occurred might often be political.

A recent study by Lane based on depth interviews with fifteen working-class and lower-middle-class men selected at random from an eastern housing development focused on how often rebellion against the parent was expressed politically.[7] Concentrating on rebel-lion against the father, he found that only four of his subjects had impaired relationships with their fathers. In none of these cases did the rebellion take a political form, and the subjects' general level of interest in politics was low. On the basis of these scant but sugges-tive data, Lane argues that, compared with other Western cultures, American culture (because it is more permissive and the father is less dominant) tends to discourage youthful rebellion against the father. Moreover, when such rebellion does occur, it tends to discour-

---

[5] Talcott Parsons, "Psychoanalysis and the Social Structure," in *Essays in Socio-logical Theory* (rev. ed.; Glencoe, Ill.: Free Press, 1954), pp. 336–347.

[6] Hyman, *op. cit.*, p. 72.

[7] Robert E. Lane, "Fathers and Sons: Foundations of Political Belief," *American Sociological Review*, XXIV (August, 1959), 502–511.

age its expression in political terms because politics is relatively unimportant to the father, making other forms of rebellion more appealing.[8]

Maccoby, Matthews, and Morton conducted a study of the circumstances under which political rebellion against the parent was most likely to occur in American society.[9] Seeking to test the hypothesis that the young tend to become radical in their political views because of adolescent rebellion against strict parental authority and discipline, they interviewed 339 first-time voters between the ages of twenty-one and twenty-four in Cambridge, Massachusetts, immediately after the 1952 presidential election. Each respondent was asked: "In your case, when you were in your teens, did your family want to have quite a lot to say about your friends and the places you went and so on, or were you pretty much on your own?" They found that there was maximum political conformity to parents among those subjects who said that their parents had "about an average amount to say." Those who reported that their parents "had a lot to say" and those who said their parents left them "on their own" were both more likely to deviate politically from their parents. The researchers thus concluded that political rebellion was correlated with the type of discipline prevalent in the adolescent's family.

On the other hand, Nogee and Levin, in a study of 314 Boston University students eligible to vote for the first time in the 1956 presidential election, found no evidence of any relationship between strict parental control in early adolescence and political rebellion: "Although a small number do 'revolt' against their parents' political views, there is no evidence that the likelihood of such revolt is related to the strictness of parental control."[10] This study, like the previous study by Maccoby, Matthews, and Morton, did not investigate whether strictness of discipline was correlated with estrangement between the youth and his parents; rather they implicitly asssumed such a relationship and concentrated on measuring the degree to which it might be expressed politically.

Previous research thus presents an incomplete and contradictory picture of adolescent political rebellion. It is generally agreed that adolescence is a period of general rebellion in American society.

[8] *Ibid.*, p. 510.

[9] Eleanor E. Maccoby, Richard E. Matthews, and Anton S. Morton, "Youth and Political Change," *Public Opinion Quarterly*, XVIII (Spring, 1954), 23–39.

[10] Philip Nogee and M. B. Levin, "Some Determinants of Political Attitudes among College Voters," *Public Opinion Quarterly*, XXII (Winter, 1958–1959), 463.

Hyman and Lane, however, are doubtful that this rebellion is likely to take a political form in the context of American culture. And when political rebellion occurs, Maccoby, Matthews, and Morton disagree with Nogee and Levin as to whether it is associated with the perceived degree of strictness of parental control.

In the present study we have attempted to investigate further some of the problems raised by the earlier studies. Are youths who are estranged from their parents no more likely to deviate from parental political views, as Lane suggests, than youths who are close to their parents? Does parental indifference to politics, as Lane further suggests, inhibit the political expression of rebellion by those who are estranged from their parents?

Our basic hypothesis is that estrangement from parents is associated with political rebellion if the parents are interested in politics, and perceived extremes of parental discipline (strict or permissive) are associated with lack of closeness between parent and child and thus with political rebellion.

METHODS

Anonymous questionnaires were administered late in 1961 to classes of students in sixteen colleges and universities in the United States. A state university, a state college, a private university, and a private liberal arts college were included in each of four regions—Far West, Middle West, Northeast, and South. Four of the institutions were church affiliated. Thus, although the individual subjects were not selected in a strictly random fashion, the sample does include a broad range of types of institutions and regions. Caution should be used in generalizing the findings on this sample to American college students in general, but analysis of the sample has not revealed any marked biases correlated with political rebellion or adolescent rebellion.

A total of 1,440 completed questionnaires was obtained from students attending the sixteen colleges and universities included in the survey. Almost all the subjects were between the ages of seventeen and twenty-two, a group in transition to young adulthood. At their age, the storms of adolescence are recent enough to be recalled, but distant enough to be viewed with a certain objectivity. Fully three-fourths of these students reported that they had fairly clear political views while still in high school, and it can be assumed that the effects of adolescent rebellion on their political beliefs are now largely complete.

There were 824 males and 616 females in the sample. Since the relations of males and females to their mothers and fathers are somewhat different—especially in psychoanalytic theory, but also in terms of culturally defined relations between the sexes—we have considered the sexes separately throughout the analysis.

Each student was asked how close he was to each of his parents (response categories: "Very close," "Fairly close," "Not very close," and "Hostile"). If a parent died early in a child's life, lack of closeness is hardly indicative of rebellion, nor is the parent likely to have had a significant influence on the child's political views. When examining the personal nexus between parent and child in relation to political rebellion, therefore, we have excluded those cases in which the parent died before the child entered high school.

In order to measure political views, each respondent was presented with a set of five political categories and asked: "Which of these political positions is closest to your own views?"

1. Socialist
2. Highly liberal
3. Moderately liberal
4. Moderately conservative
5. Highly conservative
6. I have no political views

Extensive pretesting indicated that this set of categories was meaningful to American college students, involving as it does an extremely simple left-to-right continuum, and few students experienced any difficulty in characterizing their views in terms of the categories. At the same time, this approach avoided some of the knotty methodological problems involved in the use of political party affiliation or attitudes on substantive political issues as indexes of political position.[11]

To determine whether or not the student was deviating from his parents' political views, he was also asked to use the same categories to characterize the views of his mother and his father. In many

---

[11] For a detailed discussion of the problems of measuring variations in political views and the rationale for the particular categories we have selected, see Russell Middleton and Snell Putney, "Student Rebellion against Parental Political Beliefs" (paper presented at the annual meeting of the Southern Sociological Society, Louisville, Kentucky, April 3, 1962, to be published in *Social Forces*).

cases the students' perceptions of their parents' views may have been incorrect. Yet it is precisely the perceived rather than the actual views of the parent that are of crucial importance in the present study. As the Thomas theorem states, "If men define situations as real, they are real in their consequences."

For purposes of this study a student was defined as a political rebel if he placed himself to the left or right of his parent. If the student agreed with his parent, had no political views, or simply remained unaware of the views of his parent, he was considered a non-rebel.

Each student was asked, "How close are (were) you to your father?" and "How close are (were) you to your mother?" Further, in a question patterned after that used by Maccoby, Matthews, and Morton, we asked each student to report on the strictness of his parents' discipline: "When you were in high school, did your parents want to have quite a lot to say about your friends and the places you went and so on, or were you pretty much on your own?" (Response categories: "Parents had a lot to say," "Parents had an average amount to say," and "Parents left me pretty much on my own.")

As a rough index of generalized rebellion against the parent, each student was asked: "When you were in high school, how often did you defy your parents and do things contrary to their instructions or wishes?"

Finally, each student was asked how much interest he thought each of his parents took in political matters. Parents were classified as interested in politics if the student reported that they were very much interested or moderately interested most of the time. If the student believed that they were only slightly interested or not at all interested, they were classified as not interested in politics. Once again, it is the student's perception of his parent that might influence the pattern of his rebellion, not necessarily the actual views or interests of the parents.

The χ^2 test of significance was applied throughout the analysis, and the rejection level for the null hypothesis was set at .05.[12]

---

[12] A "test of statistical significance" estimates the probability (P) that the result obtained would occur by chance alone. For no particular reason but tradition, social scientists usually take a P of .05 or less as "significant," that is, as indicative of a nonrandom result. Chi-square (χ^2) is the most diverse test of this nature. See Hubert M. Blalock, *Social Statistics* (New York: McGraw-Hill, 1960), pp. 89–96, 119–130, 212–221.—Eds.

FINDINGS

As shown in Table 1, approximately half the students hold political views different from those they attribute to their fathers, and nearly half hold political views different from those they attribute to their mothers. Male students are more likely than female students to deviate from the political views of their fathers and also from those of their mothers, and these tendencies are statistically significant beyond the .05 level ($P < .001$).

Thus our findings indicate that divergence from parental political views, as measured by our categories, is fairly common, especially among male students. The question remains as to how much of this difference between viewpoints can be attributed to the nature of parent-child relationships. If deviation from parental political viewpoints is motivated by rebellion against the parents, it might be expected that those students who have a history of conflict with the parents would deviate more often than those who do not. In Table 2, the students who report that they defied their parents often or very often while in high school are compared to those who report that they did so only occasionally or rarely. Except in the case of males students in relation to their mothers (where there is no difference), those who report frequent defiance deviate from the parental political viewpoints more often than those who do not. However, the differences observed in the sample are small, and none are significant at the .05 level. It might, nevertheless, be expected that when the parents of defiant students were interested in politics, there would be markedly more political rebellion than when the parents were indifferent to political issues. However, when the data are broken down according to the degree of perceived parental interest in politics,

Table 1:   Per Cent Rebelling from Political Views of Parents, by Sex of Student and Parent

	FROM POSITION OF FATHER		FROM POSITION OF MOTHER	
	Per Cent	N	Per Cent	N
Male students	54	781	49	812
Female students	42	584	38	605
Total	49	1365	45	1417

Table 2:   *Relation of Defiance of Parental Wishes while in High School to Political Rebellion, by Sex*

	REBELLING FROM POLITICAL VIEWS OF MOTHER		REBELLING FROM POLITICAL VIEWS OF FATHER	
	Per Cent	N	Per Cent	N
Male students				
Defied parents often or very often	56	130	49	135
Defied parents occasionally or rarely	53	650	49	678
Female students				
Defied parents often or very often	48	71	44	73
Defied parents occasionally or rarely	41	515	37	533

no consistent pattern emerges, and no statistically significant relationships are found. Our data thus lend little support to the contention that political rebellion is related to a generalized rebellion against the parents, and are consistent with Lane's contention that generalized rebellion in America is likely to be expressed primarily in non-political terms.

Nevertheless, political rebellion might occur under particular circumstances. Following Maccoby, Matthews, and Morton, we therefore examined the relation of parental discipline to political deviation (Table 3). In every case, there is a maximum of political rebellion

Table 3:   *Relation of Perceived Strictness of Parental Discipline to Political Rebellion, by Sex*

	STRICT DISCIPLINE		AVERAGE DISCIPLINE		PERMISSIVE DISCIPLINE	
	Per Cent	N	Per Cent	N	Per Cent	N
Rebelling from political views of father						
Male students	56	97	53	379	54	304
Female students	55	104	36	315	46	166
Rebelling from political views of mother						
Male students	53	102	50	393	47	318
Female students	49	106	34	331	40	168

Table 4:   Relation of Perceived Strictness of Parental Discipline
            to Closeness of Relation with Parent, by Sex

	STRICT DISCIPLINE		AVERAGE DISCIPLINE		PERMISSIVE DISCIPLINE	
	Per Cent	N	Per Cent	N	Per Cent	N
Feel close to father						
Male students	73	97	86	379	70	304
Female students	73	104	83	315	70	166
Feel close to mother						
Male students	87	102	94	392	88	317
Female students	85	106	94	331	86	167

in students who perceive their parents as having imposed strict discipline. Moreover, we find (as did Maccoby, Matthews, and Morton) that those who perceive their parents' discipline as average are least likely to rebel politically (except in the case of males in relation to their mothers). However, the association between political rebellion and parental discipline is significant at the .05 level only for females ($P < .01$ for rebellion against the father's political views and $P < .02$ for rebellion against the mother's political views). Moreover, the percentages do not differ sufficiently to suggest that parental discipline is generally a decisive factor in determining whether or not the student deviates from the political views of the parents.

Discipline, however, is likely to influence the degree of closeness between parent and child. Accordingly, we examined the relation between the student's perceptions of his parents' discipline and his degree of closeness with his parents (Table 4). The relationship revealed is non-linear,[13] with those students who regard their parents' discipline as average having stronger emotional ties than those who regard it as either strict or permissive. All of the relationships are significant at the .05 level ($P < .001$ for male students in relation to their fathers, and $P < .01$ for the other three). This finding may

[13] For present purposes, a relationship between two variables is *linear* if a change in one is regularly accompanied by a change in the other of consistent proportion and size. For instance, grade-point average may be linearly related to number of hours spent studying, such that every additional hour you spend studying raises your average another tenth of a grade-point. However, this relationship stops being linear when you study so much that it cuts into your sleep, causing grades to rise at slower rates, to level off, and even to start falling.—Eds.

explain why Maccoby, Matthews, and Morton found a maximum of political conformity among those young people who perceived their parents' discipline as average. These are the young people who are likely to be closest to their parents, and if nexus to parents is related to political conformity, there would thus be an indirect relationship between discipline and political rebellion. It must first be established, however, that closeness between parent and child is related to political conformity.

In general, there is a linear relationship between parent-child nexus and conformity to parental political views (Table 5). The associations are significant at the .05 level, except in the case of male students in relation to their mothers where it is nonlinear and not significant. The factor of parental interest in politics needs to be explored, however, inasmuch as politics is a relatively pointless instrument of rebellion unless it is of some importance to the parents.

Accordingly, the factor of perceived parental interest in politics is introduced into the examination of the relationship between parent-child closeness and political rebellion (Table 6). When the student perceives his parent as not interested in politics, no consistent relationship emerges between closeness to the parent and political rebellion, and none of the comparisons are statistically significant at the .05 level. When the student perceives his parent as interested in politics,

Table 5: Relation of Closeness to Parent to Political Rebellion, by Sex

| | PER CENT OF STUDENTS REBELLING FROM POLITICAL POSITIONS OF PARENTS | | | |
| | Father | | Mother | |
	Per Cent	N	Per Cent	N
Male student				
Very close to parent	46	210	46	311
Fairly close to parent	56	399	53	424
Not very close or hostile to parent	57	172	47	77
Female students				
Very close to parent	37	205	34	333
Fairly close to parent	43	249	41	211
Not very close or hostile to parent	50	130	49	61

*Table 6:   Relation of Closeness to Parent to Political Rebellion
by Interest of Parent in Politics, and by Sex*

	PER CENT OF STUDENTS REBELLING FROM POLITICAL POSITION OF PARENT							
	Father				Mother			
	Interested in Politics		Not Interested in Politics		Interested in Politics		Not Interested in Politics	
	Per Cent	N	Per Cent	N	Per Cent	N	Per Cent	N
Male students								
Very close to parent	44	165	53	45	50	165	40	146
Fairly close to parent	57	263	54	136	63	165	56	259
Not very close or hostile to parent	63	80	53	92	74	19	38	58
Female students								
Very close to parent	35	188	53	17	36	214	32	116
Fairly close to parent	44	193	38	56	40	108	42	103
Not very close or hostile to parent	58	76	39	54	50	22	49	39

however, a linear relationship is observed in all cases between political rebellion and estrangement of the student and his parent. Three of these four relationships are significant beyond the .05 level ($P < .01$ for male students and fathers, $P < .01$ for female students and fathers, and $P < .05$ for male students and mothers).

CONCLUSIONS

The data thus support our basic hypothesis that deviation from parental political viewpoints is associated with estrangement between parent and child—if the parent is interested in politics. This finding is consistent with Lane's contention that parental indifference to politics inhibits adolescent political rebellion. In general, the association between estrangement and rebellion is more marked in relation to fathers than in relation to mothers, perhaps because enough of the traditional male predominance in politics remains to render the father's political views a more obvious basis for rebellion than those of the mother.

Our data, moreover, generally support the conclusions of Maccoby, Matthews, and Morton (as against those of Nogee and Levin) that deviation from parental political views is related to the kind of discipline experienced in the home. However, the associations observed are not extremely high, a point consistent with Hyman's contention that political attitudes in America are not in general generated by adolescent rebellion.

Some caution should be observed in imputing a causal relationship to the associations observed between impairment of parent-child relationships and deviations from parental political views. Rebellion against the parent, arising from strained parent-child relationships, may provoke political deviation. But it may also be the case that political deviation arising from factors unrelated to the parent may be the source of alienation between parent and child. For example, one of our subjects reports that he and his father have drifted apart in large measure because he acquired different political views while attending college. When he visits home he and his father now become involved in bitter arguments over political questions, although once they were fairly close. Here the causal sequence seems clearly reversed.

One unexpected finding adds another dimension to the picture of political attitudes and parent-child relationships. Our data disclose a positive relationship between parental interest in politics and closeness of the student to the parent. In fact this tendency of students to feel closer to parents who are interested in politics is significant well beyond the .001 level in all four relationships: father and son, father and daughter, mother and son, and mother and daughter. Any interpretation of this finding is necessarily ex post facto, but a plausible explanation would be that there is a relation between frequent and rewarding parent-child communication and the student's perception of the parent as interested in politics. In many cases of alienation between parent and child there may be too little communication for the student to perceive clearly his parents' political interests, whereas when the parent and child are close, communication of political viewpoints may be facilitated.

In any case, our data suggest that, while some students express rebellion against their parents in political terms, many, if not most, do not. Family relationships are an influence on political attitudes, as Lasswell suggested, but many other factors, including education, reference groups outside the home, mass media, and perhaps even rational evaluation of issues, may influence political beliefs.

11 *The Political Socialization of State Legislators*

HEINZ EULAU
JOHN C. WAHLKE
WILLIAM BUCHANAN
LeROY C. FERGUSON

As long ago as 1925, Charles E. Merriam, viewing the promises of political research, proposed that "the examination of the rise and development of the political ideation and the political behavior of the child has in store for us much of value in the scientific understanding of the adult idea and conduct."[1] Yet, over thirty years

Reprinted from "The Political Socialization of State Legislators," *Midwest Journal of Political Science* 3 (1959) by Heinz Eulau, John C. Wahlke, William Buchanan, and LeRoy C. Ferguson by permission of the Wayne State University Press. Copyright 1959 by Wayne State University Press.
[1] Charles E. Merriam, *New Aspects of Politics* (Chicago: University of Chicago Press, 1925), p. 85.

later, we know next to nothing about "political socialization"—the process by which people selectively acquire the values, attitudes, interests or knowledge that fit them for particular political roles and make them take these roles in characteristic ways. Studies of voting behavior suggest that, under certain conditions, family tradition can be an important factor in a person's orientation towards politics, influencing the degree, kind and direction of his political involvement. We also know that religious, ethnic, and class perceptions and attitudes are formed rather early and, through time, become integrated into a system of values which tends to shape a person's social outlook and changes only slowly when it comes into conflict with opposed social values.[2] But these studies shed little light on the developmental pattern of a person's political socialization.

If little is known about the initiation to politics of the population at large, not much more is known about the initiation of those for whom politics is a matter of central concern—politicians. Biographies, of course, tell us a great deal about the political socialization of particular, usually distinguished, public figures, but they represent unique cases which cannot be generalized. On the other hand, what systematic analyses have been made of political elites, are limited to data about the social bases of political recruitment and changes in the composition of elites.[3] These studies do not include systematic information on questions such as these: When do politicians become interested in politics? How do they become oriented to politics? Who are the agents of political socialization? What political or social events seem to arouse attention to politics? What kind of predispositions seem to accompany the initial interest in politics? Are political or other social beliefs involved in the process of political socialization?

This study presents some data on the political socialization of a particular type of politician—the American state legislator. In soliciting recollections about these legislators' earliest interest in politics, we did not consider it appropriate to think in motivational terms. Motivational analysis would have required more intensive interviewing than our research design permitted.[4] Hence, even though some

---

[2] See Herbert Hyman, *Political Socialization* (Glencoe: The Free Press, 1959).

[3] See Morris Janowitz, "The Systematic Analysis of Political Biography," *World Politics*, VI (1954), 405–412, for a review of such studies.

[4] The interview question read: "How did you become interested in politics? What is your earliest recollection of being interested in it?" It should be pointed out that the problem of legislators' political socialization was only peripheral to our main research interest—the analysis of state legislatures as political role

of our respondents might use motivational language in trying to explain "why" politics interested or attracted them, we are not prepared to take such comments at face value. It seems doubtful that even those with some sense of self-awareness could accurately tell the reasons or motives that directed them to politics. We are therefore not concerned with "why" state legislators became interested in politics, but rather with "how" they perceive what happened in the course of their political socialization. Recollections of this kind, it seems to us, have a functional reality of their own in constituting a part of the situation in which state legislators define their political roles.[5]

---

systems. We did not intend to collect as full a set of data as might be desirable—the story of politicians' socialization could be the subject of a full-scale research project in its own right. This study therefore aspires to nothing more than a descriptive presentation of state legislators' perception of their political socialization, and the analysis has not been guided by specific hypotheses.

[5] It should also be pointed out that the open-ended character of the question makes it mandatory to consider the results of this study as suggestive rather than definitive. While open-ended questions have the advantage of making for spontaneity and a wide range of response, and of allowing the respondent himself to formulate or "structure" the topic under investigation, there are certain drawbacks which limit their usefulness in statistical analysis. Heterogeneous answers make statistical controls difficult, if not impossible, and they make statistical inference of doubtful validity. For instance, some respondents mentioned primary groups they considered instrumental in stimulating their first political interest; others referred to some form of activity, political or otherwise, as a source of their first interest; others described events or conditions with which they associated their political concerns; still others referred to personal predispositions accompanying their initiation to politics; and a few mentioned political beliefs. Moreover, many respondents gave more than one "reason" for their political socialization. This makes it difficult to single out any one factor as more important than any other.

Secondly, the respondents differed a great deal in a number of personal characteristics which are significant in answering open-ended questions. A few were suspicious of the interview and gave minimum, if not evasive, answers, while others, more favorably inclined, were more candid. Some were genuinely pressed for time and failed to elaborate as fully as those who were willing to devote a great deal of time to the interview. Still others—especially those with relatively little education—were unable to articulate answers to a question about which they evidently had thought little prior to the interview. Fluctuations in mood, in attitude towards the interview, in verbal facility or in self-consciousness made undoubtedly for considerable variability in answer patterns.

These differences are inherent in the open-ended type of interview question and in the interview situation. They do not allow us, therefore, to make cate-

TIME OF POLITICAL SOCIALIZATION

In a recent review of voting behavior studies, Lipset and his associates reported that "it is difficult, if not impossible, to make any reliable estimate, on the basis of empirical evidence, of the age at which politics becomes meaningful to children or youth." After examining the skimpy research evidence, they inclined to focus on the period of adolescence—"the period in the life cycle where the individual first encounters strong influence outside of his family and must proceed to define his adult role."[6] Assuming Lipset's conclusion to be correct, our data (summarized in Table 1) suggest that politicians see themselves as exposed to the political environment at an earlier stage of their personal development than the average citizen. With the exception of New Jersey,[7] about a third of state legislators recalled their childhood or the grammar school period as the time when they first became interested in or aware of politics. But only ten to sixteen per cent mentioned a period roughly coinciding with adolescence and high school. Altogether, almost one half had recollections locating their first political interest in the pre-college or equivalent age period.

---

gorical statements about the actual distribution of perceptions of factors in political socialization which we might have found if we had asked direct, closed questions about the particular factors which we were able to code. For instance, the fact that a certain percentage of our respondents mentioned some form of primary group influence does not mean that others, who did not mention this, were not possibly affected by family or friends in the process of their political socialization. In other words, the percentages of responses occurring in any particular category are, at most, suggestive indices of the extent to which legislators recalled certain socializing influences.

[6] Seymour M. Lipset, Paul F. Lazarsfeld, Allen H. Barton, and Juan Linz, "The Psychology of Voting: An Analysis of Political Behavior," in Gardner Lindzey, ed., *The Handbook of Social Psychology* (Cambridge: Addison-Wesley, 1954), II, 1145.

[7] There is reason to believe that the low percentage figure for New Jersey legislators having political recollections from childhood is not too accurate. For, as we shall see (below, pp. 139–140), New Jersey legislators, more than those from at least two other states, mentioned family influence as an important factor in their political socialization. As Table 1 shows, the low percentage of New Jersey legislators recalling the childhood period must be accounted for by the fact that, compared with the other states, an inordinately large percentage could not be coded on the time dimension. In other words, it is unlikely that New Jersey represents a special case.

Table 1:   Time of State Legislators' Earliest Recollection
of Political Interest

Time of Recollection	CAL. $N = 113$	N.J. $N = 79$	OHIO $N = 162$	TENN. $N = 120$
Childhood/grammar school	39%	23%	35%	32%
Adolescence/high school	16	10	15	11
College/equivalent period	8	10	13	7
After college	17	14	11	18
Time of entry into politics	18	15	23	13
Time not specified/codable	2	28	3	19
Total	100%	100%	100%	100%

The childhood-grammar school period is perceptually more salient for state legislators than the time of adolescence or any single later period.

Nevertheless, as Table 1 shows, a sizeable proportion of state legislators reported first paying attention to politics either after college and its equivalent period or at the very time of entry into active politics. As one legislator put it: "Well, this might come as a surprise to you, but I was never interested in politics. I first became interested in politics after I was elected." The data suggest that the process of political socialization, even for those who are most active in politics, is not necessarily restricted to the early years of the life cycle. As Talcott Parsons has argued, socialization may occur at almost any phase of a person's development and is part of a continuous process of growth.[8]

If we look at the inter-state differences with regard to the time of political socialization, no particular pattern emerges. The fluctuations from state to state in each time period are small. Apparently,

[8] "The term socialization in its current usage in the literature refers primarily to the process of child development. This is in fact a crucially important case of the operation of what are here called the mechanisms of socialization, but it should be made clear that the term is here used in a broader sense than the current one to designate the learning of *any* orientations of functional significance to the operation of a system of complementary role-expectations. In this sense, socialization, like learning, goes on throughout life. The case of the development of the child is only the most dramatic because he has so far to go." Talcott Parsons, *The Social System* (Glencoe: The Free Press, 1951), pp. 207–208.

the process of political socialization in the four states follows a relatively similar time scale.

What accounts for the fact that legislators are initiated into politics in different periods of the life cycle? The evidence suggests that differences in the time of political socialization would seem to be a function of different influences which come into play in different periods of an individual's personal development.

PRIMARY GROUP INFLUENCE
IN POLITICAL SOCIALIZATION

An interest in politics is probably related to the opportunity to hear about it or directly experience it. The opportunity to become acquainted with political life is given when significant persons in an individual's most immediate social environment are themselves in close and continuing contact with politics. Having parents, relatives or close friends in politics is likely to facilitate an individual's own awareness of and familiarity with public affairs. The strong influence exerted by primary groups on voting behavior, for instance, is a reasonably well-documented finding of recent social research.[9] Earlier research on non-political social participation has also shown that family members tend to be either all participants or all nonparticipants.[10] While precise data concerning the general population are lacking, it is plain that state legislators tend to come from families which are much more involved in politics than the average American family. As Table 2 indicates, from 41%, in the case of New Jersey legislators, to 59%, in the case of Ohio and Tennessee legislators, reported that one or more of their family had been or were in politics, although in a few cases they went back several generations to find them.

State legislators, in recalling their earliest interest in politics, indicated that they are sensitive to primary group influence and attributed their political awareness to parents, relatives or friends and associates. Between 34%, in the case of the California respondents, and

[9] See Paul F. Lazarsfeld, Bernard Berelson, and Hazel Gaudet, *The People's Choice* (New York: Columbia University Press, 1948), pp. 140–145; Angus Campbell, Gerald Gurin, and Warren E. Miller, *The Voter Decides* (Evanston: Row, Peterson and Company, 1954), pp. 199–206; Bernard R. Berelson, Paul F. Lazarsfeld, and William N. McPhee, *Voting* (Chicago: University of Chicago Press, 1954), pp. 88–109.

[10] W. A. Anderson, "The Family and Individual Social Participation," *American Sociological Review*, VIII (1943), 420–424.

Table 2:   Relatives of State Legislators in Politics

	CAL.	N.J.	OHIO	TENN.
Relatives in Politics	$N = 113$	$N = 79$	$N = 162$	$N = 120$
One or more	43%	41%	59%	59%
None	57	59	41	41
Total	100%	100%	100%	100%

47%, in the case of the New Jersey respondents, spontaneously mentioned members in their immediate circle as agents of their political socialization. But if we look in more detail at those who attributed their political interest to persons with whom they were in direct and sustained relationship, we find that many more mentioned family members than friends and associates as having been instrumental in this respect (Table 3). Moreover, in the case of two states, New Jersey and Ohio, substantial pluralities of those who mentioned primary group influence as the source of their political consciousness— 32% and 31%, respectively—recalled that their family had been more than occasionally active and attributed their own political awakening to this fact, and in New Jersey friends and associates were named more frequently than elsewhere. Whether the differences between Ohio and New Jersey, on the one hand, and California and Tennessee, on the other, are meaningful reflections of possibly differing functions of the nuclear family in the political socialization of youth in these states can only be a matter of conjecture.

Table 3:   The Influence of Primary Groups on State Legislators' Interest in Politics

	CAL.	N.J.	OHIO	TENN.
Primary Group	$N = 113$	$N = 79$	$N = 162$	$N = 120$
Family members/relatives *active* in politics	18%	32%	31%	19%
Family members/relatives interested in politics	12%	2%	8%	16%
Friends/associates active or interested in politics	7%	13%	4%	8%

Political interest is seen as a matter of family tradition or inheritance: "I was born into a political family. . . . I grew up in politics"; or, "I guess it's pretty much a combination of environment and heredity. . . . We are all sort of involved in politics," were typical comments. Others were more explicit. Familiarity with political campaigning by his father going hand in hand with earliest awareness is illustrated in this comment:

> My first recollection of politics was when I was four years old and my father was a member of the House of Representatives. I played here in this room when I was a little boy. . . . Then, too, I experienced a brief Congressional campaign when my father was a candidate. He was defeated, but the whole thing left a deep impression on me. I met lots of people in politics through my father.

The family as a source of the politician's early identification with a political party and awareness of a political issue is described as follows:

> My father was a member of the city council. He ran for Congress on the Republican ticket and was defeated. I went to political meetings with him, I was always interested in politics. I therefore always felt a close identification with the Republican Party. On my mother's side the family was Democratic. . . . And my mother's mother was a suffragette. There was much discussion about the woman franchise.

The vividness of these and many other accounts testifies to the important role played by family members in shaping the politician's orientations. Ties with a political party, consciousness of public issues, knowledge of both the serious and pleasurable aspects of political behavior, or sense of public responsibility, appear as products of political socialization in the most intimate form of primary group life.

What strikes one in reading some of the comments is the casualness of the socialization process when the agents are friends or associates. As one respondent put it, "some of the boys I was going around with were interested in politics, so I just went along." Another put it this way:

> I would say that I was catapulted into politics without any approach. My law partner has been city councilman and had held other political jobs. So I went naturally to work in his behalf in these campaigns. This I did for a number of years. So from there I was asked to run for the legislature. I didn't seek the job, I was asked.

In the first case, political interest seemed to be a by-product of one's need to be socially acceptable; in the second case, it derived from activity on behalf of a politically involved professional associate. In both cases apparent political apathy is transformed into political awareness and participation as a result of primary group contact.

POLITICAL INTEREST AS RESULT OF PARTICIPATION

Political socialization does not necessarily precede some form of political activity. A person may participate in political action of one kind or another without any previously crystallized political affect. For instance, he may find himself involved in "school politics" because his political potentialities are sensed by his peers; he may become active in political campaigns because of other social ties with other campaign workers; or he may even participate in low-level political party work, as an errand-boy or leaflet distributor, without really understanding the meaning of his activity. As Table 4 indicates, these types of participation are reported as stimulants of political interest. California respondents, in particular, mentioned these directly political forms of activity as sources of their political involvement, though New Jersey legislators exceed the Californians in the "party work" category.

Table 4:   *Political Interest as Result of Political*
and Non-Political Participation

	CAL.	N.J.	OHIO	TENN.
Type of Participation	$N = 113$	$N = 79$	$N = 162$	$N = 120$
Activity in school politics	12%	4%	4%	# %
Study of politics	20%	9%	14%	8%
Political work: general (campaigns, meetings)	20%	6%	10%	13%
Party work	12%	32%	10%	7%
Civic/community work	11%	8%	6%	8%
Activity in occupational/professional groups	8%	4%	6%	# %
Activity in ethnic/religious groups	# %	3%	—	—
Legislative lobbying	3%	1%	—	2%
Politically-related job (teaching civics; journalism; law; etc.)	8%	4%	3%	7%

Less than one per cent.

Secondly, a person may become exposed to politics by experiences which are themselves non-political in character, but which are close enough to politics to serve as agencies of political socialization. For instance, school learning, or even self-education, may stimulate political awareness; so may participation in civic or community affairs, as well as activity in occupational, professional, or minority groups. Finally, a person may come to be politically conscious by performing professional tasks which are relatively close to politics, like lobbying, newspaper work, law practice, teaching of civics, or public employment. As Table 4 shows, some of these forms of non-political participation were recalled by state legislators as avenues of their political socialization. Again, these forms of activity seem to play a somewhat more important role in California than in the other states, though inter-state differences are consistently small.

Two aspects of the distributions in Table 4 deserve special mention. First, the study of civics, politics or related subjects in school does not seem to serve as a potent lubricant of political consciousness or interest. With the exception of California, where a fifth of the legislators pointed to their formal schooling as having had relevance to their political interest, a surprisingly small percentage gave responses such as: "I guess it started with my getting interested in the study of civics in grade school and high school. I suppose this study of civics was my first inspiration."

Secondly, it seems that, for a number of the politicians who populate the four state legislatures, political or party work itself was the source of their political initiation. This seems to be particularly the case in New Jersey, and might be due, in part, to the highly politicized atmosphere characteristic of that state's metropolitan areas. In other words, party politics operates as its own socializing agent. Getting involved in political work, either occasionally in connection with a campaign, or by doing regular party work, seems for some of these politicians to have been a first stimulus of a more permanent dedication to public life. Running errands, handing out leaflets, or door-to-door canvassing work was given by some as their earliest recollection of interest in politics, usually among those whose family had been active or interested in politics before them. For others, being recruited by a party to run for party or public office seems to have been the source of a political orientation. As one legislator put it, "I got politically interested in 1938 when I became involved in county and state politics. I then became the chairman of the county committee."

Among non-political forms of participation mentioned by legislators as decisive in their political socialization, activity in civic affairs or community work ranks first in all four states. That such activity served as a direct incentive to political interest might be expressed as follows:

> This is actually an extension of my activities in the school and community. I was interested in service clubs, civic progress and community problem-solving. It was getting so I was going to meetings ten nights a week. It's only a short step from this to public office.

Activity in occupational and professional groups, or contact with politics as a result of actually non-political but politically-connected jobs, was recalled by a few legislators as influencing their interest in politics. A newspaperman would say that, of course, he became interested because of his profession. Another "became interested in political intrigue as a young cub reporter, and was hired to write publicity for a state senator." A former union leader recalled that his interest was aroused when politicians catered to him to win the support of his membership. A lawyer recalled his work for a property owners association before government bodies, or a teacher of civics suggested that his political interest was stimulated when he took his classes to visit the state capital. Finally, contacts with politicians in service jobs were reported by some as having been instrumental in developing their political interest. A number of legislators mentioned having served as pages in the state legislature while in college. As one of them recalled, "I attribute my early interest in politics to my employment in the legislature." Public employment, in administrative departments of the state government or in the elected office of county trustee, was reported by some as a source of their first political interest.

The impression one gets from these recollections is one of the great variety of agents and activities which can operate as influential stimuli of political socialization. One is struck by the great heterogeneity of the sources which stimulate a political focus of attention. Most of those who mention these stimuli became interested in politics, at least in their own definition of what it means to be "politically interested," rather late in their personal development—in support of the notion that political socialization is not restricted to the earliest years of the life cycle, but that it is a process which takes place at later phases as well. While it is likely, of course, that the foundations of political interest were laid earlier, it is the later phases which apparently stand out in these legislators' perceptions of their political socialization.

POLITICAL INTEREST AS RESULT OF PUBLIC EVENTS

Great public events, either of a periodic character, like election campaigns, or of more singular though far-reaching nature, like wars or economic depressions, may have a politically mobilizing impact on persons not previously concerned with public affairs. Similarly, relatively unimportant local or state problems become public issues which may involve people who before their occurrence had paid no attention to politics. Forty-two per cent of California, 25% of New Jersey, 21% of Ohio, and 18% of Tennessee legislators recalled particular events or conditions as stimuli of their first political interest. While the percentages in particular categories are small (Table 5), except in the case of California, in connection with political campaigns, and in New Jersey, in connection with local conditions or issues, the tenor of these recollections suggests that political socialization occasioned by public events may be accompanied by a special intensity of feeling not generally experienced under other circumstances.

The Presidential campaign, in particular, seems to have a latent socializing function in the American political system. It serves not only to activate voters, but the excitement, the turbulence, the color, the intrusion of the Presidential campaign into the routine existence of a relatively little politicized society seem to make a profound impression, so that many years later a particular election or administration may be recalled with a good deal of relish as a source of political interest—as if the election had been held only yesterday:

> In the Hughes campaign of 1916 my grandfather said to me: "My boy, I'll meet my maker. There's only one thing I regret, that

Table 5: Political Interest as Result of Particular Events or Conditions

	CAL.	N.J.	OHIO	TENN.
Events or Conditions	$N = 113$	$N = 79$	$N = 162$	$N = 120$
Presidential campaigns or administrations	14%	4%	11%	8%
Other political campaigns	19%	5%	2%	3%
War	2%	3%	2%	3%
Depression	5%	—	2%	—
Local conditions/issues	5%	15%	2%	4%
State conditions/issues	5%	—	1%	—

I voted in the re-election campaign for Cleveland's second term."
People streamed through the house to find out from the old man
how to vote.

During the Bryan-McKinley campaign I hanged a picture of Mc-
Kinley on my bedroom wall. My father took it off and I hanged
it up again. He took it off and took me to the woodshed. I've been
a Republican ever since.

Remarks made about gubernatorial, senatorial or other election
campaigns were less colorful than recollections of Presidential contests. War, on the other hand, was recalled in more intensely personal
terms by the few who ascribed their political interest to this experience. "Many of us, when we came back, had a new awakening, a
new interest in civic affairs," or, "In prison camp I decided that we
should do everything that we could on a local level instead of joining
big organizations to influence grand policy."

Some California and Ohio legislators mentioned the depression
as the origin of their political awakening. One respondent reported,
for instance, that in the thirties, while he was employed in county
agricultural work, "the plight of the farmers brought my interest."
Another said that "during the depression everybody was politically
conscious, and that interest stayed with me." For some of those who
claimed to have become politically aware in the depression, politics
seems to have meant a job. As one of them put it, "Well, during
the depression, we weren't selling any automobiles. The situation was
favorable for me to get on the ticket for county auditor." In this
case, for instance, a first interest in politics seems to have coincided
with the respondent's active entry into politics. Finally, state or local
conditions were reported by a few legislators as having been instrumental in their political socialization.

PERSONAL PREDISPOSITIONS
AND POLITICAL SOCIALIZATION

As we mentioned earlier, our research orientation was to find
out "how" state legislators became interested in politics, not "why"
they became interested. Nevertheless, it is noteworthy that half of
the California, New Jersey and Ohio legislators, and a third of the
Tennesseans, seized our question of "how" they had become interested
as an opportunity to reflect on certain personal predispositions which,
they apparently felt, preceded or accompanied their political awakening. It is possible, of course, that these recollections are nothing more

Table 6: Personal Predispositions and Political Socialization

Predispositions	CAL. $N = 113$	N.J. $N = 79$	OHIO $N = 162$	TENN. $N = 120$
Political power	3%	6%	2%	3%
Admiration for politicians	19%	3%	5%	2%
Indignation	9%	8%	5%	2%
Sense of obligation: general	15%	5%	8%	#%
Sense of obligation: to special groups	3%	6%	#%	#%
Desire for sociability	2%	5%	1%	2%
Physical handicaps displaced	#%	—	#%	#%
Long interest: unspecified	14%	24%	33%	23%

\# Less than one per cent.

than current rationalizations. Yet, even if we are not prepared to interpret these responses as anything else, they are probably quite genuine perceptions and, as such, constitute significant elements in legislators' self-definitions as politicians.

Of those who expressed themselves in predispositional terms, a good many simply said that they had always been interested in politics, and left it at that. But perhaps the most interesting finding revealed in Table 6 is that only very few of these politicians spontaneously mentioned political power, influence or authority as the kind of stimuli which predisposed them towards a political orientation. While it is, of course, impossible to say whether such power motives were really present or absent among those who admitted to them and those who did not, there is no reason to suppose that in a democratic society, where a large part of the community participates in the selection of public officials, politicians are necessarily and only recruited from power-motivated persons. Even if politicians differ from average citizens in the degree of their political involvement, values other than power are likely to bring would-be leaders to public attention.[11] The fact that only a few of these legislators indicated power as a predispositional correlate of their political socialization is, there-

[11] See Harold D. Lasswell, "The Selective Effect of Personality in Political Participation," in Richard Christie and Marie Jahoda, eds., *Studies in the Scope and Method of "The Authoritarian Personality"* (Glencoe: The Free Press, 1954), p. 221, for a discussion of political personality in democratic settings.

fore, quite understandable. Only a few were as explicit as the legislator who said that it was hard for him to explain what first interested him in politics, but continued:

> I would say that I'm the sort of person interested in doing things. I feel I should contribute from the policy point of view. I'm not a good joiner. I feel the same sort of thing carries over into government and politics. I have always some desire not to be in the crowd. I'm never content to go to meetings and just listen and go home. I like to get my oar in.

Admiration for politicians—as ego-ideals—was suggested by others as having had some influence on their developing political interest. That favorable impressions of other politicians formed at an early age have an impact on political awareness seems plausible, as the following example illustrates:

> I do remember that one summer I was staying with my uncle. I guess I was about 13. I attended an old-fashioned town meeting with him. My uncle was quite active at the meeting, and it made quite an impression on me.

While some legislators recalled having become politically interested as a result of admiring certain politicians, others reported having become interested for just the opposite reason—because they were dissatisfied with politicians or political situations:

> This is a somewhat long story. I was an officer of a club, and in this capacity I had to call upon a city councilman to speak with him about getting the use of (some facility). He promised me to look into it and have my request heard before the commission, but he never did. He just ignored me.

Sense of obligation appears, not surprisingly, as a relatively frequent category of predispositional responses. This kind of answer is, of course, part and parcel of a politician's armor of rationalizations and can hardly be taken at face value:

> Well, it came about twelve or fourteen years ago when I decided I had spent all my life tending to our business and had done nothing for the community. I looked around to see how I could help out and decided to run for the legislature. I thought my business experience would be useful in the legislature.

Yet, there is an element of genuine commitment in this response that is in sharp contrast to mere political rhetoric. In other words, a distinction must be made between the politician for whom "public service" is a convenient device of deception, of himself, his audience, or both, and the politician who really feels a sense of obligation.

A few legislators suggested that their interest in politics was stimulated by the "social" possibilities which politics seemed to offer, as, for instance, the former school superintendent who upon retirement missed the chance to meet people which his occupation had given him and who, for this reason, claimed to have become interested in politics. Finally, three legislators attributed their initial interest in politics to the existence of a physical handicap and implied that politics offered them a compensatory opportunity. As one of these pointed out, "As a kid I had a bad leg, couldn't participate in sports and developed an interest in politics. I thought a legal background qualified a fellow for anything in public life."

It requires re-emphasis that our data do not tell us "why" these legislators were "moved" to seek a political career, while others in the general population, with similar ostensible experiences, were not so moved. In other words, the perceptual data on legislators' pre-political activities, or the events surrounding their earliest political interest, or even what they described as predispositional factors, cannot be interpreted in a motivational sense. If there is a personality syndrome of which one may think as "political man," the data do not and cannot reveal its existence among these state legislators.

IDEOLOGY AND POLITICAL SOCIALIZATION

Not unexpectedly in a society like the American where politics is pragmatic rather than ideological, political beliefs seem to play a minor part in the process of political socialization. As Table 7 shows, only very small minorities in all four states linked our question of how they had become interested in politics with a discussion of political beliefs. This is all the more significant because the open-ended character of the question represented a perfect opportunity for ideological discourse if the respondent wished it. One can only guess, of course, that in a European country where ideology constitutes a more important item of political culture, a legislator would probably have seized this opportunity to express political opinions or beliefs. And those who did mention beliefs gave them only most cursory attention.

Table 7:   Socio-Economic Beliefs in Political Socialization

Beliefs	CAL. $N = 113$	N.J. $N = 79$	OHIO $N = 162$	TENN. $N = 120$
Liberal	7%	1%	2%	—
Conservative	4%	1%	1%	2%
Pro-business	—	—	#%	—
Pro-labor	3%	3%	#%	—
Pro-farmer	#%	1%	1%	—
Pro-religious/ethnic groups	—	3%	#%	—

\# Less than one per cent.

SUMMARY: MAJOR SOURCES OF POLITICAL INTEREST

If we look at a summary of the major sources of political interest as spontaneously reported by legislators themselves, some state-to-state patterns emerge. We cannot say absolutely that these patterns are not due purely to chance, but the very fact that patterns do occur suggests that inter-state differences may be genuine expressions of political socialization processes among the four states. Table 8 summarizes the responses in our major categories. The most obvious difference to be noted is between California and the other states in regard to the influence of primary groups. One possible explanation of the relatively low percentage in the California column is that primary groups are less effective as political socializing agents in California because primary group influence is predicated on a reasonably stable population structure. But California is distinguished from the other three states by the fact that it is an immigrant state, and it may be that the population movement into the state has not permitted the formation of stable primary groups which can act as effective agents of political socialization. On the other hand, New Jersey, the oldest of the states in terms of admission to the Union, shows the greatest percentage in the primary group category, with Ohio and Tennessee in close middle positions.

What California may lack by way of primary group influence, it seems to make up in the categories of participation and events or conditions as stimulants of political interest. With regard to participation, it may be suggested that social and political activity is seized upon by an immigrant population to make itself feel at home in

Table 8: Summary: Major Sources of Political Interest

Major Sources	CAL. $N = 113$	N.J. $N = 79$	OHIO $N = 162$	TENN. $N = 120$
Primary groups	34%	47%	43%	42%
Participation	70%	60%	49%	43%
Events/conditions	42%	25%	21%	18%
Predispositions	52%	53%	52%	33%
Beliefs	16%	10%	6%	3%

a new environment. In newly created communities, fewer legislators are "born into" politics, more become politically active in the process of community life. Similarly, political beliefs seem to play a slightly more important role in a state where stable political party patterns have had less a chance to crystallize than in states characterized by very definite, if different, party-system structures. In both the participation and event categories, as in the category of political beliefs, the pattern of responses ranks California first, New Jersey second, Ohio third, and Tennessee last. Moreover, Tennessee legislators were less likely to mention personal predispositions than the legislators from the other three states. Just why this should be the case we cannot say.

What do our data tell us about the political socialization of state legislators? In general, it seems that a great many sources are operative in initiating political interest. Perhaps the most significant finding is tentative support for the hypothesis that political socialization—the process by which political interest is acquired—may occur at almost any phase of the life cycle, even among men and women whose concern with public affairs is presumably more intense and permanent than that of the average citizen. But it seems to take place more often at a relatively early age. Whether the differences we found from state to state, either with regard to the agency or time of socialization, are significant as evidence of differing political sub-cultures would require more detailed and systematic inquiry than we were able to execute here.

III

Individual Political Behavior

No matter when, where, or how people acquire their orientations and predispositions to behave, the result affects their approach to politics. The selections in Part III were chosen because they illustrate and analyze the wide variety of individual dispositions which are known to affect politics. Since no theory unites them all, it would only misrepresent the current state of knowledge to impose some artificial order.

Lester Milbrath summarizes much of the questionnaire research on individual differences in feelings of social ease, self-confidence, and power motivation. He finds that few people who are low in feelings of social ease and self-confidence participate in political campaign activities. On the other hand, many—but not all—of those who score high on these feelings *do* campaign. It seems, then, that a sense of social ease and self-confidence are necessary but insufficient conditions for personal involvement in political campaigns.

A test of Lasswell's formulation of the "political personality"[1] finds it wanting. Power-hungry people appear no more likely to participate in politics than anyone else. However, this finding breaks down for "offices with high power or with a clear road to success." People who are high in power motivation are especially attracted to such offices. Rather than refuting Lasswell, these results refine his hypotheses into more specific assertions.[2]

People have a marked capacity to see and hear only what they want to. Berelson, Lazarsfeld, and McPhee provide a clear example of this in the realm of political opinion. They found that the voters of Elmira, New York, in the 1948 presidential election tended to perceive more agreement than really existed between their own stands on key campaign issues and the stands taken by their favorite candidates. This misperception varied directly with the individual's partisan involvement and inversely with his level of exposure to public communications.

As Greenstein points out, the individual's partisan involvement does more than distort his perception of candidates' stands. It also simplifies his voting choice where issues and candidates are hard to sort out. Since party identification starts in childhood, it shapes other political perceptions and is extremely hard to change. Thus, the stability of party identification—like most dispositions to which individuals are politically socialized[3]—promotes the continuity and stability of the American political system. It does this by perpetuating the two-party system through the thicket of rapidly changing issues and candidates.

More than any other factor, party identification determines how an American will vote. This does not mean, however, that important issues or exceptional candidates cannot induce voters to "defect" from their party for one or more elections. V. O. Key finds some interesting correlations between voters' opinions on issues and their voting choices

---

[1] See Part I, Selection 5.

[2] For further discussion of the validity of Lasswell's hypothesis that displaced power motivation produces a political involvement, see the introductory comments to Part I.

[3] On this point see Roberta Sigel's selection in Part II.

in presidential elections.[4] The most recent Survey Research Center evidence, however, seems to reconfirm the typically small role of issue and candidate orientations relative to party identification. Taking the distribution of party identification as the "normal vote," Campbell and his associates have erected an elaborate theory to explain election outcomes.[5]

Two individual dispositions currently under intensive study in social science are authoritarianism and sense of political efficacy.[6] Louise Harned shows that although authoritarian party workers do not differ significantly from nonauthoritarian party workers in quantity of political activity, the type of activity which they find congenial is different in predictable ways. Authoritarian party workers are more concerned with the organization of the party than are nonauthoritarian workers, and they are much less likely to agree with their party's stands on the issues of the day. Such party workers, then, are better suited to getting out the committed vote than to reinforcing marginal voters' opinions or converting voters from the opposition.

The sense of political efficacy—the belief held by the individual that he can influence public decision making—is a disposition crucial to the functioning of democratic political systems. For, as the selection from *The American Voter* shows, citizens tend to participate in politics only when they expect to accomplish something by doing so. A person who deems futile his efforts to influence policy will rarely bother to make any efforts. After all, why talk if no one listens? Yet, democracy is impossible without citizens who feel that they would be heard if they aired a grievance and who therefore are active participants in the polity.

Furthermore, a person's sense of political efficacy appears to be highest when his sense of *personal* efficacy is also high. Thus, the sense of political efficacy may be the result of (or contribute to) one's sense of effectiveness in nonpolitical affairs.[7]

[4] V. O. Key, Jr., *The Responsible Electorate: Rationality in Presidential Voting, 1936–1960* (Cambridge: Belknap, 1966).

[5] Angus Campbell, Philip E. Converse, Warren E. Miller, and Donald E. Stokes, *Elections and the Political Order* (New York: Wiley, 1966).

[6] Some of this research is summarized in the introduction.

[7] For some other possible causes of the sense of political efficacy, see George I. Balch, "The Cognitive Basis of Powerlessness," James W. Dyson (ed.), *Attitude and Action in Politics: A Reader in Political Behavior* (Boston: Blaisdell, forthcoming).

In the selection from *The Appeals of Communism,* Gabriel Almond investigates some of the ways in which neurotic needs have made communism an attractive political movement: as a dignified outlet for hostility, as a source of strong authority, as a shelter from loneliness, and as a compensation for feelings of inadequacy. Note the parallel between this and Lasswell's thesis that intense political involvement may be an attempt to compensate for one's personal deficiencies or frustrations or both.[8]

Several other studies may offer some perspective on this one. Milton Rokeach found less anxiety in a group of British Communists than in several American and British noncommunist groups. Noting that Communists spend enormous portions of their time in group political activities (a fact also noted by Almond), he suggests that "if one is constantly busy, tired, and in need of sleep, there is no time to be anxiously preoccupied with oneself and with apprehension of the future."[9]

In a study of radicals and liberals in Chicago, William Kornhauser found that an extremely high social commitment is demanded by the radical organization. The radical finds himself insulated from nonradical friends and associates, even to the point of straining the integrity of his family.[10] At the same time, this insulation from people who do not share one's views may operate to reduce anxiety by sheltering the individual from situations conducive to shame and self-doubt. To tie these facts together, we suggest that those who join the Communist Party to satisfy their neurotic needs have a good chance of getting what they came for.

[8] See Part I, Selection 5.
[9] Milton Rokeach, *The Open and Closed Mind* (New York: Basic Books, 1960), p. 347.
[10] William Kornhauser, "Social Bases of Political Commitment: A Study of Liberals and Radicals," Arnold M. Rose (ed.), *Human Behavior and Social Processes: An Interactionist Approach* (Boston: Houghton Mifflin, 1962), pp. 321–339.

12 *Political Participation as a Function of Personal Factors*

LESTER W. MILBRATH

Personality is a complicated, interrelated, and interacting system. The study of a complete personality, such as might be carried out by a psychoanalyst, is time-consuming and requires special training. Case studies of this type show rather convincingly how personality affects political behavior,[1] but the time costs of such studies are

Reprinted from Lester W. Milbrath, *Political Participation* (Chicago: Rand McNally & Company, 1965), pp. 73–78, 81–83, and 83–89 by permission of the author and publisher.
[1] M. Brewster Smith, Jerome S. Bruner, and Robert W. White, *Opinions and Personality* (New York: Wiley, 1956); Robert E. Lane, *Political Ideology: Why*

so great that it is difficult to get enough cases to arrive at generalizations that one can be confident would hold for the great mass of
people. Furthermore, the personality dynamics leading to a political
act are so complex as to defy succinct summarization. Consequently,
no attempt is made in this book to summarize psychoanalytic or depth
studies of personality and political behavior.

Personality also can be studied, in somewhat more piecemeal
fashion, by using scales to measure specific personality traits.[2] The
methods of trait psychology enable one to administer scales and tests
to large numbers of people and to establish statistical relationships
between traits and behavior patterns. The discussion to follow depends mainly on the findings of trait psychology. These are uneven
in coverage: certain traits have been well investigated, while others
are neglected. These findings also are difficult to interpret because
of the measurement difficulties mentioned above. Failure to discover
a relationship between a trait and behavior may mean that, in fact,
there is no relationship, but also it may mean that the researcher's
measuring tool does not measure what he hoped it was measuring.
If a researcher finds no correlation between a cynicism scale and
political activity, it may mean that, in reality, there is no relationship,
but it also may mean that either his measure of cynicism or his measure of activity is faulty. Conversely, finding a relationship may not
be proof of its existence; relationships can appear as an artifact of
measurement bias. . . . One must question the assumption that a
scale measures what the designer intended it to. In this section, syn-
dromes of traits are discussed rather than specific scales. If similar
results are discovered when similar, but not identical, scales are administered to different samples, one has increased confidence that
a relationship does in fact exist between a trait and political behavior.[3]

SOCIABILITY

It has been observed many times that politicians are gladhanding
extroverts. Does it follow that a sociable personality is a prerequisite

---

the American Common Man Believes What He Does (New York: The Free
Press of Glencoe, 1962).

[2] For present purposes, a "scale" is a form of personality test in which a series of
statements is presented to the individual. Responses to these statements are
assumed to reflect the individual's characteristic ways of responding to the stimuli
with which the statements deal.—EDS.

[3] Donald T. Campbell and Donald W. Fiske, "Convergent and Discriminant
Validation by the Multitrait Multimethod Matrix," *Psychological Bulletin*, LVI
(March, 1959), 81–105.

for political action? Some scholars believe that man has a social need, and that filling this need is an important motive for engaging in political action.[4] Sociability is here defined as the possession of social skills and a feeling of ease and graciousness in social relationships. *Sociable personalities are more likely to enter politics than nonsociable personalities; this is especially true of political activities that require social interaction.*[5] The studies supporting this point used similar, but not identical, measures of sociability, and the differential effects of socioeconomic status were controlled.[6] Sociable persons were significantly[7] more likely to engage in activities requiring social interaction: campaigning, contacting politicians, soliciting political funds, and being consulted on policy. Behaviors not requiring social interaction, such as being active in a party, contributing money, or attending meetings, had lower correlations (nonsignificant on one sample).

It was necessary to control for SES in these studies because there is a positive correlation between SES and sociability. A correlation between sociability and participation could be a mere artifact of the well-known correlation between SES and political participation. The relationship between sociability and participation, however, was significant even with SES controls. Sociability should be called a necessary but not sufficient condition for entering politics. Many sociable persons do not become active. The reverse is not true, however; a nonsociable person has a barrier to participation in socially interactive political behavior.

The five-nation study gathered information about the general social activity patterns of their respondents, finding cross-national differences in general social activity levels. *Nations that were high*

---

[4] James Davies, *Human Nature in Politics* (New York: Wiley, 1963), pp. 34–36.
[5] Lester W. Milbrath, *Measuring the Personalities of Lobbyists* (mimeographed); Lester W. Milbrath and Walter Klein, "Personality Correlates of Political Participation," *Acta Sociologica*, VI (fasc. 1–2), 53–66; Yasumasa Kuroda, *Measurement, Correlates, and Significance of Political Participation at the Community Level* (mimeographed).
[6] A relationship between two variables is "controlled" when it holds within categories of one or more additional variables. For instance, the authors in question have found that a higher proportion of people who get high scores on a scale of sociability also get high scores on a scale of political activity than do those who score low on sociability. This is true whether one is high, medium, or low in socioeconomic status (SES).—EDS.
[7] This refers to "statistical significance," which indicates the probability of finding a specific relationship by chance. Usually, a relationship is judged "significant" when it could have occurred by chance less than five times out of a hundred. This concept is further developed in Hubert M. Blalock, *Social Statistics* (New York: McGraw-Hill, 1960), chs. 8 and 9.—EDS.

on social activity (the United States and the United Kingdom) *also were high on the level of participation in politics by their citizenry.*[8] Nations low on social and political activity (especially Italy) had a relatively high percentage of persons who did not feel confident and safe in interacting with other persons.

A study of opinion leaders found that gregariousness was related to public affairs opinion leadership.[9] Some scholars have suggested that while the possession of social skills facilitates entry into politics, overly high social aspirations could lead a person away from politics toward more immediately gratifying social activities.[10] One study found no correlation between gregariousness and political activity.[11]

Another trait that probably belongs in the same syndrome with sociability is a sense of personal esteem; the two are highly intercorrelated.[12] It is difficult for a person who does not have a reasonably high estimation of his personal worth to interact naturally with other persons. *People who like themselves and who expect most others to like them find it easier to enter the political fray.*[13] *Such persons tend to have more "faith in people" and in politicians, which facilitates their participation in politics.*[14] Those nations which were low on social and political activity especially seemed to have many persons with very low faith in people; the latter trait, in turn, was related to political trust.[15]

EGO STRENGTH

Other terms that might apply to this syndrome are self-confidence, sense of competence, or sense of effectiveness. Traits in this syndrome are positively correlated with sociability and esteem; apparently, many

[8] Gabriel Almond and Sidney Verba, *The Civic Culture* (Princeton: Princeton University Press, 1963), ch. 10.
[9] Elihu Katz and Paul Lazarsfeld, *Personal Influence* (Glencoe, Ill.: The Free Press, 1955).
[10] Morris Rosenberg, "Some Determinants of Political Apathy," *Public Opinion Quarterly*, XVIII (Winter, 1954–1955), 349–366; and also Robert E. Lane, *Political Life: Why People Get Involved in Politics* (Glencoe, Ill.: The Free Press, 1959).
[11] Bernard Hennessy, "Politicals and Apoliticals: Some Measurements of Personality Traits," *Midwest Journal of Political Science*, III (November, 1959), 336–355.
[12] Milbrath and Klein, *op. cit.*
[13] *Ibid.*
[14] Lane, *Political Life, op. cit.*; Morris Rosenberg, "Misanthropy and Political Ideology," *American Sociological Review*, XXI (December, 1965), 690–695.
[15] Almond and Verba, *loc. cit.*

of the same environmental conditions that create sociability also create ego strength. The personal effectiveness scale[16] . . . is one example of a scale that measures this trait. The reader will recall that it correlated positively with political efficacy and also that persons who feel personally effective are more likely to become active in politics.[17]

The statistically demonstrated relationship between personal effectiveness and political participation corresponds with some earlier speculations. One scholar characterized the "autonomous character" as a person with high competence and with high affect toward politics; such a person would be more likely to be active in politics.[18] Another speculated that persons with a desire to be creative and those with a need for ego enhancement would be inclined to become active in politics.[19]

As might be expected, *persons growing up in an upper-middle or upper SES environment are more likely to develop self-confidence and feelings of competence than those from a lower SES environment. This is especially characteristic of persons who achieve the higher ranks of education.*[20] The reader is reminded of Dahl's argument . . . that environment and feelings of confidence and efficacy have interactive effects on one another. Dahl found that if the effects of feelings of confidence and efficacy were controlled statistically, the relationship between SES and political participation was no longer statistically significant.[21] This suggests that environment primarily affects political participation through shaping personality traits like sociability and ego strength.

It is also difficult to separate the effects of environment from those of heredity in developing feelings of confidence and effectiveness. The more generously endowed child, who is sensitive and analytical, learns to manipulate successfully the objects and persons in

[16] Items for this scale are in Milbrath, *Political Participation,* p. 158. The concept itself is discussed on pp. 58–60 of that work and in Selection 16, "Some Roots and Consequences of the Sense of Political Efficacy."—Eds.

[17] Lester W. Milbrath, *Political Participation, op. cit.,* pp. 58–60.

[18] David Riesman, *Faces in the Crowd* (New Haven: Yale University Press, 1952).

[19] Morris Rosenberg, "The Meaning of Politics in Mass Society," *Public Opinion Quarterly,* XV (Spring, 1951), 5–15.

[20] Angus Campbell, Phillip Converse, Warren Miller, and Donald Stokes, *The American Voter* (New York: Wiley, 1960); Robert A. Dahl, *Who Governs? Democracy and Power in an American City* (New Haven: Yale University Press, 1961).

[21] *Ibid.,* pp. 291–292.

his environment early in life. If he is also well coordinated and successful athletically, his sense of mastery will be enhanced. The rewards of successful manipulation soon build a firm personality trait of self-confidence. A child of this type who also lives in a high SES environment is given many opportunities to encounter and master different types of situations; consequently, he has little fear of social, business, or political challenge. His low SES counterpart, who may be equally gifted, will have less broad familiarity with challenging situations.

One additional bit of evidence bears on this trait. One study found that *persons who score highly on the personal effectiveness scale are less likely to resent government.*[22] One can speculate that persons who feel effective in dealing with their environment also feel effective in dealing with government and, thus, are less inclined to resent government or to feel that it does not respond to their efforts.

DOMINANCE, MANIPULATIVENESS

It is often supposed that individuals with a personal need for status and power over others naturally gravitate to politics to fulfill their craving. Hobbes and Nietzsche built their political philosophies around this central assumption. In his early writings, notably *Psychopathology and Politics,* Harold Lasswell set forth his famous formula for the developmental sequence of political man. Restating the symbolism of his formula into verbal terms, he said that the private motives, which had been nurtured in the person's early life in the family (especially the motive for power), might become displaced onto public objects. These displaced private motives would tend to be rationalized in terms of the public interest and, thus, ordinary man became transformed into political man. Later Lasswell qualified his position, suggesting that power is a nonprimary motive; considering it the sole or major motive for entering politics was too inflexible an explanation. He thought it more likely that political leaders would seek such values as respect, rectitude, and wealth. If a person did enter politics only to seek power, he would be likely to be restrained by other political actors and might not rise above a lesser position.[23]

---

[22] Donald Stokes, "Popular Evaluations of Government," in Harlan Cleveland and Harold Lasswell, eds., *Ethics and Bigness* (New York: Harper, 1962).

[23] Harold Lasswell, "The Selective Effect of Personality on Political Participation,"

The available empirical evidence on this point (for the United States only) suggests that *persons with high power motivation are not likely to enter politics* (other arenas, such as business or the military, provide better opportunities to dominate others), *and if they do, they are not likely to be very successful at it.*[24] A dominance scale was administered in three studies of political participation.[25] Only a slight trend appeared for dominants to be more likely to become active in politics, and in only one study was the relationship statistically significant, and that just barely. A study of South Carolina legislators found them only slightly more dominant than a sample from the general population.[26] A study of office-holders found no correlation between power motive and holding public office.[27] When only offices with high power or with a clear road to success were considered, the correlation was significant. The researchers also found a correlation between achievement motive and holding public office in political systems where the office had high achievement potential. In sum, the evidence suggests that a desire for dominance and power provides only a weak attraction toward general political action; only in special cases affording clear use of power (rare in politics) could power be considered a significant or primary motivation.

If additional evidence should confirm that power-hungry persons are not particularly likely to go into politics, how would one explain the lack of relationship? It is quite likely that a certain proportion of any population does develop strong motives for power and that

---

in Richard Christie and Marie Jahoda, eds., *Studies in the Scope and Method of "The Authoritarian Personality"* (Glencoe, Ill.: The Free Press, 1954), pp. 197–225. Jacob and Rosenzweig have also suggested that respect is a high motive for entering politics. Herbert Jacob, "Initial Recruitment of Elected Officials in the U.S.: A Model," *The Journal of Politics*, XXIV (November, 1962), 703–716; Robert M. Rosenzweig, "The Politician and the Career in Politics," *Midwest Journal of Political Science*, I (May, 1957), 163–172.

[24] Lane has an excellent discussion of the belief that political man seeks power and suggests why this supposed relationship is not borne out by the evidence. *Political Life, op. cit.*, pp. 124–128.

[25] Lester W. Milbrath, "Predispositions toward Political Contention," *Western Political Quarterly*, XIII (March, 1960), 5–18; Milbrath and Klein, *op. cit.*; Jack Jensen, *Political Participation: A Survey in Evanston, Illinois* (Unpublished master's thesis, Northwestern University).

[26] John McConaughy, "Certain Personality Factors of State Legislators in South Carolina," *American Political Science Review*, XLIV (December, 1950), 897–903.

[27] Rufus P. Browning and Herbert Jacob, "Power Motivation and Political Personality," *Public Opinion Quarterly*, XXVIII (Spring, 1964), 75–90.

some, but not many, do find their way into politics. A very strong power motive may be the outward manifestation of a deep need for reassurance and a cover for feelings of unworthiness and low self-esteem. We saw above that persons of low ego strength are not likely to enter politics. The person who attaches great importance to imposing his will on others is not likely to be very successful in democratic politics; he may alienate instead of attract followers. He may be unwilling to take orders or to serve menially as a way of working his way up in a political party.

Another factor is that the political arena is not a particularly fruitful place to find fulfillment for power needs; there is too little opportunity for direct satisfaction. The worlds of finance, industry, or the military may be more satisfying to a man with lust for power. For many people, the need for power is most visibly satisfied in primary relationships. Perhaps it is enough for such persons that they can be autocrats in their own homes. There are, then, many other environments, in addition to politics, where the need for power can be satisfied; many of them carry fewer uncertainties than politics.

The desire to manipulate is somewhat different from the desire for power. One study found politicals more willing to compromise than apoliticals.[28] Another found law students planning to go into politics scoring higher on a manipulative scale than those not planning to enter politics.[29] There is no evidence that political actives necessarily have a desire or need to manipulate, but the willingness to manipulate and the ability to be successful at it probably facilitates entry into politics.

CONCLUSIONS

The role of personality in attracting people to politics or keeping them out of politics probably is much more pervasive than the sketchy research evidence presented here can indicate. The available evidence suggests that persons with great neurotic or psychotic problems are not attracted to normal democratic political action. The chaotic, rough-and-tumble environment of competitive politics carries few rewards for thin-skinned, neurotic personalities. Such persons might be attracted to extremist politics under certain conditions, but there

[28] Hennessy, *op. cit.*
[29] Robert E. Agger, "Lawyers in Politics," *Temple Law Quarterly*, XXIX (Summer, 1956), 434–452.

are no data specifying such conditions. This is not to say that political actives do not have neurotic needs—probably many of them do—but they usually have their impulses under control and clothe their motives with the garb of public interest. Their defense mechanisms are strong enough to withstand political shock and disappointment. A finding from the Evanston survey, cited earlier, is relevant here: 83 per cent of the party actives said they "enjoyed the challenge of politics," but only 42 per cent of the cross-section of citizens thought they would enjoy it.[30]

The data suggest that political gladiators are persons who are particularly well equipped to deal with their environment. They feel personally competent; they know themselves and feel confident of their knowledge and skills; their ego is strong enough to withstand blows; they are not burdened by a load of anxiety and internal conflict; they can control their impulses; they are astute, sociable, self-expressive, and responsible. Although they may desire to dominate and manipulate others, political gladiators do not seem to lean any further in this direction than persons in many other roles. Gladiators seem to glory in political battle and are self-sufficient enough to withstand the rough-and-tumble of partisan politics. The political arena is not a hospitable place for insecure, timid, and withdrawn people who do not have great faith in their ability to deal effectively with their environment.

[30] Jensen, *op. cit.*

13 *Political Perception: The Candidates' Stands on Issues*

BERNARD R. BERELSON
PAUL F. LAZARSFELD
WILLIAM N. McPHEE

    . . . [P]olitical beliefs and perceptions have a strongly "normative" quality. They not only state that "this is the way things are," but they also imply that "this is their customary or natural state" and therefore what they "ought" to be. The parties are not only what their leaders do or say; the parties are also what their followers believe they are, expect them to be, and therefore think they should be.

    Once again we encounter a brief glimpse of the spiral of cause and effect that constitutes political history—in this case the history of political issues: What the parties do affects what the voters think they are and what the voters think they are affects what they subsequently do. Out of this interaction between subjective perception and objective reality, mutually affecting one another over decades, emerges not only our definition but the reality of a political party's role. The popular image of "what Republicans (or Democrats) are like" helps to define and determine what they "really" are. Today's subjective unreality in the voters' minds affects tomorrow's objective reality in the political arena.

About thirty years ago an analyst of public opinion gained lasting distinction by elaborating the differences between "the world outside and the pictures in our heads." Walter Lippmann discussed what many theorists—philosophers, psychologists, sociologists, political scientists, anthropologists—have noted and documented before and since: subjective perception does not always reflect objective reality accurately. Selective perception—sampling the real world—must be taken into account. The mirror that the mind holds up to nature is often distorted in accordance with the subject's predispositions. The "trickle of messages from the outside is affected by the stored-up images, the preconceptions, and the prejudices which interpret, fill them out, and in their turn powerfully direct the play of our attention, and our vision itself. . . . In the individual person, the limited messages from outside, formed into a pattern of stereotypes, are identified with his own interests as he feels and conceives them."[1] Another student of public opinion put it similarly: "Each looks at, and looks-for, the facts and reasons to which his attention points, perceiving little, if at all, those to which his mind is not directed. As a rule, men see what they look for, and observe the things they expect to see."[2]

The world of political reality, even as it involves a presidential campaign and election, is by no means simple or narrow. Nor is it crystal-clear. Over a period of six months, and intensively for six weeks, the electorate is subjected to a wide variety of campaign events. Even if all the political events were unambiguous, there would still be a problem of political perception; but, as it is, the campaign is composed (often deliberately) of ambiguous as well as clear elements.

Just how clear was the objective field to be perceived in 1948?

[1] Walter Lippmann, *Public Opinion*, p. 21.
[2] A. Lawrence Lowell, *Public Opinion in War and Peace*, p. 22.

Table 1:   Positions Taken by Dewey and Truman
on Four Issues During the Campaign

	Dewey	Truman
Price control	Causes of high prices were war, foreign aid, the administration's discouragement of production, governmental mismanagement Remedies: cut government spending, reduce national debt, increase production No reference to imposition of controls Only one major reference	Republicans would not act against inflation in Eightieth Congress or special session; they rejected the administration's program Called for price controls or anti-inflation measures on several occasions
Taft-Hartley Law	Referred to it as "Labor-Management Relations Act of 1947," never as "Taft-Hartley Law" Made abstract remarks about "labor's freedoms" which would be "zealously guarded and exextended" Approved the law in general ("will not retreat from advances made") but left door open for improvements ("where laws affecting labor can be made a better instrument for labor relations . . .")	Made the "shameful" and "vicious" law a major issue; recalled that Republicans passed it over his veto: "It ought to be repealed" Took this position in at least ten major campaign speeches during October
Policy toward U.S.S.R.	Took a strong anti-communism position; linked communism to administration Made this a major issue in about seven campaign speeches	Took an anti-communism position; major references twice
Public housing	Only minor references to need for more housing (Republican platform called for housing financed by private enterprise, with federal "encouragement" when private industry and local government were unable to fill need)	Republicans "killed" Taft-Ellender-Wagner Bill Called for public housing sponsored by government in at least ten major campaign speeches

Some propagandists, and some students of propaganda, believe that ambiguity often promotes effectiveness, since each subject is then free to define the matter in terms satisfactory to himself. While a sharply clear statement may win some friends by its very decisiveness, it may also lose some people for the same reason. Now Truman and Dewey had both been public figures for some time and had taken public stands on many political matters; yet their positions on the issues in the campaign were not equally clear.

In 1948 Truman took a more straightforward and more aggressive position on these issues than Dewey (Table 1). The latter spoke to a large extent on the need for unity, peace, and freedom, while Truman specified his position *for* price control and public housing and *against* the Taft-Hartley Law. And Truman used quite vigorous language in stating his position, whereas Dewey employed a more lofty rhetoric. Except perhaps for the Russian issue (which became involved with the spy and domestic Communist issue), there can be no question but that, objectively, Dewey's position was more amenable to misperception than Truman's.

And this is reflected in the extent of nonperception of the candidates' stands.[3] On the four issues the proportion of respondents who do not know the candidates' stands average about 10 per cent for Truman and about 25 per cent for Dewey. (This also reflects the fact that Truman's official position brought him before the public on such issues on numerous occasions; but a counterconsideration is that Dewey's position as governor of New York made him especially familiar to Elmirans.)

Perception and Party Preference

More importantly, the voter's perception of where the candidates stand on the issues is not uniformly affected by partisan preference—only selectively so (Chart I). It is not marked on the central issues of price control and the Taft-Hartley Law. Republicans and Democrats agree that Truman is for price control and against the Taft-Hartley Law and that Dewey is for the Taft-Hartley Law and against price control (although on this last there is by no means a clear perception of where Dewey stood). On public housing (and, as we

[3] The questions followed this form: "From what you know, is Truman (Dewey) for the Taft-Hartley Law or against it?" The respondent could say "Don't know" or state that the candidate had not taken any stand on the issue. The perception questions were asked in August, before the campaign proper; replies may have been different in October.

saw earlier, on the Russian problem) the difference between the parties was greater.

Why should the partisans agree in perception on some issues and disagree on others? For one thing, of course, perception varies with the ambiguity of the situation. The less ambiguous the objective situation (e.g., Truman's position on price control), the less disagreement. But, for another, perception seems to vary with the degree

Chart I: *Party Preference Does Not Particularly Affect Voter's Perception of Where Candidates Stand on Some Campaign Issues*

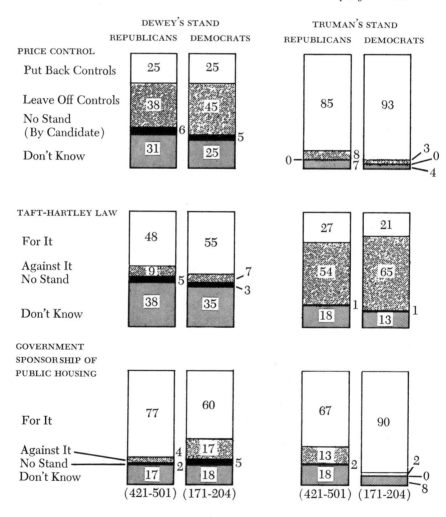

of controversiality of the issues in the community. On price control and the Taft-Hartley Law the respondents with opinions divided about 60–40; on the other two issues (including firmness toward Russia), in Elmira the split is about 90–10. In the latter case, then, there is virtual agreement within the community—which means that one side of the issue is considered "right" and the other side "wrong." Hence there is, so to speak, a standard to guide misperception—and each side pulls its own candidate toward the "correct position" and pushes the opponent away from it. On the two central issues, however, the controversy is too visible to allow a designation of "rightness" for one or the other side, and as a result there is less motive for or gain in misperception. If the voter gets nothing for his misperception (e.g., being "right"), there is less reason for him to engage in it. Deviation or misperception requires a certain degree of ambiguity in the objective situation being perceived, but it also requires a psychic indulgence for the misperceiver. Where this opportunity is not present, perception is likely to be more accurate.

Perception and Own Stand

This suggests that perception of the candidates' stands on issues may be affected by the respondents' own stands on them. The voters can thus manage to increase the consistency within their own political position, or at least the apparent consistency. And this is clearly the case. In almost every instance respondents perceive their candidate's stand on these issues as similar to their own and the opponent's stand as dissimilar—whatever their own position (Chart II). For example, those Republicans who favor price control perceive Dewey as favoring price control (70 per cent), and few who oppose price control perceive Dewey as favoring controls (14 per cent). And the Republicans who are against controls perceive Truman as favoring them somewhat more than the Republicans who are for them. As with their perception of group support, so with their perception of the issues: the partisans manage to "pull" their own candidate and "push" the opposing candidate with considerable consistency. Overlaying the base of objective observation is the distortion effect—distortion in harmony with political predispositions. As Schumpeter says, "Information and arguments in political matters will 'register' only if they link up with the citizen's preconceived ideas."[4]

---

[4] Joseph Schumpeter, *Capitalism, Socialism, and Democracy,* p. 263.

Chart II: *The Voter's Own Stands on the Issues Affect Their Perception of the Candidates' Stands**

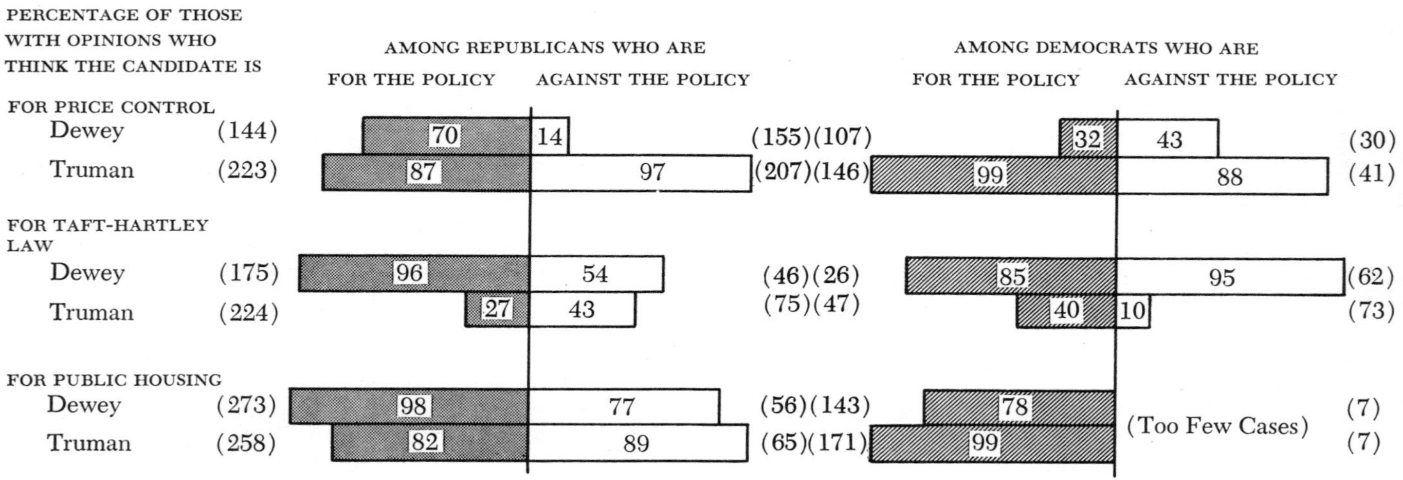

PERCENTAGE OF THOSE
WITH OPINIONS WHO
THINK THE CANDIDATE IS

AMONG REPUBLICANS WHO ARE

AMONG DEMOCRATS WHO ARE

FOR THE POLICY   AGAINST THE POLICY   FOR THE POLICY   AGAINST THE POLICY

FOR PRICE CONTROL
Dewey   (144)   70   14   (155)(107)   32   43   (30)
Truman   (223)   87   97   (207)(146)   99   88   (41)

FOR TAFT-HARTLEY
LAW
Dewey   (175)   96   54   (46)(26)   85   95   (62)
Truman   (224)   27   43   (75)(47)   40   10   (73)

FOR PUBLIC HOUSING
Dewey   (273)   98   77   (56)(143)   78   (Too Few Cases)   (7)
Truman   (258)   82   89   (65)(171)   99   (7)

* For simplification and clarity, the "No stand" and the "Don't know" responses have been omitted from this chart. This ommission does not affect the point of the data.

At the same time, some voters maintain or increase their perceptual defense on political issues by refusing to acknowledge differences with one's own candidate or similarities to the opposition candidate. Such denial of reality, a defense utilized against uncongenial aspects of the environment, is well documented by case studies and laboratory experiments in the psychological literature of neurosis. Here we have evidence on its operation in the midst of a political campaign where motivation is less strong.

Take the two major issues of price control and the Taft-Hartley Law, on which the candidates took relatively clear positions. Objectively, an observer would say that Truman was for and Dewey against

Chart III: *Partisans Tend Not To Perceive Differences with Their Own Candidate or Similarities to the Opposition Candidate*

PERCENTAGE WHO "DON'T KNOW" THEIR OWN CANDIDATE'S STAND

PRICE CONTROL

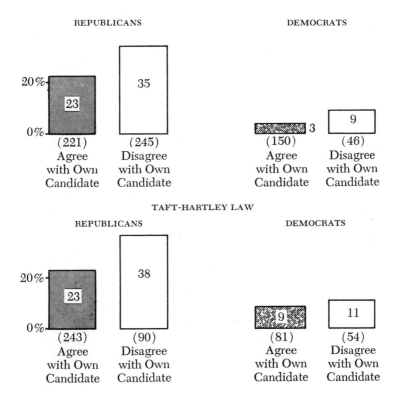

price control and that Truman was against and Dewey for the Taft-Hartley Law. Yet, when our respondents are asked where the candidates stand, a certain proportion of them do not know or profess not to know. But—and this is the point—the "Don't knows" are more frequent among partisans who themselves take a different position from their own candidate or the same position as the opponent (Chart III).

Perception and Strength of Feeling

This tendency to "misperceive" issues in a favorable direction does not operate in a uniform fashion within the electorate. The degree of affect attached to the election, in the form of intensity upon one's vote intention, also influences perception. Those voters who feel strongly about their vote intention perceive political issues differently from those who do not feel so strongly about the matter (Chart IV). With remarkable consistency within each party, the intensely involved "pull" their own candidate and "push" the opponent more than the less involved. (Incidentally, it is probably not too much to suggest that this "pull" and "push" are equivalent to the psychological defense mechanisms of generalization and exclusion.)

For example, when objectively they are *not* in agreement with their own party, *strong* Republicans and Democrats perceive their candidate's stand on the issues as more in harmony with their own stand than do weak Republicans and Democrats in the same situation. But, by no means is this a general tendency to see everyone in agreement with themselves. When they objectively disagree with the *opposition* candidate, the strong partisans are quickest to perceive that disagreement. The stronger the partisanship, the *greater* the (mis)perception of agreement with one's own side and the *less* the (mis)perception of agreement with the opposition. Presumably, misperception makes for partisanship, and the reverse. Thus, the people strongest for a candidate—the ones most interested in and active for his election, the ones who make up the core of the party support—are the ones who take the least equivocal position on what their party stands for. And, at the same time, those who favor the party position as they see it are more likely to support the candidate strongly.

In the course of the campaign, then, strength of party support influences the perception of political issues. The more intensely one holds a vote position, the more likely he is to see the political environ-

Chart IV: *The Stronger the Political Affiliation, the Greater the Tendency to Perceive Political Issues Favorably to One's Self**

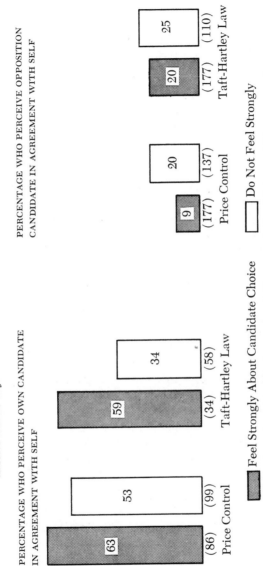

AMONG THOSE OBJECTIVELY IN DISAGREEMENT WITH THE GIVEN CANDIDATE

PERCENTAGE WHO PERCEIVE OWN CANDIDATE IN AGREEMENT WITH SELF

PERCENTAGE WHO PERCEIVE OPPOSITION CANDIDATE IN AGREEMENT WITH SELF

Price Control
63 (86)
53 (99)

Taft-Hartley Law
59 (34)
34 (58)

Price Control
9 (177)
20 (137)

Taft-Hartley Law
20 (177)
25 (110)

▨ Feel Strongly About Candidate Choice   ☐ Do Not Feel Strongly

* Analogous results are obtained for the housing and "firmer with Russia" issues. This same tendency appears in the case of perception of the support given the candidates by various socioeconomic and ethnic groups. In almost every case strong partisans "pull" approved groups more than weak partisans.

ment as favorable to himself, as conforming to his own beliefs. He is less likely to perceive uncongenial and contradictory events or points of view and hence presumably less likely to revise his own original position. In this manner perception can play a major role in the spiraling effect of political reinforcement.

Necessarily, such partisanly motivated perception increases the recognized or believed differences between the parties. Strong Republicans and Democrats are farther apart in perception of political issues than weak Republicans and Democrats; they disagree more sharply in their perception of campaign events. Among the strongly partisan, then, the process of perception operates to make the opponent into more of an "enemy" and thus to magnify the potential for political cleavage.

But all this should not be taken to exaggerate the effect of perception (or issues). Regardless of their perception of the issues, important social groups still follow their own voting tradition.[5] An index of agreement was constructed between the position of each respondent and the position he perceived each candidate to be taking. Here again Catholics vote more strongly Democratic regardless of the degree of their ideological agreement with Truman or Dewey (Chart V). But why does agreement with Dewey make more differences for Catholics, and agreement with Truman for Protestants?

Now when these two indexes of agreement are combined into one, this curious effect of perceived agreement sharpens. If Protestants and Catholics agree with "their own group's" candidate and disagree with the opponent, then the vote is overwhelmingly for one's own candidate; and, if the situation is reversed, so is the vote—though not so strongly (see Chart VI). But what of those people who agree with both candidates, as perceived, or with neither? The answer is that voters who *disagree* with both candidates' stands on the issues, as they perceive them, end by supporting their group's "proper" candidate (more strongly than those who agree with both). If they disagree with both candidates, they seem to have no alternative. So they remain loyal, "at home." If they *agree* with both, however, they are more likely to try the other side. When the grass is green in *both* yards, it seems a little greener in the other fellow's!

---

[5] Nor was perception related to *changes* in voting. We hypothesized that voters might maintain stability by means of misperception, but there were no differences in the data on voting changes subsequent to the asking of perception questions. If perception questions had been repeated, then one would expect perception to adjust to vote more often than the reverse.

Chart V: Social Differences in Voting Remain regardless of Perceived Agreement with Candidates

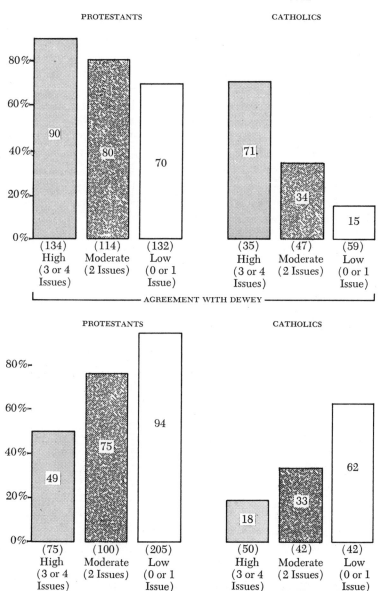

PERCENTAGE REPUBLICAN OF TWO-PARTY VOTE

PROTESTANTS   CATHOLICS

	PROTESTANTS			CATHOLICS		
%	90	80	70	71	34	15
(N)	(134)	(114)	(132)	(35)	(47)	(59)
Agreement	High (3 or 4 Issues)	Moderate (2 Issues)	Low (0 or 1 Issue)	High (3 or 4 Issues)	Moderate (2 Issues)	Low (0 or 1 Issue)

———— AGREEMENT WITH DEWEY ————

PROTESTANTS   CATHOLICS

	PROTESTANTS			CATHOLICS		
%	49	75	94	18	33	62
(N)	(75)	(100)	(205)	(50)	(42)	(42)
Agreement	High (3 or 4 Issues)	Moderate (2 Issues)	Low (0 or 1 Issue)	High (3 or 4 Issues)	Moderate (2 Issues)	Low (0 or 1 Issue)

———— AGREEMENT WITH TRUMAN ————

ACCURACY OF PERCEPTION

The question of "correct" and "incorrect" perception has been implicit in our discussion thus far, since differentiation in perception requires a degree of misperception on the part of some perceivers (assuming a definition of objective reality). But the question has not been given explicit consideration. Without retracing our steps, let us now summarize from this vantage point.

Analysis of the perception that occurs during a presidential campaign requires a definition of what is "correct" perception. In the case of political issues, perceiving the candidates' stands as they predominantly appear in the campaign speeches should serve. Since some stands are ambiguous, or at least contain an element of propagandistic vagueness, we use here two stands of Truman and Dewey that are reasonably straightforward and clear—those on the Taft-Hartley Law (with Truman against and Dewey for) and on price control (with Truman for and Dewey against). The index of correct perception on the issues is based upon the number of correct responses given out of the four possible.

In the first place, the amount of correct perception in the community is limited. Only 16 per cent of the respondents know the correct stands of both candidates on both issues, and another 21 per cent know them on three of the four. Over a third of the respondents know only one stand correctly or none at all. And these are crucial

Chart VI: Protestants and Catholics

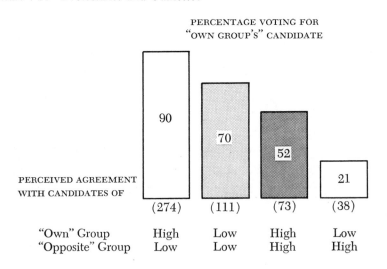

PERCENTAGE VOTING FOR
"OWN GROUP'S" CANDIDATE

	90	70	52	21
PERCEIVED AGREEMENT WITH CANDIDATES OF	(274)	(111)	(73)	(38)
"Own" Group	High	Low	High	Low
"Opposite" Group	Low	Low	High	High

Chart VII: Several Characteristics Are Associated with Accurate Perception of the Candidates' Stands on Issues*

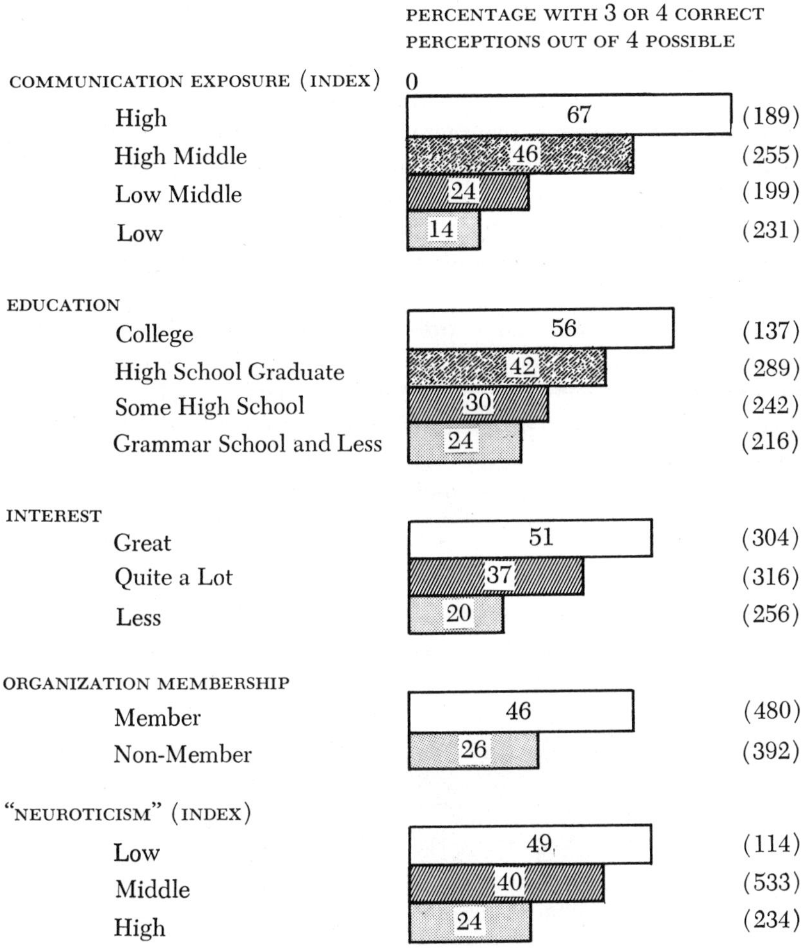

PERCENTAGE WITH 3 OR 4 CORRECT
PERCEPTIONS OUT OF 4 POSSIBLE

COMMUNICATION EXPOSURE (INDEX)

High	67	(189)
High Middle	46	(255)
Low Middle	24	(199)
Low	14	(231)

EDUCATION

College	56	(137)
High School Graduate	42	(289)
Some High School	30	(242)
Grammar School and Less	24	(216)

INTEREST

Great	51	(304)
Quite a Lot	37	(316)
Less	20	(256)

ORGANIZATION MEMBERSHIP

Member	46	(480)
Non-Member	26	(392)

"NEUROTICISM" (INDEX)

Low	49	(114)
Middle	40	(533)
High	24	(234)

* Each of these characteristics works independently of the others.

issues in the campaign, much discussed in the communication media. Thus, a good deal less than half the political perception in the community is reasonably accurate, by such definitions.[6]

---

[6] To repeat: these figures apply to the early campaign period of August. Similar data for October, at the end of the campaign, would almost certainly raise these estimates.

But any such arbitrary measure is less useful for its absolute than for its relative value. Who are the people more and less likely to perceive political issues correctly? For example, what of attention to the campaign in the press and radio? Do the people who read and listen about politics more than others perceive more correctly, or does selective perception get in the way? It seems that communication exposure clarifies perception probably more than any other factor (Chart VII). This is an important consideration: the more reading and listening people do on campaign matters, the more likely they are to come to recognize the positions the candidates take on major issues. It is as though the weight of the media is sufficient to "impose" a certain amount of correct perception, regardless of the barrier presented by the voter's party preference (and despite the fact that those who do most of the reading and listening also feel most strongly for their candidate and are hence more amenable to selective perception). The more that people are *exposed* to political material, the more gets through.

Other characteristics also make for accurate perception. The intel-

Chart VIII: Percentage with 3 or 4 Perceptions Correct

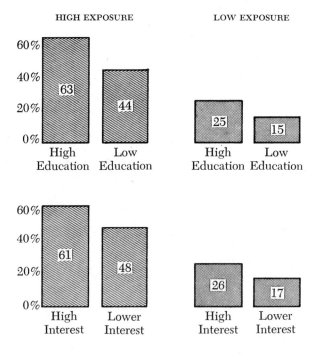

lectual training received in the classroom enables the voter to make clearer discriminations in the political arena. And, despite greater affect toward campaign affairs, the interested people manage to maintain a clearer view of the issues (see Chart VIII). In addition, accuracy of perception is a function of cross-pressures. Voters cross-pressured on class and religion are less accurate than those not so cross-pressured (34 per cent high to 41 per cent); and voters cross-pressured (inconsistent) on price control and Taft-Hartley are less accurate than those not so cross-pressured (42 to 65 per cent). But, of all these factors, the strongest is communication exposure. It is more effectively related to accurate perception of where the candidates stand then either education or interest. Reading and listening must make a difference.

INFERENCES: PSYCHOLOGICAL AND POLITICAL

What are the implications of this perceptual situation? Broadly speaking, there are two sets of conclusions which can be drawn.

The first deals with the psychology of political perception. For perceptual selection must serve a definite psychological function for the individual voter. As in other spheres of activity, so in the political: one function must be to avoid potential stress. The voter must do this, even though unconsciously, by using his perceptual opportunities as a defense or protection against the complexities, contradictions, and problems of the campaign. Indeed, the extent and nature of misperception suggests that the voter may even be aware of the attitudinal cross-pressures to which the campaign subjects him and from which he gains escape through perceptual processes. For the greater his affect toward the election (in terms of strength of feeling toward the candidates), the greater the degree of psychic protection. The voter tends to oversee or to invent what is favorable to himself and to distort or to deny much of what is unfavorable. This must leave him fewer internal conflicts to resolve—with, so to speak, a favorable balance of perception. In any event, the voters manage to use the materials of politics, even of a presidential campaign, for their own psychological protection—for the avoidance of some inconsistencies in their beliefs that otherwise would be manifest.

Then there are certain political implications of the patterning of perception. First, there are in a sense two political campaigns. One is the objective campaign that is carried on in the "real" world, and the other is the campaign that exists in the voter's mind, that is, the "real" campaign as perceived. There is no one-to-one correspondence between them. Given the chance, some voters transform the objective campaign into a subjective one more satisfying to them. The campaign waged by the candidates—even when deliberately unambiguous—is not the one perceived by all the voters, but this does not make it any less "real" for the voters themselves. "If men define situations as real, they are real in their consequences."

Second, there is the meaning of perception for rational political judgment. Here its role must make the voter's political judgment *seem* more rational to him because it maximizes agreement with his own side and maximizes disagreement with the opposition. In other words, perception often operates to make the differences between the parties *appear* greater than they actually may be—and thus to make the voter's decision *appear* more rational (in one sense) than it actually is. In this way, paradoxical though it may seem, misperception contributes to a seeming "rationality" in politics.

Third, perception must reduce or even eliminate certain political cross-pressures before they come to the level of visibility—before they start pressing. If the voter finds himself holding opinions championed by opposing parties, it has been thought that he could do one of two things: remain in this "inconsistent" position (which is, of course, altogether legitimate) or remove the "inconsistency" by changing one opinion to fit the other. But he has another out: he can perceptually select, out of the somewhat ambiguous propaganda of the campaign, those political cues which remove the problem by defining it away. He can "see" that the candidates do not disagree on the issue at hand or that his candidate really agrees with him or that the opponent really disagrees or that he cannot tell where his candidate stands. Just as the process may reduce the voter's level of psychological tension, so may it reduce his political inconsistency.

Finally, this serves to introduce the major political implications of our perceptual material—its implications for the problem of cleavage and consensus in the democratic community. . . . The over-all effect of political perception is to increase the amount of political consensus *within* the parties and to increase the amount of political cleavage *between* the parties—once again, homogeneity within and polarization between. Both are achieved by something like the mechanisms of generalization, exclusion, and denial—through the perceptual enlargement of the area of agreement with one's own candidate (generalization); through the misperceived rejection of the opponent's position (exclusion); and through the professed lack of knowledge of one's candidate's stand where disagreement is likely (denial).

Let us close this chapter by comparing it briefly with the chapter on the perception of groups.[7] In each case the perceptions are likely to help voters to maintain their own position, without being too much concerned by contradiction. In the social case it is harmony with people; in the present case it is a harmony with ideas. With groups the matter was fairly simple: each respondent is surrounded by a primary group in which the large majority thinks like himself. No wonder, then, that he infers that "everyone" will vote as he does. (Of course, this tendency is tempered by a strong sense of reality; misperception is only superimposed upon it.) In the case of the candidates' stand, the voter gets his information from reading, listening, and discussion. This is subject to *selective* gathering of information, forgetting of disturbing elements, reinterpretation of what the candidate "really" means—all mechanisms familiar in social psychology. Probably, even, social selection reinforces the selective collection of information, as a result of discussion between like-minded people.

In a way, both phenomena can be subsumed under one heading. Voters cannot have contact with the whole world of people and ideas; they must *sample* them. And the sampling is biased. People pick the people and the ideas to suit their personal equilibrium and then project that sample upon the universe. First, selective perception, then misperception, then the strengthening of opinion, and then, in turn, more selective perception. Fortunately, there are realities, competing concerns, and corrosion of existing beliefs that, under normal circumstances, do not permit this process to get far out of bounds.

In sum, then, the actual operation of political perception during a presidential campaign decreases tension in the individual and increases tension in the community—one might almost say, *by* increasing tension in the community. The voters, each in the solitude of his own mind, wish to see the campaign in a favorable way, and they use their perception of where the candidates stand to this end. "Democracy in its original form never seriously faced the problem which arises because the pictures inside people's heads do not automatically correspond with the world outside."[8]

[7] Bernard R. Berelson, Paul F. Lazarsfeld, and William N. McPhee, *Voting*, chap. 5.
[8] Walter Lippman, *Public Opinion*, p. 21.

SUMMARY

Perception and Voting

1. Party preference does not particularly affect the voter's perception of where the candidates stand on the issues.

2. The less ambiguous the objective situation, the more agreement in perception between the two sides.

3. Partisans tend to perceive the candidate's stand on the issues as favorable to their own stand. (1) They perceive their candidate's stand as similar to their own and the opponent's stand as dissimilar. (2) They tend *not* to perceive differences with their own candidate or similarities to the opposition condidate.

4. Voters who feel strongly about their choice are more likely to misperceive the candidates' stands on the issues as favorable to their own positions.

5. Social differences in voting are largely maintained regardless of perceived agreement with the candidates.

6. Voters who disagree with both candidates' stands, as perceived, support their own candidate more strongly than those who agree with both.

Accuracy of Perception

7. Only about one-third of the voters are highly accurate in their perception of where the candidates stand on the issues.

8. Accuracy of perception is affected by communication exposure, education, interest, and cross-pressures—with communication exposure probably the strongest influence.

14 *The Significance of Party Identification*

FRED I. GREENSTEIN

ORIENTATIONS TOWARD ISSUES AND ELECTORAL CHOICE

The voter who is highly issue-oriented gathers information and weighs the policy alternatives posed in a campaign, making his choice on the basis of agreement or disagreement with the candidate's expressed views on the burning problems of the day. This citizen doubtless fits best into the standard civics-book conception of how voters *should*

From Fred I. Greenstein, *The American Party System and the American People*, © 1963. Reprinted by permission of Prentice-Hall, Inc., Englewood Cliffs, New Jersey.

make their choices. By and large, he will be an "ideologue." That is, he will have a reasonably explicit overarching view of the good life, usually expressed in the form of a liberal or conservative philosophy.

Ideology provides a remarkably keen tool for assessing new political issues as they arise—the liberal or conservative ideologue will quite readily be able to decide where he stands on policies as diverse as parity price supports, off-shore oil reserves, free trade—and possibly even free love. His pressure to be consistent will lead him to abandon a traditional party or a once-supported candidate if they stray from the path of purity. But voting research suggests that ideologues are rare in the United States. Even people who simply *tend* to view the political world in liberal or conservative terms probably make up little more than a tenth of the electorate.

Nevertheless, orientations toward issues of a less thoroughgoing sort are sufficiently widespread to affect election outcomes significantly. In Table 1, for example, we can see how voters who agreed with the general policy stance of the Truman Administration differed in their 1952 vote from those who disagreed. More of the voters who agreed with the Democratic view that the government should do more to deal with unemployment, education, and housing voted

*Table 1: Relationship between Issue Position
and Eisenhower-Stevenson Vote in 1952*

Some people think the national government should do more in trying to deal with such problems as unemployment, education, housing, and so on. Others think the government is already doing too much. On the whole, would you say what the government has done has been about right, too much, or not enough?

1952 vote	Pro-Democratic Should Do More	About Right; Qualified Answer; Don't Know	Pro-Republican Should Do Less
Eisenhower	43%	48%	85%
Stevenson	52	49	14
Other	5	3	1
Total	100	100	100

Source: Angus Campbell *et al., The Voter Decides* (Evanston, Ill.: Row, Peterson, 1954), p. 118; and Angus Campbell *et al.,* "Political Issues and the Vote: November, 1952," *American Political Science Review,* Vol. 47 (June, 1953), 383–384.

for Stevenson than for Eisenhower. More of the voters who rejected this view backed Eisenhower. But the correlation between issue position and vote was low. Forty-three per cent of the voters taking a pro-Democratic view on this issue nevertheless voted for the Republican candidate. Fourteen per cent of those with pro-Republican views about the expansion of governmental activity still found it possible to support Stevenson.

In the 1952 election the Survey Research Center found particularly strong relationships between a few simple clusters of issues and electoral behavior. The Republicans drew votes especially from citizens who were concerned with "the management of government" (i.e., the charges of corruption and dishonesty which were widespread late in the Truman administration) and foreign policy (especially the Korean War). The Democrats, on the other hand, were kept from being even more severely trounced by the popularity of their approach to domestic policy. In 1960 the *sub rosa* issue of religion evidently influenced a considerable number of voters.

ORIENTATIONS TOWARD CANDIDATES
AND ELECTORAL CHOICE

Few readers will be surprised to learn that the personal attractiveness (or unattractiveness) of a candidate may have a considerable effect on the behavior of voters—an effect which is independent of the policies espoused by the candidate. In recent years the appeals of Presidents Roosevelt and Eisenhower were especially potent. The Eisenhower attraction has been carefully studied through examination of the many "trial heat" presidential surveys conducted during the years before he had stated a party affiliation and avowed an interest in running for office, and of voter response during the two Eisenhower campaigns. Liking Ike seems to have resulted to a remarkable degree from perception of the General's personal attributes. The appeal of these qualities reached many of the groups (e.g., high school graduates) which ordinarily tend to support the Democrats.[1] The Survey Research Center's analyses of voter motivation have consistently shown relationships between candidate orientation and voting.

It normally is far easier to distinguish *analytically* between candi-

[1] Herbert Hyman and Paul Sheatsley, "The Political Appeal of President Eisenhower," *Public Opinion Quarterly*, Vol. 17 (Winter, 1953–1954), pp. 443–460.

date and issue orientation than it is to disentangle the two classes of criteria in the "real world." To what degree, for example, can F.D.R.'s great personal electoral appeal be separated from the attraction for the electorate of his New Deal? In fact, a voter's candidate response often will influence his issue response and vice versa. Thus the voter who likes Ike will ordinarily be predisposed to like what Ike likes. The reverse is also true. In 1960 the SRC found that Mr. Nixon's personal qualities were much more highly valued by Protestant voters who attended church regularly than by those whose allegiance tended to be more nominal. It seems reasonable to assume that the issue of Catholicism was far more salient to active than to inactive Protestants and that the former therefore found it easier to see Kennedy's opponent's good points.[2]

It is part of our political mythology that Americans generally "vote for the man." Actually this statement is in need of a good bit of qualification. If electoral choices were made simply on the basis of candidates' personal characteristics, there probably would be very little continuity between elections in the voting of various groups, as shown, for example, by the election returns from high- and low-income precincts, or urban and rural sections of a state. But actually the continuities are impressive, except . . . when political parties are not a part of the electoral process. In 1896, for instance, the Democratic party virtually repudiated the conservative policies of its President, Grover Cleveland, and nominated William Jennings Bryan, a man who was close to being Cleveland's antithesis. Nevertheless, a large proportion of Bryan's support came from precisely the same Democratic areas which had backed Cleveland four years earlier.[3] Evidently virtually any candidate named by the Democrats would have been supported by these areas.

IDENTIFICATIONS WITH PARTIES AND ELECTORAL CHOICE

The candidate- and issue-oriented voter is to a considerable extent basing his vote on short-run factors tied to a specific election cam-

---

[2] Donald Stokes, "1960 and the Problem of Deviating Elections," paper delivered at the 1961 Annual Meeting of the American Political Science Association.
[3] Lee Benson, "Research Problems in American Historiography," in Mirra Komarovsky (ed.), *Common Frontiers of the Social Sciences* (Glencoe, Ill.: The Free Press, 1957), 162–163.

paign. It is, after all, not until summer of the presidential election year that the candidates are formally designated, even though occasionally (especially when there is an incumbent) one party's nominee may be fairly well set in advance of the nominating conventions. Similarly, although there will have been a four-year issue debate between the politically active segments of the community, only when the nominees have been selected will it be clear *which* issues are to be emphasized by the candidates in what ways. Yet a remarkable proportion of voters regularly report that they make up their minds *before* the presidential nominating conventions and many additional voters decide immediately after the conventions—i.e., before the campaigns "officially" begin.[4]

On what basis are such election decisions made? The answer is that for many citizens a vote is—in V. O. Key's words—a "standing decision" to support one political party. Party identification—the third of the criteria for electoral choice—is by far the strongest of the lot. If we were able to learn where a voter stood on just one of the three criteria—issues, candidates, and party—the latter would enable us to make the most accurate prediction of his vote. In any election some party identifiers—especially those whose loyalties are not strong—will vote for the opposing party, normally on the basis of issue or candidate preferences. But it is considerably more likely that a voter's choice on election day will be inconsistent with either of these two preferences, than it is that he will bolt his party.[5]

By party identification we mean no more than the degree to which an individual considers himself a Republican or a Democrat (or, in the case an infinitesimal proportion of the electorate, a supporter of some minor party). Unlike many European parties, the major American parties have no formal membership procedures, or initiation ceremonies; there are no card-carrying Republicans or Democrats. Yet, in spite of the informality of the party tie in the United States and the low level of citizen involvement in politics, a large majority of the electorate—about 75 per cent—identifies with one or the other of the major parties. Most party identifiers report that

---

[4] For example, in the 1952 election, 31 per cent of a sample of voters reported that their minds were made up before the conventions. Another 34 per cent decided at the time of the conventions. Angus Campbell, *et al.*, *The Voter Decides* (Evanston, Ill.: Row, Peterson, 1954), p. 18.

[5] Angus Campbell and Donald E. Stokes, "Partisan Attitudes and the Presidential Vote," in Eugene Burdick and Arthur J. Brodbeck (eds.), *American Voting Behavior* (Glencoe, Ill.: The Free Press, 1959), pp. 356–357.

never in their lives have they identified with a different party, and a majority of them state that they never have deserted their party on election day.[6]

To a considerable extent party identifications are traditional. Like affiliation in a religious denomination, they are passed on by parents to their children. In 1952, 72 per cent of the Survey Research Center respondents who reported that both their parents had been Democrats were themselves Democrats; 63 per cent of the children of Republican parents were Republicans.[7] The author, in a study of the political orientations of grade-school children, found that by as early as fourth grade (nine years of age) a majority of New Haven children had party preferences. At this tender age, children are familiar with the names of a few conspicuous public officials (mainly the President), but are otherwise almost totally without information about politics, government, and the issues of the day. Thus party seems to be one of the first links formed by the individual to the political system.[8] The remarkable stability of party identifications in recent years is shown by the findings of the seven national surveys, covering an eleven-year span, summarized in Table 2.

For the young child, party identification is so barren of supporting information that it is even possible to know that "I am a Republican" or "I am a Democrat" without knowing the party of the incumbent President. It was not until seventh grade that a few New Haven children could be found who differentiated between the parties in terms of what they stand for. Some adults—but only a very few—manage to stay in this state of blissful ignorance. The meanings people learn to attribute to the parties are to a considerable degree consistent

[6] In all, 50 per cent of the total electorate claims always to have voted for the same party's candidate in presidential elections. The considerable effect of party preferences is suggested by the fact that only 5 per cent of the self-styled independents report such consistency. (For the proportion of the electorate which is uncommitted to either party, see Table 2.) Campbell, *et al.*, *The Voter Decides*, pp. 88–111.

These exceedingly influential orientations are elicited in the University of Michigan voting studies simply by asking: "Generally speaking, do you usually consider yourself as a Republican, a Democrat, an independent, or what?" Following this, the voter is asked if he considers himself a strong Republican (Democrat); if he describes himself as an independent he is asked if he "leans" toward one of the parties.

[7] *Ibid.*, p. 99.

[8] Fred I. Greenstein, "The Benevolent Leader: Children's Images of Political Authority," *American Political Science Review*, Vol. 54 (December, 1960), pp. 934–943.

Table 2:   *Distribution of Party Identification:*
Findings from Seven National Surveys

	Oct. 1952	Sept. 1953	Oct. 1954	Oct. 1956	Oct. 1958	Oct. 1960	Oct. 1962
Strong Republican	13%	15%	13%	15%	13%	14%	11%
Weak Republican	14	15	14	14	16	13	13
Independent Republican	7	6	6	8	4	7	5
Independent	5	4	7	9	8	8	10
Independent Democrat	10	8	9	7	7	8	9
Weak Democrat	25	23	25	23	24	25	21
Strong Democrat	22	22	22	21	23	21	26
Apolitical, don't know	4	7	4	3	5	4	5
	100%	100%	100%	100%	100%	100%	100%
	1614	1023	1139	1772	1269	3021	1474

Source: Survey Research Center studies reported in Donald E. Stokes, "1960 and the Problem of Deviating Elections," paper delivered at the 1961 Annual Meeting of the American Political Science Association, St. Louis, Missouri. The 1962 data were supplied by Professor Stokes.

Table 3:   *Voters' Views of Which Party Serves*
Their Group Best: January 1962

As you feel today, which political party—the Democratic or Republican—do you think serves the interests of (business and professional people; white-collar workers; skilled workers; unskilled workers) best? (Asked of members of each group.)

	Business and Professional	White Collar	Skilled	Unskilled
Democratic	22%	38%	59%	58%
Republican	51	23	13	12
No difference	13	25	16	13
No opinion	14	14	12	17
	100%	100%	100%	100%

Source: AIPO Releases, January 12, 14, and 17, 1962. Of the groups listed above, all but white-collar workers showed considerable stability in their perceptions of the parties as revealed by Gallup polls during the decade from 1952 to 1962. The latter moved by slow stages to the division indicated above from the following 1952 division: Democratic, 28%; Republican, 44%; No difference, 12%; No opinion, 16%.

with . . . group voting regularities. . . . As Table 3 shows, the Democratic and Republican voting groups tend to see the appropriate party as "best" for their group.

When they are actually asked what they like about each party, most voters show an awareness—with varying degrees of sophistication—of the kinds of party differences we noted in the congressional voting on the Housing Act of 1961. Only about 12 per cent of the electorate presents well-developed, issue-based descriptions of the parties on a liberal-conservative basis, associating the Democrats with high levels of government spending and welfare policies, the Republicans with budget-cutting and lack of government regulation. But another 42 per cent sees the parties as differentiated on a group basis—linking the former to "poor people" or "common folk" and the latter to business. Still another 24 per cent has some fragmentary way of characterizing the parties—often in terms of the goodness and badness of the times when one or the other party is in office. (The Democrats are seen as the party of prosperity by many voters— but also as the party of war. One of the greatest Republican assets, on the other hand, is the widespread belief that the GOP is the peace party.) Even among the remaining voters party preferences may be consistent with group membership, simply because they are acquired in a group milieu—namely, the family.[9]

An individual's attitudes on issues may, as we have seen, predispose him to prefer a particular candidate, just as the candidate's attraction may influence the voter's views on issues. Similarly, identifying with a party will often contribute to favoring both the party's issue position and its candidates. *But it is rarely true that either issues or candidates will lead a voter to change his traditional party loyalty.* Although there probably is always a minor ebb and flow of party loyalties, particularly among members of groups which are not solidly located in either the Democratic or Republican constituencies,[10] only a cataclysmic political or social event produces rapid, widespread shifts in party preference. The only event of this magnitude in the twentieth century seems to have been the Great Depression of the 1930s, which saw unemployment levels as high as 25 per cent of the work force. During this period many traditional Re-

[9] Angus Campbell, *et. al., The American Voter* (New York: Wiley, 1960), pp. 216–265.
[10] See, for example, the fluctuation in evaluations of the parties by white-collar workers reported in the note to Table 3.

publican voters, especially in the low-income and unskilled occupational groups, moved into the Democratic party.[11]

Party identifications seem to have such great impact on electoral behavior because they are, in effect, first on the scene. When new issues and candidates emerge, the voter already has in his mind a handy instrument with which to organize his perception and evaluation of them. Thus party is not only a criterion for voting. It also is a criterion for shaping the other voting criteria. When asked to explain our vote, we rarely do so in party terms. Instead, we say that candidates and the election issues were the criteria by which we determined our choice. But we rarely appreciate the degree to which party preferences (and the group experiences which reinforce them) are "behind" these consciously expressed views.

SOME CONCLUSIONS

Just as voting on the basis of issue orientation seems to many Americans to be closest to the ideal in citizen participation, so party voting seems to be furthest from that ideal. To many observers, party is a blind criterion for political choice—one which leads merely to "brand label" voting. Yet, if there is truth to the following observation of Bryce's, the pervasive influence of party in voting may not be unfortunate in terms of maintaining democracy and promoting political stability.

> To the great mass of mankind in all places public questions come in the third or fourth rank among the interests of life, and obtain less than a third or fourth of the leisure available for thinking. It is therefore rather sentiment than thought that the mass can contribute, a sentiment grounded on a few broad considerations and simple trains of reasoning; and the soundness and elevation of their sentiment will have more to do with their taking their stand on the side of justice, honour, and peace, than any reasoning they can apply to the sifting of the multifarious facts thrown before them, and to the drawing of the legitimate inferences therefrom.[12] . . .

[11] This accounts for the greater tendency noted above for voters whose parents were Democrats still to identify with the parental party. On elections leading to party realignment see V. O. Key, Jr., "A Theory of Critical Elections," *Journal of Politics*, Vol. 17 (February, 1955), pp. 3–18.

[12] James Bryce, *The American Commonwealth*, 3rd ed. (London: Macmillan, 1904), Vol. II, pp. 250–251.

Bryce's observations *are* to a considerable degree true—public evaluations of government and politics do tend to be confined to "broad considerations" and "simple trains of reasoning." That one of the most important of these considerations is party is probably of great consequence both for the political system and for the voter.

For the voter, party labels simplify the task of political choice to a remarkable degree. They enable him to respond to the infinitely complex events of the contemporary political world in terms of a few simple criteria. Without such criteria, detailed research on the issues of the day would be necessary to make any sort of meaningful electoral choice. Perhaps even more important than the usefulness of party labels as devices to simplify issue questions is their usefulness for sorting out candidates and public officials. Given the vast complexity of American government, with its divisions between executive and legislature and between the federal, state, and local levels, there is immense value to an instrument which enables the voter, in one burst of exertion, to evaluate all the public officials he must select. Without party labels choice becomes almost impossible, especially at the state and local levels, where dozens of public officials—down to the tax collector and the county sheriff—may be on the ballot.

Although party labels, and voting on the basis of party identifications, are great political simplifiers, they are not complete blinders. Where powerful issues and striking candidates have not emerged and broken through to the focus of public attention, most of the electorate votes on a party basis. Under such circumstances, elections will be decided by the underlying distribution of party identifications in the population. For example, in contemporary America, Democrats outnumber Republicans by about 3 to 2. When one accounts for the greater political apathy of Democrats (due largely to the lower educational and occupational level of their core supporters), it has been estimated that there is a "natural" Democratic majority of about 53 per cent in any election which involves a ratification of party preferences.[13] Democrats are especially likely to win in the off-year congressional elections, since these contests rarely raise burning issues, or attract a great deal of attention. However, the Democrats received only 45 per cent of the two-party vote in 1952, 42 per cent in 1956, and little more than a bare 50 per cent in 1960. Thus, although the dead weight of voters' "standing decisions" has a major effect on

[13] Philip E. Converse, *et al.*, "Stability and Change in 1960: A Reinstating Election," *American Political Science Review,* Vol. 55 (June, 1961), pp. 269–280.

election outcomes, the nation's electoral decision is also dependent on evaluations of current issues and candidates. Furthermore, the various elements in the equation of voting behavior—party identification, differential group turnout, response to current issues and candidates—are such as to make any single election a matter of sufficient uncertainty to keep politicians on their toes and to stimulate the more politically interested and active members of the electorate to pay attention to the spectacle and drama of the campaign.

The outcomes of national elections are ordinarily in doubt, but one result of the stability of party identifications and of their underlying bases in group voting differences is that many aspects of politics become predictable. In the present era, Democrats—or at least northern Democrats—can be sure that the core of their support will come from citizens in the lower educational and blue-collar occupational levels. Republicans may generally be confident of their business, professional, college-educated, and small-town stalwarts.[14] Out of a desire to maintain the backing of the groups which make up the cores of their constituencies, politicians in both parties are led to advance policies consistent with group interests and needs. This results in a degree of differentiation in the policies supported by leaders of both parties.

Each of the parties is dependent for support not only on its core voters but also on less committed groups (such as white-collar workers and farmers) and on groups in the other party's coalition. Therefore the differentiation between the parties is not likely to be so sharp that changes in party control of government will produce radical reversals of governmental policy. Neither the Republican return to office in 1953 after 20 years in the wilderness, nor the Democratic return 8 years later, led to momentous shifts in the nation's domestic or international programs. The cross-cutting nature of the party appeals also keeps political cleavage from becoming so substantial that some elements of the public or leadership will consider it preferable to replace ballots with bullets in order to prevent intolerable policies from being put into effect by their opponents.

[14] Recent research makes it clear that the rapid rise and fall in France of new political movements (many of them hostile to the democratic political order) is related to the weakness of voters' party ties. Less than 45 per cent of the French voters (in contrast to the 75 per cent of Americans) identify with parties. Philip Converse and Georges Dupeux, "Polarization of the Electorate in France and the United States," *Public Opinion Quarterly,* Vol. 26 (Spring, 1962), pp. 1–23.

As reasonable as these concluding statements about the consequences of parties for the behavior of the electorate and the workings
of the political system may seem, they are of necessity somewhat
speculative. The present state of our knowledge does not enable us
to document them with the confidence with which we can say that
75 per cent of the electorate holds party identifications, or that college-educated voters consistently turn out at the polls more often
than grade-school-educated voters. However, we do know enough
about the dynamics of voter motivations to assert with great confidence that wherever party becomes an element in the electorate's
deliberations, the nature of politics will be altered substantially. . . .

15 *Authoritarian Attitudes and Party Activity*

LOUISE HARNED

If the essence of an organization is partly determined by the motives and aspirations of its members, the question of why men and women participate actively in political parties, even in modest positions, has meaning for the nature of the party system. Both fiction and factual analyses have noted that local party organizations are often staffed by people who join in search of such rewards as social outlets, jobs, or increased clientele. Obviously, the essentially nonpo-

From Louise Harned, "Authoritarian Attitudes and Party Activity," *Public Opinion Quarterly* 25 (1961), pp. 393–399. Reprinted with permission of the author and publisher.

litical nature of these motives has profoundly shaped the operation of parties and political life in the American local community by extending the functions of parties into realms theoretically unconnected with government.

These categories of reward for participation by no means exhaust the possible attractions of party activity, even for people who have no particular ambition for elected office or a policy-making role in government. The significance of different specific rewards may vary for people of differing personality structures. Although no single component can be considered as the sole, or most important, psychological influence upon political action, the California study on authoritarianism has provided a method for the analysis of the effects of at least one aspect of personality.[1] Moreover, the authoritarian syndrome analyzed by the California investigators seems particularly relevant to an inquiry into participation in hierarchical organizations, such as parties. In brief, the constellation of attitudes considered to characterize an authoritarian personality are as follows: the tendency to conform, to adhere rigidly to conventional values, complemented by a tendency to condemn others who violate such values (this can be related to general hostility toward out-groups and positive attitudes toward in-groups); the tendency to submit uncritically to, to identify with, the strong leaders of in-groups, accompanied by a desire to dominate those considered weaker than oneself (this involves a general preoccupation with power relationships); the tendency to concentrate on externals, to be "anti-intraceptive" in relation to one's own experience, to blame one's troubles on a hostile and threatening environment; the tendencies to think in terms of stereotypes and superstitions, to be cynical about other people's motives; and the tendency to be fearful and suspicious of sexual impulses.[2] Of particular relevance to the present analysis are those characteristics pertaining to power and submission. Activity in political parties may have special appeal to those with authoritarian traits, owing both to the parties' hierarchical structure and to their relationship to the agencies of political power in the community.

THE STUDY

The present paper is a report on some data relating authoritarian attitudes to rewards and satisfactions gained by party work. It is

[1] T. W. Adorno, Else Frenkel-Brunswik, Daniel J. Levinson, and R. Nevitt Sanford, *The Authoritarian Personality*, New York, Harper, 1950.
[2] *Ibid.*, pp. 102–150, 222–279.

based on material gathered in 1953–1954 by interviews of a random sample of forty-one ward committee chairmen in New Haven, Connecticut. A control group of twenty-seven men and women inactive in politics was also interviewed. This group paired with politicians in terms of sex, education, occupation, income, religion, race, and ethnic background.

The examination of authoritarian characteristics of New Haven committeemen was based on their responses to three of the projective questions devised by Daniel J. Levinson as part of the California study:[3]

1. We all have impulses and desires which are at times hard to control but which we try to keep in check. What desires do you have difficulty in controlling?
2. We all have times when we feel below par. What moods or feelings are the most unpleasant or disturbing to you?
3. What great people living or dead do you admire most?

In selecting these questions, care was taken to see that the responses to them would represent most of the psychological qualities found by Levinson to characterize ethnocentric (authoritarian) and anti-ethnocentric (equalitarian) subjects.

The method of categorizing the responses was the same as that described in Levinson's chapter on projective questions in *The Authoritarian Personality*.[4] Each politician was given an authoritarianism score based on assigning one point for each response with a low authoritarian content, two points for a neutral answer, and three points for a response high in authoritarian content.

In general, there is no evidence that more people of high than of low authoritarian tendencies are likely to work for political parties, but authoritarianism does seem to be associated with some political attitudes and opinions that appear relevant to the satisfactions certain ward leaders may derive from party work.[5]

---

[3] *Ibid.*, pp. 545–600. In Levinson's terminology these particular questions were specifically designed as a measure of ethnocentrism. However, since the responses to them can be interpreted as revealing most of the authoritarian (or equalitarian) attributes, it is feasible to use them for that purpose here.

[4] *Ibid.*, pp. 548–595.

[5] Of the 27 matched committeemen, 55.5 per cent had authoritarian scores of 8 to 9, as compared to 62.9 per cent of the 27 matched nonpoliticians. This percentage difference is not of statistical significance.

Emphasis on Party Organization

The committeemen with the highest authoritarian scores appear to place more emphasis on the importance of party organization per se. Table 1 compares high authoritarianism scores with scores on the "organizational emphasis scale," based on responses to the following questions:

> 1. If you wanted to ask someone for information about political affairs, to whom would you turn?
> 2. What do you think is the most important aspect of your job as committeeman?
> 3. Why do you think letters to Congressmen are effective?

One point was added to each committeeman's organizational emphasis score if he would seek information or advice from a member of the party hierarchy who was not his friend, whose importance to him was based on rank in the party; if he thought that the most important aspect of his job was limited to its organizational side (e.g. involving his position of leadership in the ward apparatus); and if he thought that Congressmen took cognizance of letters because of his official position and not because of his personal and friendly experience with his elected representative.

It appears that for those with relatively substantial authoritarian tendencies the formal organization of the party hierarchy and their own position in it are of primary importance. Authoritarian ward leaders seem to derive special satisfaction from a dominant role in their ward organization and from a submissive status in relation to

Table 1:   Percentage of Ward Chairmen with High and Low Organizational Emphasis Scores Who Rate High or Low in Authoritarianism

Organizational Emphasis Score	AUTHORITARIANISM SCORE			
	Low (3–7)	High (8–9)	Total	(N)
Low (0–1)	60	40	100	(20)
High (2–3)	28.6	71.4	100	(21)
Total group of ward chairmen	43.9	56.1	100	(41)

$\chi^2 = 4.06$; $.02 < p < .05$[6]

[6] See note 12, p. 127.—EDS.

party superiors, to whom they turn for information and help not because they know them personally but in frank acknowledgment of their sanctified position. This is fully consistent with the general conception of authoritarian attitudes toward dominance and submission.

Number of Organizations Participated In

The material also suggests that political activity may play a more important role for authoritarian ward leaders than it does for equalitarians. Although there is no difference between the two groups with respect to the number or types of organization other than parties to which they belong, there is a definite tendency on the part of chairmen with lower authoritarian ratings to consider themselves active participants in more associations. Only 26.1 per cent of the committeemen with high authoritarian scores, in contrast to 72.2 per cent of those with lower ratings, stated that they were active in two or more organizations other than parties ($\chi^2 = 8.6$; $p < 1\%$). This difference is in partial conflict with the observations of Robert E. Lane, who found that authoritarians tend to belong to more organizations than do equalitarians,[7] but it appears to be in harmony with some of Fillmore Sanford's conclusions. The New Haven data can be interpreted to reflect Sanford's findings that authoritarians "do not get themselves involved in group activities nor readily accept responsibility."[8] In his concluding analysis, Sanford hypothesizes that authoritarians "will be found in leadership positions where appointment has come from above and where . . . responsibility is primarily to . . . superiors rather than to followers."[9] While this is not strictly true of the position of ward chairman, those aspects of the job to which this description applies may be particularly important to authoritarian politicians. Although there is machinery for the election of chairmen, in fact there is rarely a contest and the practice of co-option seems to be frequent. Second, the responsibility of a ward leader to "deliver the vote" to his superiors is the most obvious duty he has to perform. His obligation to his followers as chairman of the ward committee and representative of his district is a relatively minor one and certainly can be interpreted as such if the chairman feels so inclined. Thus,

[7] Robert E. Lane, "Political Personality and Electoral Choice," *American Political Science Review*, Vol. 49, 1955, p. 179.
[8] Fillmore Sanford, *Authoritarianism and Leadership*, Philadelphia, Institute for Research in Human Relations, 1950, p. 178.
[9] *Ibid.*, p. 181.

the nature of the job can at least partially explain why authoritarian men and women may be active in political parties while comparatively apathetic in other types of organization.

Ideological Partisanship

One characteristic of parties which clearly distinguishes them from other community organizations appears to be particularly unimportant to committeemen with authoritarian tendencies. Except for a limited number of independent political associations, parties are the community organizations most directly concerned with the issues of the day. Without overemphasizing the importance of ideology as a factor precipitating participation in party work, it is nevertheless reasonable to assume that people gain satisfaction from belonging to an organization which represents an ideological position similar to their own.[10] However, the New Haven data suggest that such ideological partisanship is not of paramount importance to authoritarian men and women. One section of the study involved a detailed examination of some of the ideological attitudes of ward workers. In connection with this, an ideological partisanship scale was devised based on whether or not the responses to questions of policy favored the position of the chairman's own party.

The scale was based on the following questions:

1. Some people think the national government should do more in trying to deal with such problems as unemployment, education, housing and so on. Others think that the government is already doing too much. On the whole would you say that what the government has done has been about right, too much, or not enough?
2. Some people think that since the end of the last world war this country has gone too far in concerning itself with problems in other parts of the world. How do you feel about this?
3. Some people feel that it was our government's fault that China went communist—others say there was nothing that we could do to stop it. How do you feel about this?

[10] Whether the ward chairmen's ideological positions were developed before they became active in politics or whether they were "created" by their party work is a question that will not be considered here. It should be noted, however, that the investigation showed a relationship between number of years of party activity and degree of ideological partisanship, indicating that party work itself tends to generate such attitudes.

Table 2:   *Percentage of Ward Chairmen with High and Low*
Authoritarianism Scores Who Score High or Low
on the Ideological Partisanship Scale

Authoritarianism Score	IDEOLOGICAL PARTISANSHIP SCORE			
	Low (0–3)	High (4–6)	Total	(*N*)
Low (3–7)	27.8	72.2	100	(18)
High (8–9)	65.2	34.8	100	(23)
Total group of ward chairmen	48.8	51.2	100	(41)

$\chi^2 = 5.72$; $.01 < p < .02$

4. Do you think we did the right thing in getting into the fighting in Korea three years ago or should we have stayed out?
5. Some people think that the national government can reduce taxes now and still keep up an adequate military defense. Others say it would be impossible. How do you feel about this?
6. Some people think that the constitution of Connecticut is too clumsy and that therefore the state government is inefficient. Others think that the constitution is all right as it is. How do you feel about this?[11]

As can be seen from the data in Table 2, there appears to be a definite association between high authoritarian ratings and low scores on the ideological partisanship scale. Only 34.8 per cent of the twenty-three chairmen with authoritarian scores of 8 to 9 had partisanship ratings of 4 or over, as opposed to 72.2 per cent of the ward leaders with authoritarian scores of 7 and under.[12]

[11] The general approach and four of the questions used were devised by the Michigan Survey Research Center in its study of the 1952 elections. See Angus Campbell, Gerald Gurin, and Warren Miller, *The Voter Decides*, Evanston, Ill., Row, Peterson, 1954, pp. 116–123, and Angus Campbell, Gerald Gurin, and Warren Miller, "Political Issues and the Vote: November, 1952," *American Political Science Review*, Vol. 47, 1953, pp. 359–385. The responses of the New Haven sample were categorized in the same way as those of the Michigan survey (*ibid.*, pp. 383–385). One point was added to the "ideological partisanship" score of each respondent if his position on a given issue represented that generally taken by his party. For further details on methodology, see Harned's unpublished dissertation, *Participation in Political Parties: A Study of Party Committeemen* (Yale University, 1927), pp. 102–105.
[12] Space does not permit detailed examination; however, it should be noted that this relationship persists despite pressures tending to its modification. What

DISCUSSION

The significance of these findings in terms of the wider context of the American party system may basically be that the presence of people with authoritarian attributes within the organizations' ranks tends to accentuate those familiar aspects of the system that involve well-oiled, disciplined hierarchies and action largely devoid of ideological content. It is true that these characteristics of the "game of politics" as played in the United States are accepted as inevitable facts of life. Nevertheless, ward chairmen operate on a strategic level in American cities, for they represent a group that can serve as a transmission point between the party superstructure and the ordinary citizen. To the degree that democracy is based on the necessity for an informed electorate, ideally such ward politicians could perform a useful job as opinion leaders on issues in their neighborhoods. If local chairmen are uninterested in issues, as those with authoritarian tendencies appear to be, it goes without saying that they will not effectively fulfill this function. Moreover, if parties organized on a democratic basis are desirable, it would seem regrettable to have the lower echelons staffed with men and women more concerned with approval from above and their personal control over well-organized ward committees than with communicating their own desires to their leaders and in turn responding to the ideas of their followers. That there are a substantial number of chairmen whose participation in party activity is largely limited to these concerns is certainly not surprising to anyone familiar with the literature on city politics. The data discussed in this report would seem to indicate that those who are so restricted and who therefore may themselves limit the role and shape the operation of parties tend to be people with psychological characteristics that can be labeled "authoritarian."

---

relationship there is between authoritarianism and opinions on any of the specific issues on which the partisanship score was based appears in an association between pro-Democratic opinion on internationalism and intervention in Korea and a low authoritarianism score. Significantly, the relationship between intervention and equalitarianism was due to Republican, not Democratic, ward chairmen. The latter, with only two authoritarian exceptions, took the party line. This suggests that, in a situation where party position was easily perceived, authoritarian Democrats showed no hesitation in conforming. This display of loyalty may be allied less with fundamental beliefs than with a tendency on the part of more authoritarian people to submit to the established leadership of their party as an in-group with which they are identified. For further details on this point, see *ibid.*, pp. 153–155.

16 *The Sense of Political Efficacy: Some Roots and Consequences*

ANGUS CAMPBELL
PHILIP E. CONVERSE
WARREN E. MILLER
DONALD E. STOKES

PERSONALITY AND VOTE PARTICIPATION

. . . The sheer fact of participation in the political process—whether it be in the form of voting or in further actions—tokens some inner motivational state much more clearly than the case of simple professions of partisanship. To be sure, some people seem to go to the polls through direct social pressure, despite little personal interest. By and large, however, the conceptual characteristics of political

From Angus Campbell, Philip E. Converse, Warren E. Miller, and Donald E. Stokes, *The American Voter* (New York: John Wiley & Sons, Inc., 1960), pp. 104–105 and 515–519. Reprinted with permission of the authors and publisher.

Table 1:   Relation of Sense of Political Efficacy
           to Voting Turnout, 1956

	SENSE OF POLITICAL EFFICACY[a]				
	Low				High
Voted	52%	60%	75%	84%	91%
Did not vote	48	40	25	16	9
	100%	100%	100%	100%	100%
Number of cases	263	343	461	501	196

[a] Respondents were classified according to the strength of their sense of political efficacy on the basis of a cumulative scale formed from responses to four questions.

action are quite different from those involved in expressions of partisan preference. A person may accept a party rather automatically from his social milieu and remain within its clientele for long periods of time. But direct political participation cannot be accomplished for the individual by others. There must be some sources of energy that are entirely personal and that must be activated afresh with each ensuing election.

Hence it seems reasonable to look for some influence of personality organization on the inclination to participate politically. . . .

An important aspect of the individual's response to politics as a general area is the degree to which this response is passive in character. To some people politics is a distant and complex realm that is beyond the power of the common citizen to affect, whereas to others the affairs of government can be understood and influenced by individual citizens. We have assessed the effectiveness the individual feels in his relation to politics by using answers to several questions probing attitudes of this sort to develop a cumulative scale, on which we could array our samples.[1] The influence this dimension of attitude has on the turnout decision is shown by Table 1 for the election of 1956. The rate of voting turnout was found to increase uniformly with the strength of the individual's sense of political

[1] For a detailed discussion of the construction of cumulative scales to measure sense of political efficacy and sense of citizen duty see Appendices A and B in Angus Campbell, Gerald Gurin, and Warren E. Miller, *The Voter Decides* (Row, Peterson and Co., Evanston, Ill., 1954), pp. 187–199.

efficacy, and more than 40 percentage points separated those whose sense was least developed from those whose sense of effectiveness was strongest.

. . . Variables of this sort, in contrast to measures of involvement in the current election, may be conceived as lying at a relatively "deep" level in any hierarchy of dispositions. That is, they represent highly generalized orientations toward the world of politics and could be expected to remain rather stable over a period of time. In this sense, they are approaching "personality" status. If we wished to think in terms of "political personality," they would warrant prominent attention. However, it may be worthwhile to conceive of them as dependent in part on aspects of underlying personality in a more general sense and to seek their roots in full-blown personality terms.

The measure of political efficacy is designed to capture differences between individuals in a basic sense of control over the workings of the political system. The politically efficacious individual feels that his vote counts in the operation of government and feels furthermore that there are other reasonable ways in which he can influence the progress of the system beyond going to the polls. What underlies the sense of political efficacy? To some degree, we would suppose that simple past experience with political matters would play an important role in its determination. That is, an individual who finds himself on the losing side in election after election is likely to feel less politically potent than the individual who contributes regularly to the tide of victory. Similarly, the person who finds himself constantly tormented by decisions of local government without perceived redress of grievances may come to feel that his capacity for political control is weak indeed.

At the same time, a belief in political efficacy may be determined in part by broader personality trends than those which reflect immediate political experience. The sense of control or mastery over the environment is an important component in modern personality theory. A term like "the ego" is often used as a shorthand for the many adaptive mechanisms that the individual develops as a means of reconciling his basic needs with the limitations of the physical and social environment. The ego functions that may be posited are extremely various. One of the more summary dimensions that may be abstracted to reflect individual differences at this level has to do with "ego strength," or the integration and efficiency of the individual's characteristic adaptive patterns. Although the individual is not presumed to be entirely aware of the dynamics of his ego functioning, he is aware in a general way as to how successful he is in transactions with his environment. We may speak, then, of a "sense of personal effectiveness," representing feelings of mastery over the self and the environment. The person lacking such a sense of mastery may either be tense and anxious about the course of his personal life, or may be resigned in a fatalistic way to a succession of events with which he does not feel that he can cope adequately.

It seems reasonable to suppose that, political experiences aside, differences in ego strength should influence beliefs in personal efficacy *vis-à-vis* the political process. Therefore we have attempted to measure this general sense of personal effectiveness with a set of eight items, none of which has any manifest political content.

Table 2 summarizes the expected relationship between the generalized sense of effectiveness of ego strength and the belief in personal political efficacy. . . . [Since] political efficacy is strongly related to education . . . [and] since ego strength is also related to education, it is important to indicate the conceptual status that we accord to these three terms.

The evidence suggests rather clearly that the sense of political efficacy is a product of an interplay between education and ego strength. We have already argued that education fulfills one of its primary functions in providing tools with which the individual can cope more effectively with the environment. Hence, education appears to lead to increased ego strength. On the other hand, it has been shown that adolescents with a stronger sense of personal competence are more likely to have higher social aspirations and, undoubtedly,

Table 2:   Relation of Sense of Personal Effectiveness
to Sense of Political Efficacy, 1956

Political Efficacy	SENSE OF PERSONAL EFFECTIVENESS				
	Low	Med. Low	Medium	Med. High	High
Low	33%	29%	23%	16%	4%
Medium	26	24	18	19	27
High	41	47	59	65	69
	100%	100%	100%	100%	100%
Number of cases	92	112	151	159	68

Table 3:   The Relation of Sense of Personal Effectiveness to Political
           Involvement and Vote Turnout, by Education

| | SENSE OF PERSONAL EFFECTIVENESS | | | |
Education	Low	Low Med.	High Med.	High
Grade school				
Per cent voting	43%	47%	72%	82%
Per cent involved	32%	34%	48%	41%
Number of cases	47	47	60	22
High school				
Per cent voting	67%	79%	80%	82%
Per cent involved	48%	45%	62%	57%
Number of cases	67	61	136	34
College				
Per cent voting	—	90%	90%	88%
Per cent involved	—	76%	73%	86%
Number of cases	[a]	29	52	22

[a] Nine cases involved in this column have been merged with the next adjacent
column to give a sufficient number of cases.

are likely to pursue their education farther as a result.[2] Thus education
and ego strength show a substantial statistical relationship and may
be considered as interacting factors in a causal nexus.

At the same time, the intercorrelation of these two factors is
lower in magnitude than the correlation of either with political
efficacy, a fact that suggests that both education and ego strength
make independent contributions to the development of a sense of
political efficacy. Among individuals with a similar sense of competence, the better educated are significantly more likely to rate high
in political efficacy. And within levels of education, higher ego
strength leads to higher efficacy. Therefore, neither component is
superfluous in our understanding of the manner in which a sense
of political efficacy develops.

As we would expect from our knowledge of political efficacy,
differences in the sense of personal effectiveness are related to expressions of political involvement and to vote turnout, even within categories of education (Table 3). In this instance, the control exercised

[2] Elizabeth Douvan and Joseph Adelson, "The Psychodynamics of Social Mobility
in Adolescent Boys," Journal of Abnormal and Social Psychology, LVI (January
1958).

on education is in many senses an "overcontrol," since we see education as part of the sequence leading through ego strength to political efficacy and on to increased political participation. With such a control, we see that relationships are least distinct among the college educated, in contrast to the pattern of findings where authoritarianism was involved. There appears to be more social pressure toward voting and involvement in higher-status milieus. At lower levels, the individual is more dependent on personal motivations, and hence personality becomes a more visible discriminant.

The fact that aspects of personality organization affect political participation is congruent with theory underlying the ego functions. Political affairs are, for most people, peripheral to their day-to-day lives. The efficiency of ego functioning bears directly on the way in which the individual can or must allocate his energies in dealing with the environment. Where such functioning is chaotic, more energy is drained off in the maintenance of the psychological economy and less remains to initiate and create beyond the immediate emotional necessities. Where the ego is strong, however, the individual can maintain a higher level of involvement in these secondary areas of behavior.

17 *Types of Neurotic Susceptibility*

GABRIEL A. ALMOND

In this section, Professor Almond reports the results of intensive interviews with ex-Communists from four nations. Most of the non-American examples have been cut for convenience. However, two caveats are in order here: (1) In the chapter prior to this one, Almond notes that there are reasons other than the satisfaction of neurotic needs for joining the Communist Party. In France and Italy, for instance, the Communist Party was a major source of opposition to the Nazis and Fascists, respectively. Moreover, the percentage of

From Gabriel A. Almond, *The Appeals of Communism* (Princeton: Princeton University Press, 1954), pp. 258–294. Reprinted by permission of Princeton University Press. Copyright © 1954, by Princeton University Press.

people who belonged to the Party for the gratification of neurotic needs rises as rank in the Party declines. The higher echelons are much less neurotic and much more ideological about membership. (2) Neurotic needs propel individuals toward a variety of political ideologies other than Communism. Indeed, most of the data gathered by social scientists deals with the marked tendency of ultra-conservatives or members of the "radical right" toward such neurotic attributes as authoritarianism.[1]—Eds.

It would be tempting to suggest that some particular type of emotional maladjustment or some unique pattern of psychological development lies at the basis of neurotic susceptibility to Communism. What actually appears to be involved in this type of susceptibility is the presence of any one or any combination of the common types of disturbances of personal relationships, occurring in conjunction with certain intellectual and moral patterns, and occurring in a setting in which there is an exposure to the party. Thus two college students may be affected by economic circumstances in the same way, and both may perceive politics in the same terms. They may both be confronted by the same student organizations, and both approached by party representatives and asked to join. If one of these students is unconsciously hostile and destructive, there is a higher probability that he will join the party than that his more "normal" friend will do so, since the party appeals not only to his conscious, rational, political interests, but to his unconscious feelings as well. Similarly, during a party crisis resulting from a change in line, as between two party members, one neurotic and one normal, the "normal" one will feel freer to withdraw from the party if it no longer adheres to the position it held at the time of joining, while the neurotic one will tend to be held to the party by his underlying destructive feelings.

The problems of interpersonal relationships most commonly manifested among the former Communist respondents were hostility and withdrawal; in other words, there was a relatively high incidence of persons who were chronically rebellious and antagonistic, and of persons who were poorly related to others and to their surroundings. The case material submitted by the psychoanalysts who cooperated with the study brought to light other patterns, such as excessive submissiveness and dependence in personal relations, and feelings of self-rejection of one kind or another (e.g., guilt feelings, inferiority feelings, etc.).

If we take both our interviewing material and our psychoanalytic

[1] The landmark study of this subject is Adorno, *et. al.*, *The Authoritarian Personality*.

case histories, it is evident that any of the common patterns and problems of personal maladjustment can contribute to joining the party. The interviews with former party members, since they represented self-portraits and appraisals, tended to reveal only the grosser forms of behavioral maladjustment—a record, for example, of constant rebelliousness or of constant withdrawal from personal relationships. The psychoanalytic cases, on the other hand, consisted of clinical appraisals, and hence tended to bring to light types of feelings and attitudes which would be held in repression or suppression. Thus the two types of data are complementary and suggest the range of different kinds of emotional problems which can be "solved" by joining the party.

A further point as to the uses of the two types of data may be made. The interviews with former party members suggest hypotheses as to the distribution of different types of emotional problems among different types of party members. The psychoanalytic cases cannot be used for purposes of estimating distributions since they are such an unusual group of Communists. However, they are of great value for illustrative purposes, as studies in depth of the ways in which neurotic difficulties contribute to joining the party. In general, the percentage figures cited in the material which follows should be taken with considerable caution. While the coding was conservative, a depth interview is hardly a satisfactory basis for making clinical appraisals.[2]

---

[2] The psychoanalytic material consisted of 35 cases contributed by 22 analysts in New York, Los Angeles, Washington, D.C., and New Haven during the period of October 1950 to June 1951. The analysts were mainly orthodox Freudian in their approach, although several from the Washington School were included. Typically, the presentation of a case involved a two-hour session with the analyst, with an open-ended interviewing guide which covered the patient's life history and personality problems, the political history of the patient, and appraisals by the analyst of the functions of Communist affiliation in the personality system of the patient. The 35 cases included 20 men and 15 women. Eight were from the medical profession, 6 were social workers, 6 were in the theatrical professions and the fine arts, 5 were academic people, 5 in the applied sciences (mainly engineers), and 5 miscellaneous. Twenty-nine of the 35 were of foreign-born parents. In almost all cases, the analyses took place after the end of World War II. Twenty-six were party members at the time of their analyses, and 9 were ex-members. Of the 26 who were in the party at the time of their psychoanalytic treatment, 15 withdrew from the party during their analysis, and 11 remained. For a more detailed description of this selection of case histories and for a more detailed analysis of the role of hostility, see Herbert E. Krugman, "The Role of Hostility in the Appeal of Communism in the United States," *Psychiatry*, August 1953, pp. 253 ff.

HOSTILITY

In the areas outside the Communist orbit, the most common, if not universal, feeling related to joining the party is that of resentment. In the discussion of the ways in which the party is perceived, it has already been pointed out that the great majority of our respondents account for their decision to join by referring to some aspect of the party's militance, its trade union militance, its militance in the interest of minority groups, its militance in striving for a variety of different kinds of political and ideological objectives. Affiliation with a "militant" political movement almost by definition implies conditions, situations, or groups which are negatively appraised or "resented." We have also seen that militance is the attribute of the party which is most frequently stressed in the party classics and other media of communication. In particular, the analysis of the American *Daily Worker* showed the enormous emphasis which the party places on the evils of society, and the relatively slight emphasis given to constructive themes. It was there suggested that the first stage in assimilation to the party, if one were to accept the party's own picture of itself, involved the adoption of the Communist exoteric demonology in whole or in part, far more than the acceptance of positive and explicit goals. In other words, the party on the mass level appeals almost entirely to resentments, or tries to create them where they do not already exist, and in either case tries to focus these resentments on particular objects.

Given this enormous emphasis on rejection, resentment, and militant combat against evil antagonists, it should hardly occasion surprise that the feeling most commonly manifested among respondents was resentment, antagonism, rebelliousness, and hatred. In the majority of cases the resentment appeared to be situationally induced and in conformity with community patterns. But in a substantial number of cases it appeared to be a pattern of chronic and unconscious hostility resulting from family and childhood experiences. While the incidence of neurotic hostility was relatively higher among the British and American cases, the middle-class respondents, and in the lower echelons, it also occurred with some frequency among the French and Italian respondents, the working-class respondents, and in the higher echelons (see Table 1).

It is also of interest that in 20 out of the 35 psychoanalytic cases, the psychoanalysts explicitly related unconscious hostility in their patients to the attraction of the Communist Party. A number of illustra-

Table 1:   *The Incidence of Neurotic Hostility among Different*
Party Groupings (in per cent)

Country	
United States	33
England	34
France	20
Italy	24
Social Class	
Middle class	41
Working class	16
Echelon	
Rank and file	33
Low echelon	34
High echelon	13

tive cases taken from the interviews and the psychoanalytic material will show how neurotic hostility may contribute to susceptibility to Communism.[3]

The Case of Maureen

[T]he case of Maureen . . . was one of extreme rebellion against the family. Maureen was born in a medium-sized New England town in 1910. Her mother and father were badly matched; they quarreled and were quite unhappy together. Maureen was exposed to several different kinds of conflict in her childhood. There was especially intense hostility and misunderstanding in her relationship with her father. Her own parents were aggressively atheistic, while other members of her family with whom she lived after the death of her mother were pious Catholics.

When Maureen was eight, her mother died and she went to live with relatives. Her memories of her childhood were acutely unhappy. Confronted by the strong and clashing personalities of her mother, father, and other members of her family, she took refuge in aesthetic interests. She began reading at four years of age and wrote her "first novel" at nine. When she was fourteen she ran away

[3] In order to protect the anonymity of the respondents, certain of the facts pertaining to place and similar points of information have been scrambled.

from home and never returned to her family. "Father's policy was that if I came home he'd support me, but not before. We get along fine now, though when I was young I used to go without food at times."

She worked her way through high school and college, and from her own account was rather difficult to handle. "I never paid much attention to rules. I was the terror of the university." After leaving college she went to Chicago, where she got a job as a reporter. It was while working as a reporter (and a very successful one) during the first years of the depression that she became interested in politics. She attributes her conversion to Communism to her experiences with suffering and chaos in the Chicago of the depression. Having made up her mind to act, she sought out the party. She was in favor of doing something violent about the depression and thought the party would offer such an opportunity. When she finally made contact with the party, she asked that she immediately be assigned to underground and dangerous tasks. The party had other plans for her. It wanted to use her as an underground member in a front organization. She fought bitterly with the party officials, begged to be permitted to leave her journalistic work and be given some active and tough assignment, but she was prevailed upon to use her talents in her own field.

Though Maureen's tenure in the party was long, she was constantly resigning or threatening to resign, and then going back since she had committed herself so deeply and had acquired a husband who was a party functionary. She said about her antagonist in one party quarrel: "I would have shot him if I had had a gun at the time." At the same time, she got a great sense of security out of being in the party. "I never had a real family and, though you didn't have to like the CP family, at least you were all together against the world. Persecution won't drive them away from the party; it only makes them closer."

The Case of Max

Max was born in 1895, the child of poor French peasants. His parents abandoned him when he was four years old and he was brought up by a neighbor. He had only three years of schooling and then was put to work by other farmers. His childhood was hard and barren of affection. He found work in a factory after the end of World War I. He had moved to a part of France which was traditionally left and in which the newly formed Communist Party was successful in recruiting. In explaining his decision to join, he said that his ". . . unhappy childhood had produced in me an implacable hate for all those who from their childhood had enjoyed all the good things of life and who never experienced what hunger, cold, and poverty meant. I never tried to think why I hated them so much. I gave myself up to these feelings without reasoning, and instead put all my cunning and the shrewdness of a wild animal at the service of an idea that promised me vengeance." His reputation for violence is reflected in the fact that his party nickname was "The Fist." He served a prison sentence between 1930 and 1939 for violence done to a member of the *Croix de Feu*.

In 1942 Max joined the *Maquis* and had the command of a small group of partisans. His unit was known for its coldbloodedness. Max himself was assigned to punitive action against the collaborationists. He carried out a number of night raids. "Several times I was forced to kill these individuals when they offered resistance or when they called me a thief and assassin. I always had a sense of satisfaction in killing the rich, the Fascists."

Apparently Max was not too careful in his selection of victims. After the war, the mother of one of the men whom he had killed accused him of the murder. The party provided him with legal defense, and got him off with a one-year sentence. At the end of his prison term, he was called to the federation headquarters of the party and told that the party would have to expel him because of his criminal record. He was expelled with the understanding that the party would call on him whenever they needed his special talents. He considers himself a loyal Communist and holds himself in readiness for "violent days."

It is evident that in both the case of Maureen and that of Max, feelings of hostility were of an extraordinary intensity. Maureen was barely capable of controlling her rage reactions and had as unstable a career in the party as out of it. Max's indoctrination appeared to be the simplest veneer over violence and other forms of criminality. Despite the militance of the Communist movement, extreme hostility in a member would appear to come into conflict with the need for a stable controllable organization and a disciplined policy. As long as the party needed a desperate and courageous executioner Max had a place in it. But in the more subtle and law-abiding days of peace he was a dangerous man to have on the party rolls. Maureen could remain in the party for a very long time, since she was able to control her resentment and found it possible to discharge some of her hostile feelings in the writing of articles for the Communist press and in the training schools of the party. Often the party is the factor which makes it possible for individuals to control their hostility, by offering opportunities to express it under "socially acceptable" terms, by permitting hatred to be discharged in speech and in writing, and providing occasions for incurring danger, such as passing out leaflets at points where violence might occur, haranguing workers outside plants, and the like. Sometimes the party is the factor which keeps people from flying apart because of the intensity of the hatred pressing for discharge.

The Case of Jack

Such a case was Jack, of whom his psychoanalyst said, "He was defending himself against violent impulses—all his gentleness is a struggle against hostility. . . . He had no inner authority over himself. The party gave him something he never had—consistent authority. It gave him a way of looking on the world as an orderly place. Otherwise, he would regard it as chaotic and violent." His analyst hazarded the guess that if it were not for the party he might have been ". . . a criminal, a ruthless big-time swindler, or something of the sort." Jack came to his psychoanalyst suffering from great anxiety, spells of unjustified rage, and inability to sleep or work. The analyst described him as "a very disturbed person—at times on the verge of psychosis and at times on the verge of violence."

The analysis brought out the following picture. Jack was first-generation native-born of Eastern European Jewish parents. His father was pathetically ineffective as a wage earner and as a family authority. He had two brothers, one older and one younger, toward whom he felt extremely rivalrous and hostile in childhood, and whom he still holds in complete contempt. He grew up in a poor, foreign section of a large city. There was always the danger of attack from other non-Jewish groups of boys who lived in nearby neighborhoods. He was always afraid until he learned to fight well. He failed to finish high school because he wanted to be independent and make money.

At around this time he decided to become a playwright, and moved to New York. He refused to take help from his family and spent several hard years breaking into the theater. He married a woman with independent means. Much of the time in the analysis was taken up with therapeutic work on his rages, which were directed against his wife, superiors, and literary agents. If he did not think he was being treated fairly, he had to hold himself in to keep from attacking the man in authority. Most of the time, on the surface, he was mild, quiet, gentle. His rage would break out suddenly after an accumulation of irritations. For example, his wife was a poor house-keeper. After a period of household neglect, Jack would suddenly become violently angry. "He was always under tension, always on the point of rage, and a little detail might set it off."

In the party Jack thought of himself as a master of the ideology, ". . . arrogant and aggressive about correcting others for ideological slips." His fantasies about his political role were completely ruthless. His analyst pointed out that the party made it possible for him to impersonalize his hatred. "His need for the party is very great. He has no faith in anything else, no other community ties. He doesn't fit into society in any way except through the party, and through its ideology."

A number of points may be made as to the ways in which the party meets the needs of neurotically hostile people. In the first place, the party is a hostile organization; it is an "outlaw," an organization which fights established authority. The mere act of affiliating with it may be an act of defiance, and hence satisfying to persons who have these needs. Within the party there are many opportunities to express hatred, to discharge the tensions resulting from pent-up hostil-ity. The tone of the party press, the atmosphere of party discussions and mass demonstrations, serve to drain off and discharge this hostil-ity. Furthermore, the party makes it possible to dignify and ennoble these hostile impulses and hence make them "fit" for expression. Since the feelings are often extremely powerful and directed originally at quite inappropriate objects, such as mothers, fathers, and siblings, most individuals feel the need to displace these feelings, to direct them upon other and safer targets, to rationalize them in political, intellectual, and moral terms, to project the hatred upon other objects, which thus makes one's own hatred permissible. The party offers a hostile person an attractive self-image of one who understands the cause of evils and the effective ways of combating them. Thus it permits a man to transform himself from a hating and hence hateful in-dividual into a person whose hatred is based upon and supported by knowledge. It also tends to allay the guilt feelings that are usually associated with hostility: one can not only hate with "reason" but for morally good reasons. The psychoanalytic data were especially revealing on this point. In many cases the analysts referred to the

ways in which party membership took care of these guilt feelings.
A few quotations may serve to make the point. The party supplied
one person with "the opportunity to be ruthless without guilt"; it
gave another "his one and only outlet for aggression without guilt";
it provided a third with "the right to hate without guilt"; a fourth
was permitted "to destroy without guilt, to commit aggression without
responsibility." Such comments occurred with great frequency in the
psychoanalytic cases and in many of the interviews with party members.

The party is also of use in allaying the anxiety that is usually
associated with neurotic hostility. Persons who are constantly under
the pressure of hostile feelings ordinarily suffer from anxiety over
the destructiveness of their feelings and the dangers of retaliation.
It is dangerous to them to have such feelings. The party provides
group support, and hence a certain safety.

Thus the party is hospitable to neurotic hostility and to the feelings and emotional needs which are often associated with it. It satisfies
the need to express hostility even when the hostility is unconscious,
and when the general pattern of the individual's overt behavior is
genial, compliant, dependent, and passive.

In his analysis of the place of hostility in the appeal of Communism which is based upon our psychoanalytic interviews, Krugman
points out that in a number of these cases, hostility was a latent
rather than a manifest pattern.[4] These particular individuals had
found it impossible in their childhood to carry off revolt successfully.
The patterns of family life to which they had been exposed had
made it necessary for them to repress their hostility and to adopt
conciliatory approaches in their relations with parents and other persons. They had resolved the problem of how to respond to cruel,
exploitative, or unloving parents not by attacking, defying, or breaking
away, but by repressing these dangerous impulses and by developing
a yielding or detached overt behavior pattern. But the hostility continued to influence behavior in subtle ways—through not giving one's
self in personal relations, through lying and cheating, evading and
thwarting, rather than attacking and rebelling. After joining the party,
these individuals remain passive. In fact, the authoritarian pattern
of the party permits them to be passive at the same time that it
satisfies their unconscious needs for rebellion and defiance.

The theme of hostility is so pervasive in all this material that

[4] Krugman, *op. cit.*, pp. 259 ff.

its crucial role in neurotic susceptibility to Communism is inescapable. It is also true that hostility is a central factor in all neurosis, even when the overt behavior manifestations do not appear to be hostile at all. This would seem to suggest that any neurotically hostile person is susceptible to Communism. But this would be as incorrect as saying that any person resentful because of some damage to his position and status is susceptible. In the case of the situationally resentful person, as well as in that of the neurotically hostile one, the mediating factors which make for susceptibility are the adaptive patterns which require an intellectually and morally satisfying solution, and a perception and exposure to the party which is congruent with these feelings and patterns. In the case of the neurotically hostile person, the mechanisms of defense are of special importance, since the individual is responding not so much to problems outside of himself but to needs which are within and which press him antagonistically against his environment. The man who joins the party because he is unemployed or employed at an inadequate wage, or because his father has been killed in a war, may try to adjust himself to his external situation by joining the party. The mechanisms of learning and reality-testing are central in this adjustment. If the party fails to deal with the external situation in accordance with his expectations, then he may leave it and seek adjustment by other means. The party appears to be a way of getting employment or eliminating war by social and political reforms of one kind or another. The man who joins the party because of neurotic hostility or other neurotic needs is dealing with a threat which is inside himself, as well as with threats and problems which are external. Hence his political orientation represents a jerry-built structure of adjustive and defensive measures. The apparent threat may be a depression, a war, or social and religious discrimination, but there may be available in the situation a variety of devices and instrumentalities to deal with these problems. If a man is neurotically hostile, he may select the Communist Party because it satisfies his unconscious need to express extreme and integral hatred. This will involve displacing his hatred from such objects as parents, siblings, spouse, or individual authorities, impersonalizing it and focusing it on capitalism, the ruling class, and the like. It may also involve projecting onto the political arena his unconscious conception of personal relations as being unamenable to mutuality and compatibility, as involving integral incompatibility, the destruction or absorption of one antagonist by the other. It will also involve rationalization. Thus, instead of recognizing hostile and destructive feelings in himself, he may create an image of an alert and militant leader chastising evil and rewarding virtue.

ISOLATION

While hostility and resentment appear to be all-pervasive themes in the appeal of Communism, the attractions of the party typically involve other emotional problems and needs. Rossi makes much of the community aspect of the Communist movement.[5] In the classics and in the Communist media of communication there is constant emphasis on organization, community, relatedness. The ideal image of the Communist conveys the impression of a man who has his place in the meaningful progression of time, and who is surrounded by steadfast and loyal comrades. The Communist militant is not only related to a group; he also shares in a kind of mystical body, he merges himself in the *corpus mysticum* of the party, acquires a larger identity from it and even a sense of immortality. This stress upon union and unity, sharing in communion and community, has an especial impact upon those who are unrelated or inadequately related to their fellowmen, upon the lonely and the isolated. It can appeal to the one whose loneliness is situational—for example, to the college freshman away from home for the first time, who may lack the necessary introductions and contacts—as well as to the one whose loneliness is self-imposed, who rejects and withdraws from others because of some deep distrust of men, some fear of being improperly used and hurt.

That the party appeals to such withdrawn people is reflected in Table 2, which reports the incidence of neurotic isolation among the various groupings in the party. As might be anticipated, the incidence of neurotic isolation was higher among the American and British respondents, among the middle-class and intellectual respondents, and among the rank and file and the low echelon. If there is a kind of detachment in the role of the intellectual, it might be expected that persons who already have these withdrawn and alienative tendencies would be more likely to opt for intellectual professions. Persons whose relationships are more or less impaired may find science, philosophy, and the arts a possible way of relating themselves to life and purpose.

In contrast with neurotic hostility, which had some incidence

[5] A. Rossi, *A Communist Party in Action*, trans. by Willmoore Kendall (New Haven: Yale University Press, 1949), pp. 230 ff.

Table 2:   *The Incidence of Neurotic Isolation among Different Party Groupings (in per cent)*

Country	
United States	27
England	26
France	18
Italy	8
Social Class	
Middle class	32
Working class	5
Echelon	
Rank and file	25
Low echelon	29
High echelon	2

among the high-echelon respondents, isolation seems to be almost non-existent at this level. This may be due to the fact that the high-echelon Communist is under pressure to produce a high output of energy; he has constantly to deal with people, manipulate them, give them orders, inspire them, and the like. He can be antagonistic, autocratic, sadistic, but he cannot be shy, withdrawn, fearful. The neurotic isolate is more likely to be in the rank and file, or to occupy some low-echelon position involving routine actions.

How withdrawal may enter into the appeal of Communism is the theme of a number of illustrative case histories.

The Case of Julia

Julia grew up in a small Ohio town, the daughter of two professional musicians who were quite temperamental and unstable. "My parents have been warring for forty years. From the early days, my sister and I were both very maladjusted, especially me. I never went out with anyone at school, but rushed home to play the piano. . . . Our parents' rivalry almost wrecked us. It's a wonder we didn't have nervous breakdowns. . . . I took my father's side and sister took my mother's. However, father pushed me away because I was a girl, and mother pushed me away for siding with him."

After leaving school, Julia came to New York, where she got a job playing in a small hotel orchestra. Some of her fellow musicians were party members and sympathizers. She was asked to help in a strike which was then going on, and got great satisfaction out of working in the soup kitchens or helping the men in other ways. After this experience she joined the party. She said, "The attraction was heavily emotional. A group of friends attracted me—a need to belong—a feeling that perhaps I would do something to improve conditions, to be a hero of some kind. . . ."

She was always attracted to simple people, ". . . seamen, garage mechanics. . . . Maybe it's due to some inferiority of my own—probably so." These were the only types to whom she could relate herself. For a short while she was in a party cell with intellectuals. "We were mighty glad to get rid of each other. They were mighty stuffy." She was too shy to do recruiting or sell the *Daily Worker*. "My usual reaction was to give my own money, and give the newspapers away. I couldn't go out like the others and make speeches while selling the *Daily Worker*."

Julia's way of dealing with difficult situations was to run away. She wanted to divorce her first husband, but was afraid to face him and ran away to Chicago where she became a waitress. She returned to New York several years later and went back into the party. Throughout her interview she emphasized her loneliness. She had had no friends before joining the party, and apparently did not acquire any real friends after joining. Although she joined because of loneliness along with many others who joined for the same reason, she claimed ". . . it doesn't solve loneliness problems at all."

The Case of Alvin

Alvin came to his analyst complaining of great insecurity in his relations with people, a problem which he had had from childhood on. He was the second of three boys, the son of a foreign-born Jewish painter and decorator. The family lived on the "West side" of Chicago in a "tough" neighborhood. He avoided getting into fights by running away; he was very nimble and fast. His parents quarreled constantly. The father was worried about business, and the mother was bitter toward those in the block who had more than they had. There was no tenderness between the parents; after the birth of the children they no longer slept together. The mother gave Alvin no tenderness at all, no care, not even when he was sick. She would not let him play with other children or visit their homes. Alvin viewed his father as a failure, a flop. His older brother had rebelled a little and gotten hit for it. Alvin learned to get along by being compliant, by keeping his mouth shut.

Alvin was good in school, but recalls that he used to lie about his grades (said he got "B's" or "C's" instead of "A's") in order to deprive his mother of satisfaction. Until he became involved in the Communist movement, Alvin never joined anything. It was out of loneliness that he became a member of the Communist Party. He felt no resentment against society or his family. The hostility was deep underneath, but he protected himself from it and from outside hurts by the techniques of withdrawal. The few friends he had were either persons who went out of their way to be friendly toward him, or persons who were unhappier than he. One of these friendships was with a Communist who was very bitter and very aggressive. Alvin got a vicarious kick out of his friend's aggressiveness, but would not dream of behaving that way himself. He was quiet and often rude, but never antagonistic. If he could not think of a direct answer to a question he would say nothing. He had no life goals, no desire to get ahead. His hostility was held in repression, and affected his behavior mainly through withdrawal and "negativism," i.e., hurting himself and depriving others of himself rather than attacking others. His analyst summarized his case history as "simple schizophrenia—just a lonely, isolated, bitter, self-defeating person."

The chief defense mechanism involved in withdrawal is repression. The neurotically aggressive person strikes back, attacks, not only when he is situationally threatened but in most relationships. The withdrawn person represses his hostility and in a sense anesthetizes himself and defends himself against his feelings. Hostility was often reported in our withdrawn cases, but the withdrawn person may have been confronted with a family situation in which attack and retaliation were simply impossible. Hence the only possible way of dealing with his rages and hostilities was to drive them below the level of consciousness. His hostility, instead of pressing against others, presses in a subterranean way against himself, pulls him out of contact with people, and to a considerable extent out of contact with his own feelings. The withdrawn person is a "shell," lacking in spontaneity and direction. In the ultimate catatonic state of schizophrenia, the withdrawn person comes close to being emotionally dead.

But, short of these extreme states, the neurotic isolate feels some need to relate himself to people and to events. He knows he is alone and lonely, and tries to overcome this situation. But as long as his feelings are repressed, his efforts to relate himself are futile. He goes through the motions, but he just is not there. He may be led to the choice of Communism through his unconscious feelings of hostility and self-rejection, and through his external adjustive problem. The party is not only a community; it is a hostile community, and it is a community for outcasts. In most of the cases of neurotic withdrawal, the party was the first real group which was joined. The party can offer such an individual the illusion of being related. It prescribes tasks for him, gives him a role, gives him comrades, prescribes the mode of his relationships to the outside world as a whole. It helps him keep his hostile feelings in repression, by being hostile for him. This may involve the mechanisms of displacement and projection. It helps him evade his own anesthesia by giving him goals and the illusion of purposeful action. And this may involve the mechanisms of reaction formation, and of rationalization. The stronger the need to withdraw, and the greater the impairment of the capacity to feel, the more likely is such a person to be a passive rank and filer in the party. At best, such persons tend to hold low-ranking offices or perform functions which require little initiative.

SELF-REJECTION

Thus we have seen that Communism may appeal to persons who are overtly hostile toward or resentful of their environments, to persons who are neurotically passive and dependent, and to persons who are withdrawn from or isolated in their environments. It would also appear that Communism may appeal to persons who feel rejected or are rejected by their environments. The image of the Communist militant is of a dignified, special person, dedicated, strong, confident of the future, a man who knows his objectives, does his duty without hesitation. These aspects of Communism have an obvious attraction for persons who carry within themselves feelings of being weak and unworthy as a consequence of early childhood experiences, as well as for persons who have been objectively rejected by their environments. The Negro, the Jew, the foreign-born, and the first-generation native-born, the unemployed, the native intellectual in a colonial country, may respond to their social situation by feeling rejected, unworthy, lacking in dignity and esteem. In this sense, any negatively discriminated status may contribute to susceptibility. Throughout the interviews, even when neurotic problems were not indicated, this theme of rejection occurred with some frequency. In some cases, the emphasis was on weakness and inadequacy; in others, on ugliness, unworthiness, unassimilability. In either case, the basic provocation was rejection, either rejection in the situation, such as the Negro who is deeply hurt by an experience in school or college, or rejection in early childhood which has left inner and chronic doubts of one's strength and worth. The healthy child or adult who experiences some rejection at the hands of the environment may respond to such provocations by adjustive behavior. The neurotic adult whose damaging experiences occurred in early childhood may carry with him permanently the consequences of such mistreatment in the form of feelings of inadequacy and inferiority, confusions of identity and of role, feelings of worthlessness and of sinfulness. Regardless of his objective situation, he is constantly under pressure to defend himself against the defects which he feels inside himself.

As has already been pointed out, these self-rejective feelings were manifested with far greater frequency in the psychoanalytic case histories than in the interviews with former party members. Twenty-one of the 35 psychoanalytic case histories (or 60 per cent) indicated the importance of feelings of weakness in the attraction of Communism, and 16 (or 46 per cent) stressed unworthiness. On the other hand, Table 3 shows that only 11 per cent of the former Communist respondents manifested feelings of weakness and inadequacy, and 10 per cent feelings of unworthiness.

The incidence of these feelings follows roughly the same pattern as was the case for feelings of hostility and isolation—relatively high

Table 3:   *The Incidence of Neurotic Feelings of Weakness*
            and Unworthiness among Different Party Groupings
            (in per cent)

	Weakness	Unworthiness
Country		
United States	19	14
England	18	8
France	5	7
Italy	2	8
Social class		
Middle class	14	14
Working class	8	5
Echelon		
Rank and file	14	9
Low echelon	11	12
High echelon	6	6
Total for all interviews	11	10

among the American and British, the middle class, and the lower echelons, and relatively low among the French and Italian, the working class, and the high echelon.

The reason for the relative infrequency of reference to these feelings of self-rejection in the self-appraisals of former Communists would appear to be clear. These are the very feelings which many of them are fighting against, which they are unwilling to admit, and which they hold in repression. In many of the rebellious cases, it was quite evident that the hostility represented a kind of compensation for and defense against inner feelings of weakness and dependence. And in many of the "withdrawn" cases, it was evident that the withdrawal represented a defense against feelings of hostility, inadequacy, and unworthiness. Thus one would expect that clinical but not self-appraisal would bring to the surface the "weakness and vulnerability" aspect of hostility, and the hostile and self-rejective aspect of withdrawal. Then again, hostility and withdrawal are overt behavior manifestations. In describing one's career and social relations it is hard to conceal a chronic pattern of antagonism or withdrawal. And, in addition, these qualities are not necessarily negative ones. One can speak of being "shy," "proud," a "lone wolf," or "tough" and "hard-boiled," without creating the impression of being "queer." On the other hand, for men to speak of feeling passive, weak, or feminine, of feeling morally worthless or perverse, does involve an admission of being queer. Hence, it may be a safe inference that the incidence of these feelings of weakness and unworthiness was higher among the respondents than was manifested in their interviews, but that they were in some measure unconscious feelings, or the respondent was unwilling to speak of them.

The Case of Alice

Alice was the child of foreign-born Jewish parents who grew up in an anti-Semitic community. In her childhood she "wanted to be accepted by all," and went to great lengths to deny her Jewishness and foreignness by taking on the interests and mannerisms of the Gentile children. She was mainly interested in sports and was a cheerleader. But she apparently always suffered from a lingering feeling that there was some fraudulence in her credentials. In addition to feeling "out" because of Jewishness, the family went through economic "ups and downs," sometimes well-off, and sometimes at the point of dispossession. There was much conflict in the home. The need for acceptance and recognition appeared to be dominating themes in her efforts at adjustment.

In college she went through the typical process of being "developed." She found the Communist boys had a sense of direction. They brought her problems down to size. She was able to solve her problem of Jewishness by denying its importance, by assimilating the problem itself into much larger, "truer" problems. To still the feeling of being without roots, she developed a sense of having roots in something that was world-wide, meaningful, and powerful. "I had been running away from my Jewishness before college. . . . There was the pain of being Jewish and the hurts suffered at home. . . ." She described her mechanism of escape from the Jewish problem in the following terms: "If you can't belong to any country, then belong to no country, and then nobody should belong to a country. . . . If you are not accepted by Gentiles, why not join the most different group, give it some meaning . . . revel in your isolation?"

The role of feelings of inferiority and unworthiness, as well as the developmental patterns and emotional problems which give rise to them, are brought out with greater sharpness in the psychoanalytic cases. To be sure, this material stresses the importance of sex-role conflict. And it is important to point out that feelings of inferiority and of unworthiness may arise out of situations of social discrimination and rejection, particularly if these problems impinge on a person in early childhood, and in situations where the family is particularly vulnerable—in the case, for example, of Jews who live in unfriendly Gentile neighborhoods, or of children who grow up in families which deviate from the neighborhood patterns. The problem in these cases may not be a family one. The relations within the family may be comparatively sound. Similarly, organic defects such as lameness, blindness, ugliness, exceptional clumsiness, may result in feelings of inadequacy and unworthiness which lead to a potential susceptibility. In other words, the inferiority may be objective, the consequence of social ratings or of organic shortcomings, or it may be the consequence of an inner conviction of inferiority owing to some early laming experiences.

The Case of Walter

Walter came for treatment because of a general dissatisfaction with his personal relations. He felt that he got along with people by being a phony, that nobody really liked him, and that he didn't really like anyone either. His father was a successful businessman, emotionally dependent on his wife, who ruled him through martyrdom and tears. The father was greatly concerned with what people thought of him, constantly tried to maintain appearances. There was no real warmth in the family, no strength or stability. He had no admirable father to identify with, and his mother's hysteria made him distrustful of women, a pattern which led to difficulties in marriage and to promiscuity.

He had many friends, but his relationships with them were over-anxious. He was constantly worried about whether he was good enough for them. "He is always acting as though trying to prevent them from finding out how unworthy he is. They visit him, he thinks, because they can't think of any excuse to get out of it." In depressed moments, he thought of himself as a dirty, loathsome, and unpleasant person, essentially unlovable. At other times, he conceived of himself as very powerful, capable of taking any blow, capable of manipulating any situation. He had a dreadful need of being loved and approved by people, but at the same time felt that he could obtain their approval only by fooling or tricking them into it. He did not feel he could be liked spontaneously and for his own sake.

In college Walter was identified with all the extremist groups— the gamblers, the bohemians, and the Communists. His affiliation with the party was based upon a belief in the fundamental evil of the present "system" and of himself. He had few thoughts about the future of Communism. He mainly saw it as a powerful and cunning force with which to fight the evil of the world.

These feelings of self-rejection, of inadequacy, of moral depravity, are often, but by no means always, associated with conflict and confusion in sex roles. The developmental pattern which seems to be involved in these cases is that of a family situation in which the child's efforts to use his parents as images after which to model himself are thwarted. Thus, in the American culture, which stresses success and conformity in the outside world as the proper male role, many of the families described involved weak fathers and dominating mothers. Neither fathers nor mothers had the capacity to develop in their sons any confidence in their ability to fulfill male roles in relation to other males, or in relation to women. The individual's capacity to develop and sustain in later life warm and responsive relationships with persons of the same sex, or of the opposite sex, are crucially influenced by the "rehearsals," so to speak, of childhood relationships in the family. A strong and stable father may provide a son with a bridge to later relationships with authority and with other males. A warm and stably loving mother may give him confidence in women, and lay the basis of good relationships with women and a sound marriage.

A common pattern among the psychoanalytic cases and American respondents was the impairment of family relationships as a consequence of culture conflict.[6] Thus a large proportion of both groups were children of foreign-born parents. In these families, it often happened that the foreign-born fathers failed or did poorly in business and were inadequate in other respects. They spoke with foreign accents; they were extremely insecure in their social positions; they tried to prevent their sons from conforming or adjusting to the outside culture patterns, or made fools of themselves in trying to conform to these patterns themselves. Often the mother led in deprecating the father, urging her sons on to achieve what the father obviously could not attain. In other words, the mothers minimized the fathers and exploited the sons, pushing them beyond their capacities, using them, rather than permitting them to find their own levels. Thus a quite common pattern in our case material was the boy who had contempt for his father, and who distrusted his mother, who felt cheated by his family, and cheated by his society because of his foreign origin.

For such individuals as these, joining the party may represent an escape from an inner role confusion into something that is strong, integrated, dignified, and confident. If there is real internal doubt of one's capacity to behave as a male, joining the party may on the one hand serve as an act of defiance against a world which has denied him a secure sense of his role, and on the other hand provide a spurious sense of strength and maleness. The party and its authorities, such as Lenin, Stalin, or the national party leaders, or the individual Communists who recruited these people, often appeal to them as substitutes for the good, strong fathers whom they never had. And by giving their loyalty to these new fathers they allay the grief and guilt which those who reject their fathers cannot escape.

The Case of Arthur

Arthur's father was born in Europe and never really learned to speak English. He was a meek man who always looked as though he were about to cry. Arthur hated his father for his weakness, and refused

[6] See the discussion of the ethnic factor in the American party in Gabriel A. Almond, *The Appeals of Communism* (Princeton, N.J.: Princeton University Press, 1954), chap. 7, and the analysis of family structure and role conflict in Krugman, *op. cit.*, pp. 255 ff.

to take presents from him. The mother always won arguments in the family. She spoke English and was intelligent. She was hard on Arthur, refused to give him sympathy when he got involved in fights, told him to fight his own battles. In his adolescence Arthur began to avoid his mother. He became furious when she cooked his favorite dishes. He was afraid she wanted to dominate him, and he refused to give an inch.

He never developed any lasting friendships, but he was always a good boy and did what he was supposed to do in school. He had no confidence in his ability to be adequate with women, and was unmarried at the time of his analysis. He was afraid of women, feared they would dominate and destroy him, just as his father was destroyed by his mother.

His analyst commented about the meaning of the party to Arthur in these terms: "His personality is dominated by confusion. For example, he thinks he wants to get married, but when you get closer you find that he can't imagine what it's like to be a father or a husband. The party is the group that knows what's right and what's wrong. He became a Communist because men were humiliated and dominated by women. He hated his mother for her domination and his father for permitting it. He felt helpless." He defended himself against feelings of inadequacy and impotence by intellectual snobbery which had no real basis in fact. He really was not interested in intellectual problems. In college the sophisticated people were Communists. They made an "equal" out of him.

Arthur was typical of many of the male psychoanalytic cases for whom joining the party represented an effort to remedy defects in themselves, such as an incapacity to assert themselves professionally or to obtain satisfactory love and friendship relations. The basic problem appeared to arise out of role conflict and confusion, which in turn was attributable to a family situation in which neither parent played his nor her proper role as parents or as husband and wife, and in which the child was unable to develop a stable and secure sense of identity.

The Case of Frances

The family pattern among some of the female psychoanalytic cases was similar. Frances came to analysis in a state of acute anxiety. She said that she disliked her parents intensely, and wanted to leave home but was terrified of doing so. She was afraid at night, terrified of being alone, had feelings of unreality and moments in which she could not remember who she was.

Her father was a successful businessman who was very dependent on his wife. The strong partner was the mother, who viewed Frances as a competitor for her husband's affection. She was envious and vain, and in a subtle way a complete tyrant. Frances both feared and hated her mother, and viewed her father as a poor weak man in the control of her mother. By the time Frances was seven, her parents considered her a problem child. She was deviant and rebellious. In school she associated only with the lonely and queer children.

After puberty she began to develop a hatred and contempt for women and for being a woman herself. She loathed and feared her own body. In her fantasies she thought of herself as being without a body. She fought her own sexual feelings since they always reminded her that she was a woman. She had no confidence that men could love her, since she felt that she was a disgusting object.

Joining the party made it possible for Frances to have sex relations, not because they gave her satisfaction, but because she could show contempt for the ordinary laws of society. The Communist doctrine of sex equality helped her reject her femininity. Being a party member also meant that she could wear blue jeans, do common labor, in fact, do everything that was prohibited to middle-class girls. After she left school she went to work in a factory.

She liked art, music, bohemia, and periodically had intense attachments to one or two neurotic girl friends, bound to them by a common hatred. The party provided her with a supporting structure for her self-rejection and hatred. Though on the surface she was defiant and assertive of her views, underneath she was tormented by doubts about everything. The party gave her absolute answers to everything. There was no need for decisions, for doubt; it gave her real relief.

Being in the party supported Frances' effort to deny that women are different from men, and in particular it made it possible for her to think of herself as a strong male. The party enabled her to project her distrusts and hatreds into politics. She could interpret the world in terms of dog-eat-dog, struggle, and violence, without feeling irrational. The party in a sense confirmed and elaborated and justified her private paranoid ideas. In the words of her analyst, "There is violence and hatred everywhere and every act, no matter how small, can be interpreted in terms of the struggle. Her affiliation provided a chance to deny personal failure and make it world failure. She could identify herself with a group of underdogs—the mistreated ones . . . who have the right to counterattack. It took care of her conscience. . . . You don't have to consult your conscience, but only your memory for slogans and manifestoes." Frances' way of dealing with her hatreds and confusions was defiant and rebellious. She sought to destroy herself—her social class and her sex—and bring the whole world down in the process.

The pattern manifested in Frances' case represents in extreme form the impulses which lead individuals to go bohemian. Promiscuity and iconoclasm are means of defying rigid and rejective parents and of overcoming inner feelings of inadequacy and shame. As in the case of Frances and a number of others, an important aspect of this bohemianism is to be understood as an effort to humiliate one's parents by rejecting their class, their manners, their entire code. But it is also to be understood as an effort to find and establish an identity. And since one's internal appraisal of the self is low, it is possible to attain identity and relatedness only among similarly fallen persons. Bohemia is a kind of society of rejects and outcasts seeking for standards and ideals which will resolve and satisfy impulses which are in full conflict with one another—impulses to conform and be related, impulses to reject and withdraw, impulses for health and integrity, impulses to demean and debase the self. Often the party can serve as a kind of resolution of these conflicting impulses by appearing to satisfy the destructive and constructive impulses at the same time. For individuals unable to escape from these cruel dilemmas and confusions, the party makes possible a positive and constructive image of the self: for the wounded and aggrieved, a day of reckoning; for the lonely, community; for the weak, strength; for the humiliated, dignity; for those who have lost their way, certainty and clarity; for those burdened down with guilt, safety and redemption.

CONCLUSIONS

Thus the presence of alienative feelings which have resulted from serious deprivations and thwarting of expectations in early life may contribute to susceptibility to Communism. These feelings may be "engaged" and to some extent satisfied by joining the party and participating in its activities. At the same time, it would be a great mistake to believe that the mere presence of such alienative feelings creates susceptibility. Other aspects of the individual's orientation, such as his information and knowledge and his values, as well as the particular manifestation of the party to which he is exposed, may enhance or reduce the probability of his joining.

If it is incorrect to argue that all emotionally maladjusted persons are susceptible to Communism, it would be equally inaccurate to say that a particular type of maladjustment or developmental pattern is congruent with the appeal of Communism. If anything can be said along this line, it would be that among the various patterns hostility, if amenable to discipline, may contribute to the kind of motivation which leads to rapid and successful assimilation in the party. In other words, if the individual is overtly aggressive but not to the point of being incapable of a stable interpersonal role, he would appear, on the basis of our data, to have possibilities for party leadership. The same cannot be said for persons who are primarily withdrawn or self-rejective and whose hostility rarely, if ever, comes to the surface or, when it comes to the surface, takes on explosive proportions.

It did not appear from these data that any particular "oedipal" pattern contributed to susceptible personality tendencies. There were family situations in which the father was authoritarian and the mother weak, where it appeared that the party symbolized a revolt from the father. Among the American first-generation native-born of foreign-born parents a quite frequent constellation was one in which the father was weak and the mother dominant, and in which joining the party appeared to symbolize a revolt from the mother and a search for a strong father. And there were cases in which intense sibling rivalry appeared to be the main focus of family conflict.

A number of aspects of the developmental pattern appeared to be significant. One of these was whether or not the individual was able to mobilize and express his hostility. This would in part be determined by temperamental and constitutional factors, and in part by the possibilities within the family and other primary institutions of expressing this hostility. If the childhood pattern was such that the major direction which the maladjustment took was rebelliousness and antagonism, such an individual might find the party congenial to his emotional needs and gravitate to a responsible post. Other feeling patterns might lead to joining the party, but rarely to high-echelon status. In addition, the cognitive and value patterns of the family, the community setting, and the individual's own orientation are crucial to the whole problem of susceptibility. If the family cognitive pattern placed a premium on intellectuality—that is, knowledge and the capacity to generalize—or if the individual himself developed this mode of relating himself to the world in the absence of such a family pattern, and if the family moral pattern set obstacles to the more direct and simpler methods of expressing hostility, then such an individual might find the "moral militance" and the "theoretical" properties of the party congruent with his needs. The party supplies the supporting intellectual structure which for neurotics can transform hostility and antagonism into "fighting intelligently and with knowledge for good goals."

This factor of emotional maladjustment affects not only susceptibility to Communism, but also the process of adjusting to the party and the process of defection from it. Thus persons who find affiliation a means of coping with emotional difficulties may cling to the party long after it conflicts with their ideals, their career, and other personal interests, or when leaving the party may experience the most extreme suffering and disorientation.

IV
Components
of Personality
and Political
Systems

Part IV offers some examples of how each of the three components of personality can affect not only individual political decisions, but also the policies of important groups and entire political systems. The reader will remember that the behavior of the individual is influenced by his very humanity, by the groups to which he belongs, and by his unique organization of predispositions.[1]

One kind of group which seems to shape individuals' personal predispositions is the nation. We are all familiar with the traveler who, after a two-day stopover in Paris, tells us what "the French"

[1] See the Introduction.

are like. Indeed, some of the most insightful observations on American politics and character come from a French traveler, Alexis de Tocqueville.[2] Following the perceptive Frenchman, David Riesman has described Americans as essentially "other-directed" people whose opinions reflect no deep personal convictions and who are easily swayed.[3] Alternative portrayals of American character and political styles abound, as they do for other nations.[4]

The fact remains, however, that there is little careful research in this area. So sketchy are most analyses that J. Milton Yinger feels justified in asking, "*When* does it make sense to talk of national character?" He then sets forth a list of tentative answers which deftly exploit the complex interactions among social structure, culture, and individual character. He concludes that "it is impossible to speak with any confidence on this question because, despite hundreds of commentaries, there are few rigorous measurements."

This serves as a useful caveat for Fromm's analysis of Nazi Germany in *Escape from Freedom*. For Fromm, social character is an essential part of the glue that holds societies together by ensuring that people will do what is needed for the maintenance of the system.[5] It also makes life easier for the individual to *want* to do what he *has* to do. At the same time, social character may catalyze social change when the structure or culture or both fail to provide for the satisfaction of the needs which individuals have learned to feel under the old structure. Such unrequited demands may account for the allure of a new ideology to a nation's masses. (A microcosm of this phenomenon is the attractiveness of Communism to lonely, authoritarian, hostile, and insecure people.[6]) And the ideology, in turn, may

---

[2] Alexis de Tocqueville, *Democracy in America*, Phillips Bradley, ed. (New York: Knopf, 1945).

[3] David Riesman, *The Lonely Crowd* (New Haven: Yale University Press, 1950).

[4] Two of the most famous studies of American national character are Geoffrey Gorer, *The American People: A Study in National Character* (New York: Norton, 1948) and Margaret Mead, *And Keep Your Powder Dry: An Anthropologist Looks at America* (New York: Morrow, 1942). A list of useful studies of national character in other nations is J. Milton Yinger, *Toward a Field Theory of Behavior: Personality and Social Structure* (New York: McGraw-Hill, 1965), p. 96, n. 44.

[5] Riesman, among others, shares this explanation of social character. Both he and Fromm agree that modern industrial societies are likely to produce "other-directed" or "marketing-conformist" men. Fromm's position on this is in *Man for Himself: An Inquiry into the Psychology of Ethics* (New York: Holt, Rinehart and Winston, Inc., 1947).

[6] See the introductory comments to Part III and Selection 17.

generate behavior which reshapes the society. Nazism, for instance, appealed to the presumably authoritarian German character structure far better than did the democratic socialist ideal of the Weimar Republic. All the world knows the results of this appeal.

Although social character is mostly learned, human nature is not infinitely plastic. Fromm postulates a set of "higher" needs—creativity, self-expression, knowledge, and others—which emerge when the "lower" (physiological) ones have been met. Other theorists, notably Abraham Maslow and Carl Rogers, would agree with him, with the explicit addition of a need for self-respect.[7]

Viewed in this light, black nationalism in the United States may be an attempt by some Negroes to satisfy their basic human need for self-respect. In his study of the subject, Professor Essien-Udom observes that the chiliastic teachings of Elijah Muhammad foster pride in being black, whereas the prior experience of American Negroes has engendered shame and self-hatred.[8] Of course, there are other ways in which Negroes can achieve self-respect and racial pride, ranging from killing whites to winning elections. It is tantalizing—but inconclusive—to note that self-reported rioters from a probability sample of riot-torn census tracts in Newark and Detroit were more likely to exhibit racial pride than those who reported no involvement in the summer riots of 1967.[9] It remains the urgent task of our time to explain fully why people choose one mode of respect enhancement over others.

A few brief words are in order about the theories of Fromm, Maslow, and Rogers just referred to. Despite some philosophical and

---

[7] Fromm develops this thesis more fully in his later works: *Man for Himself; The Sane Society* (New York: Holt, Rinehart and Winston, Inc., 1955); and *Marx's Concept of Man* (New York: Ungar, 1961). Maslow's theory is set forth most clearly in his *Motivation and Personality* (New York: Harper & Row, 1954) and Rogers' theory is most concisely expressed in Carl B. Rogers, "A Theory of Therapy, Personality, and Interpersonal Relationships," in Sigmund Koch (ed.), *Psychology: A Study of a Science* (New York: McGraw-Hill, 1959), Vol. III, pp. 184–256. For a brief summary and critical review of all of these theories and their political implications, see George I. Balch, "On Self-Actualization: Clarification of a Political Goal," in James W. Dyson (ed.), *Attitude and Action in Politics* (Boston: Blaisdell, forthcoming).

[8] A convincing and exciting example of this is the life of Malcolm X, who was converted to Islam in jail by Elijah Muhammad. He later became a Muslim minister and one of Muhammad's chief assistants. See Malcolm X, *The Autobiography of Malcolm X* (New York: Grove, 1964).

[9] *Report of the National Advisory Commission on Civil Disorders* (New York: Bantam Books, 1968), pp. 133, 176.

empirical weaknesses, there is strong evidence for their main contention that drives for exploration, activity, and self-respect emerge in
physically sated people. This implies that economic abundance alone
will not satisfy people; they must also have opportunities to fulfill
the "higher" urges. A system which fails to provide constructive chan-
nels for these drives risks harnessing them to destructive or wasteful
activities like chiliastic and totalitarian political movements, riots, drug
addiction, gossip, superstition, the consumption, of gadgets, and total
submission to the will of others.[10]

Finally, we come to the "idiosyncratic" component of personality,
where observation and prescription start and end. Here an incisive
biographical study of former Secretary of the Navy James V. Forrestal
offers a look at the organization of predispositions over the life span
of a prominent American policy maker. Professor Rogow introduces
us to a man whose personality affected the course of American foreign
and defense policy as well as the course and violent end of his own
life. Although few politicians are psychotic and fewer commit suicide,
we must nonetheless be aware that brutal pressure is one of the personal costs of high political responsibility.

In James Forrestal we have a detailed example of an influential
"political personality" who displaces his personal motives upon the
unstructured, ambiguous domain of foreign policy.[11] His "toughness"
was a compensatory reaction against the passive, almost feminine nature which his domineering mother demanded of him. It meshed
rather nicely with the hawkish policies Forrestal favored in the cold
war. Note, too, the hints of authoritarianism[12] in Forrestal: "For those
in authority whom he regarded as weak he generally had contempt;
those who were strong he tended to dislike and resent."

At the same time, Rogow is careful to point out that Forrestal's
reactions changed hues with the situation. In a hot war he appeared
to be a strong soldier. In the cold one he rigidly supported the same

---

[10] These themes are more fully treated and documented in Balch's article cited
above. For an elaboration of the thesis that social systems should be judged by
their fulfillment of human needs, see the selection by Christian Bay in Part I.

[11] On the etiology and political recruitment of "political personalities," see the
selection by Lasswell in Part I. Implications and limitations of his formulation
are summarized in the introductory comments to Parts I and III and in Selection 12. Also, see Scott's article in Part I on the fertility of foreign policy as a
political arena for the displacement of personal motives.

[12] On authoritarianism and foreign policy, see the discussion of "Empirical
Grounds" in the Introduction.

policies, as if his opinions were based more on personal involvement than on the demands of the new situation. In this case, these personal factors were influential in the formulation of national policy.[13]

[13] A similar case from the perspective of the influence of idiosyncratic dispositions on American foreign policy is the behavior of President Woodrow Wilson regarding the Treaty of Versailles. A perceptive study of this is Alexander L. George and Juliette L. George, *Woodrow Wilson and Colonel House: A Personality Study* (New York: Dover, 1956).

18 *Modal Character*

J. MILTON YINGER

Expressed in extreme form, in which it is rarely found but which may be a useful point of departure here, the basic personality concept can be stated in this way: The influence of culture is so powerful and is experienced so uniformly by the members of a society that they have many basic character traits in common. Know the culture to which an individual has been socialized and you know how he will behave in many situations.

As a common sense idea, there is a great deal of stereotypy in this notion. It becomes easy, as a substitute for knowledge, to speak of "the" Frenchman, "the" Russian, or with reference to smaller, preliterate groups, "the" Kwakiutl, or "the" Trobriand Islander. A moment's thought leads to qualifications, of course. Role differences are recognized; status variation and individual contrasts appear. But the idea that many important similarities underlie these differences is a pervasive one.

Specifying the opposite point of view will indicate the theoretical range of judgments, although this extreme would also rarely be defended: As a result of biological variation, role differentiation,[1] accidental experiences, the range of permissiveness in cultural requirements, and other factors, the amount of character shared by the members of a society is minimal; the impressive fact is the extent of the differences in character among persons socialized to the "same" culture.

Relying on "logic" and selective evidence, one can make a good case for either of these extremes. Such a fact indicates the need for more careful specification of the conditions under which shared tendencies are numerous and those under which they are few.

Before noting what appear to be such conditions, we need to make clear which of several possible meanings of "basic" or "modal" or "national" character is being used. *First,* it should be emphasized that even under maximum conditions of cultural influence, the tendencies shared by the members of a society make up only one "layer" of character. For a complete description of any individual, one must add those tendencies he shares with subsocietal groups and his unique characteristics as well.

Second, reference to character indicates that we are dealing with a property of individuals, not of cultures. The basic or modal patterns are not necessarily the culturally required or ideal patterns.[2]

Third, we make no a priori assumption that shared tendencies must be basic, in the sense that they are the product of early experience (infant training) and are at the foundation of personality development.[3] Shared tendencies as a result of common infant experiences, "basic personality structure" . . . may be an outcome of life in

[1] J. Milton Yinger, *Toward a Field Theory of Behavior,* McGraw-Hill, 1965, chap. 7.
[2] This is to disagree with Emily M. Nett, "An Evaluation of the National Character Concept in Sociological Theory," *Social Forces,* May, 1958, pp. 297–303.
[3] For an empirical study of some of the effects of infant experiences, see William H. Sewell, "Infant Training and the Personality of the Child," *American Journal of Sociology,* September, 1952, pp. 150–159.

a homogeneous, slowly changing society; but if so, they are only part of national or societal character. Later experiences in the occupational or educational world, or in the communication network, may be more widely shared and equally influential. This necessity for the separation of "shared" and "basic" tendencies is related to the need for a shift of attention from culture alone to the sociocultural complex. Norms can affect behavior only as they are factors that influence the patterns of interaction. Even highly patterned child-training norms reach the infant only through his interactions with adults; that is, social structure as well as culture is involved.

It is important to recognize this third distinction, because culture and structure may vary independently; persons may be involved in similar structures of interaction even though cultural guidelines vary, and vice versa. A large majority of persons in industrial societies, for example, are affected by bureaucracies. Such social structures bring certain common influences to bear on individuals despite variation in cultural content. That is, there are *some* common elements in the interactions experienced in a hospital, a university, an industrial plant, an army base, the national office of a church—or, to change the base of comparison, in a Russian industry, a Japanese industry, and an American industry—despite the wide range in cultures. The division of labor, the impersonality, the size of the interacting group and the consequent complexity of the communication network, and the like, are structural elements of formal organizations that are not tied to specific cultural content.[4]

Fourth, "national character" must not be thought of as a system of almost identical tendencies found among almost all members of the society. Even in small and relatively homogeneous societies, there are significant variations around the shared qualities. This fact has led Inkeles and others to use the term "modal personality" and to suggest that in heterogeneous societies multi-modal distributions may be the rule.

On the basis of these four criteria, one readily accepts the definition of Inkeles and Levinson: "National character refers to relatively enduring personality characteristics and patterns that are modal among the adult members of a society."[5] I would modify it only

---

[4] See Alex Inkeles, "Some Sociological Observations on Culture and Personality Studies," in Clyde Kluckhohn and H. A. Murray (eds.), *Personality in Nature, Society, and Culture,* Alfred A. Knopf, Inc., 1948; 2d ed. with David M. Schneider, 1953, pp. 577–592.

[5] Alex Inkeles and Daniel J. Levinson, "National Character: The Study of Modal

slightly by adding a *fifth* criterion . . . : National character refers to shared tendencies, not to behavior. Since behavior is situational, knowledge of tendency does not suffice for prediction of behavior. . . . If we take on some of the appearance of the enemy, whether or not we wish to (and certainly our behavior may be affected much more by interaction with friends whom we wish to emulate), it is clear that explanations of behavior on the basis of character alone are inadequate. Therefore critics of the national-character concept cannot refute it by reference to changes, however drastic, in behavior (e.g., Japan, 1944, versus Japan, 1954). There is danger here, to be sure, of constructing an irrefutable concept. This can be avoided only by designing independent measures of tendencies that are applied at several periods of time, to discover the degree to which the tendencies are constant despite changing situations.

The need for distinguishing tendency from behavior is demonstrated by comparisons in space as well as time. It is possible, paradoxically, that behavior will be different *because of* similarities in tendencies. Insofar as American Negroes share the same values and aspirations as other members of the society but face discriminatory barriers to their achievement, any differences in behavior can be accounted for in part by reference to the shared qualities. (It is also true that there can be behavioral similarities in spite of differences in tendency—in values, motives, goals. Virtual unanimous support of a nation by its people in time of war is no proof of similarities of character. Modern societies require a great deal of cooperative and common behavior which does not demand identity of norms. Some core of agreement is implied—i.e., that in general, the given activity is worthwhile—but extensive dissimilarity is also possible.)

On the basis of these five criteria, I shall use the following modification of the Inkeles-Levinson definition: *National character refers to relatively enduring tendencies that are modal among the adult members of a society.*

We can return now to the attempt to specify the conditions under which shared tendencies are numerous and when they are few. There would be substantial agreement, I believe, on the following list. It is not made up of analytically distinct variables, for there is much interdependence among the items; but listing them in this way may

Personality and Sociocultural Systems," in Gardner Lindzey (ed.), *Handbook of Social Psychology*, Addison-Wesley Publishing Co., Inc., 1954, vol. 2, chap. 26.

Table 1:   Variables Related to National Character

Conditions Promoting Many Shared Tendencies	Conditions Associated with Few Shared Tendencies
Few contacts with other societies	Many contacts
Slow rate of sociocultural change	Rapid sociocultural change
Small population	Large population
Slight status differentiation	Extensive status differentiation
Little division of labor	Extensive division of labor
Extensive social mobility	Closed class system
Extensive physical mobility within society	Little physical mobility
Few racial, religious, or national groups with distinctive subcultures	Many groups with subcultures
Communication system reaches all members	Gaps in communication network; many small networks
Homogeneity among major socializing institutions—family, school, church	Heterogeneity among major socializing institutions

help us to shift from the question "Does national character exist?" toward a scale which can be applied to any society.

If such a list has validity, it is clear that there are more shared tendencies in a small, preliterate group than in a contemporary nation. But the list should also warn us against assuming an inevitable reduction of shared tendencies in the modern world. Compared with a large feudal society, for example, an open-class, mobile society with an elaborate communication network may produce more "national character."

Unfortunately it is impossible to speak with any confidence on this question because, despite hundreds of commentaries, there are few rigorous measurements. . . . Better samples and additional measuring instruments are needed. As Inkeles and Levinson note, the measurement of national character requires examination of large and representative samples studied individually.[6] But most research examines cultural products and norms, then infers character from them. More extensive comparisons are required to identify those tendencies that are pan-human (under equivalent conditions) or class-oriented ("Is there a 'poverty character' that shows the imprint of the culture of poverty?"), as well as those that are modal to the members of a society.

[6] *Ibid.*, p. 981.

19 *Character and the Social Process*

ERICH FROMM

In studying the psychological reactions of a social group we deal with the character structure of the members of the group, that is, of individual persons; we are interested, however, not in the peculiarities by which these persons differ from each other, but in that part of their character structure that is common to most members of the group. We can call this character the social character. The social character necessarily is less specific than the individual character. In describing the latter we deal with the whole of the traits which in their particular configuration form the personality structure of this or that individual. The social character comprises only a selection of traits, the essential nucleus of the character structure of most members of a group which has developed as the result of the basic experiences and mode of life common to that group. Although there will be always "deviants" with a totally different character structure, the character structure of most members of the group are variations of this nucleus, brought about by the accidental factors of birth and life experience as they differ from one individual to another. If we want to understand one individual most fully, these differentiating elements are of the greatest importance. However, if we want to understand how human energy is channeled and operates as a productive force in a given social order, then the social character deserves our main interest.

The concept of social character is a key concept for the understanding of the social process. Character in the dynamic sense of analytic psychology is the specific form in which human energy is shaped by the dynamic adaptation of human needs to the particular mode of existence of a given society. Character in its turn determines the thinking, feeling, and acting of individuals. To see this is somewhat difficult with regard to our thoughts, since we all tend to share the conventional belief that thinking is an exclusively intellectual act and independent of the psychological structure of the personality. This is not so, however, and the less so the more our thoughts deal with ethical, philosophical, political, psychological or social problems rather than with the empirical manipulation of concrete objects. Such thoughts, aside from the purely logical elements that are involved in the act of thinking, are greatly determined by the personality structure of the person who thinks. This holds true for the whole of a doctrine or of a theoretical system as well as for a single concept, like love, justice, equality, sacrifice. Each such concept and each doctrine has an emotional matrix and this matrix is rooted in the character structure of the individual.

We have given many illustrations of this in the foregoing chapters.[1] With regard to doctrines we have tried to show the emotional roots of early Protestantism and modern authoritarianism. With regard to single concepts we have shown that for the sado-masochistic char-

---

[1] E. Fromm, *Escape From Freedom*, Holt, Rinehart and Winston, Inc., New York, 1941.

acter, for example, love means symbiotic dependence, not mutual affirmation and union on the basis of equality; sacrifice means the utmost subordination of the individual self to something higher, not assertion of one's mental and moral self; difference means difference in power, not the realization of individuality on the basis of equality; justice means that everybody should get what he deserves, not that the individual has an unconditional claim to the realization of inherent and inalienable rights; courage is the readiness to submit and to endure suffering, not the utmost assertion of individuality against power. Although the word which two people of different personality use when they speak of love, for instance, is the same, the meaning of the word is entirely different according to their character structure. As a matter of fact, much intellectual confusion could be avoided by correct psychological analysis of the meaning of these concepts, since any attempt at a purely logical classification must necessarily fail.

The fact that ideas have an emotional matrix is of the utmost importance because it is the key to the understanding of the spirit of a culture. Different societies or classes within a society have a specific social character, and on its basis different ideas develop and become powerful. Thus, for instance, the idea of work and success as the main aims of life were able to become powerful and appealing to modern man on the basis of his aloneness and doubt; but propaganda for the idea of ceaseless effort and striving for success addressed to the Pueblo Indians or to Mexican peasants would fall completely flat. These people with a different kind of character structure would hardly understand what a person setting forth such aims was talking about even if they understood his language. In the same way, Hitler and that part of the German population which has the same character structure quite sincerely feel that anybody who thinks that wars can be abolished is either a complete fool or a plain liar. On the basis of their social character, to them life without suffering and disaster is as little comprehensible as freedom and equality.

Ideas often are consciously accepted by certain groups, which, on account of the peculiarities of their social character, are not really touched by them; such ideas remain a stock of conscious convictions, but people fail to act according to them in a critical hour. An example of this is shown in the German labor movement at the time of the victory of Nazism. The vast majority of German workers before Hitler's coming into power voted for the Socialist or Communist Parties and believed in the ideas of those parties; that is, the range of these ideas among the working class was extremely wide. The weight of these ideas, however, was in no proportion to their range. The onslaught of Nazism did not meet with political opponents, the majority of whom were ready to fight for their ideas. Many of the adherents of the leftist parties, although they believed in their party programs as long as the parties had authority, were ready to resign when the hour of crisis arrived. A close analysis of the character structure of German workers can show one reason—certainly not the only one—for this phenomenon. A great number of them were of a personality type that has many of the traits of what we have described as the authoritarian character. They had a deep-seated respect and longing for established authority. The emphasis of socialism on individual independence versus authority, on solidarity versus individualistic seclusion, was not what many of these workers really wanted on the basis of their personality structure. One mistake of the radical leaders was to estimate the strength of their parties only on the basis of the range which these ideas had, and to overlook their lack of weight.

In contrast to this picture, our analysis of Protestant and Calvinist doctrines has shown that those ideas were powerful forces within the adherents of the new religion, because they appealed to needs and anxieties that were present in the character structure of the people to whom they were addressed. In other words, *ideas can become powerful forces, but only to the extent to which they are answers to specific human needs prominent in a given social character.*

Not only thinking and feeling are determined by man's character structure but also his actions. It is Freud's achievement to have shown this, even if his theoretical frame of reference is incorrect. The determinations of activity by the dominant trends of a person's character structure are obvious in the case of neurotics. It is easy to understand that the compulsion to count the windows of houses and the number of stones on the pavement is an activity that is rooted in certain drives of the compulsive character. But the actions of a normal person appear to be determined only by rational considerations and the necessities of reality. However, with the new tools of observation that psychoanalysis offers, we can recognize that so-called rational behavior is largely determined by the character structure. In our discussion on the meaning of work for modern man we have dealt with an illustration of this point. We saw that the intense desire for unceasing activity was rooted in aloneness and anxiety. This compulsion to work differed from the attitude toward work in other cultures, where people worked as much as it was necessary but where they were not driven by additional forces within their own character structure. Since all normal persons today have about the same impulse to work and, furthermore, since this intensity of work is necessary if they want to live at all, one easily overlooks the irrational component in this trait.

We have now to ask what function character serves for the individual and for society. As to the former the answer is not difficult. If an individual's character more or less closely conforms with the social character, the dominant drives in his personality lead him to do what is necessary and desirable under the specific social conditions of his culture. Thus, for instance, if he has a passionate drive to save and an abhorrence of spending money for any luxury, he will be greatly helped by this drive—supposing he is a small shopkeeper who needs to save and to be thrifty if he wants to survive. Besides this economic function, character traits have a purely psychological one which is no less important. The person with whom saving is a desire springing from his personality gains also a profound psychological satisfaction in being able to act accordingly; that is, he is not only benefited practically when he saves, but he also feels satisfied psychologically. One can easily convince oneself of this if one observes, for instance, a woman of the lower middle class shopping in the market and being as happy about two cents saved as another person of a different character may be about the enjoyment of some sensuous pleasure. This psychological satisfaction occurs not only if a person acts in accordance with the demands springing from his character structure but also when he reads or listens to ideas that appeal to him for the same reason. For the authoritarian character an ideology that describes nature as the powerful force to which we have to submit, or a speech which indulges in sadistic descriptions of political occurrences, has a profound attraction and the act of reading or listening results in psychological satisfaction. To sum up: the subjective function of character for the normal person is to *lead him to act according to what is necessary for him from a practical standpoint and also to give him satisfaction from his activity psychologically.*

If we look at social character from the standpoint of its function in the social process, we have to start with the statement that has been made with regard to its function for the individual: that by adapting himself to social conditions man develops those traits that make him desire to act as he has to act. If the character of the majority of people in a given society—that is, the social character—is thus adapted to the objective tasks the individual has to perform in this society, the energies of people are molded in ways that make them into productive forces that are indispensable for the functioning of that society. Let us take up once more the example of work. Our modern industrial system requires that most of our energy be channeled in the direction of work. Were it only that people worked because of external necessities, much friction between what they ought to do and what they would like to do would arise and lessen their efficiency. However, by the dynamic adaptation of character to social requirements, human energy instead of causing friction is shaped into such forms as to become an incentive to act according to the particular economic necessities. Thus modern man, instead of having to be forced to work as hard as he does, is driven by the inner compulsion to work which we have attempted to analyze in its psychological significance. Or, instead of obeying overt authorities, he has built up an inner authority—conscience and duty—which operates more effectively in controlling him than any external authority could ever do. In other words, *the social character internalizes external necessities and thus harnesses human energy for the task of a given economic and social system.*

As we have seen, once certain needs have developed in a character structure, any behavior in line with these needs is at the same time satisfactory psychologically and practical from the standpoint of material success. As long as a society offers the individual those two satisfactions simultaneously, we have a situation where the psychological forces are *cementing* the social structure. Sooner or later, however, a lag arises. The traditional character structure still exists while new economic conditions have arisen, for which the traditional character traits are no longer useful. People tend to act according to their character structure, but either these actions are actual handicaps in their economic pursuits or there is not enough opportunity for them to find positions that allow them to act according to their "nature." An illustration of what we have in mind is the character structure of the old middle classes, particularly in countries with a rigid class stratification like Germany. The old middle class virtues—frugality, thrift, cautiousness, suspiciousness—were of diminishing value in modern business in comparison with new virtues, such as initiative, a readiness to take risks, aggressiveness, and so on. Even inasmuch as these old virtues were still an asset—as with the small shopkeeper—the range of possibilities for such business was so narrowed down that only a minority of the sons of the old middle class could "use" their character traits successfully in their economic pursuits. While by their upbringing they had developed character traits that once were adapted to the social situation of their class, the economic development went faster than the character development. This lag between economic and psychological evolution resulted in a situation in which the psychic needs could no longer be satisfied by the usual economic activities. These needs existed, however, and had to seek for satisfaction in some other way. Narrow egotistical striving for one's own advantage, as it had characterized the lower middle class, was shifted from the individual plane to that of the nation. The sadistic impulses, too, that had been used in the battle of private competition were partly shifted to the social and political scene, and partly intensified by frustration. Then, freed from any restricting factors, they sought satisfaction in acts of political persecution and war. Thus, blended with the resentment caused by the frustrating qualities of the whole situation, the psychological forces instead of cementing the existing social order became dynamite to be used by groups which wanted to destroy the traditional political and economic structure of democratic society.

We have not spoken of the role which the educational process plays with regard to the formation of the social character; but in view of the fact that to many psychologists the methods of early childhood training and the educational techniques employed toward the growing child appear to be the cause of character development, some remarks on this point seem to be warranted. In the first place we should ask ourselves what we mean by education. While education can be defined in various ways, the way to look at it from the angle of the social process seems to be something like this. The social function of education is to qualify the individual to function in the role he is to play later on in society; that is, to mold his character in such a way that it approximates the social character, that his desires coincide with the necessities of his social role. The educational system of any society is determined by this function; therefore we cannot *explain* the structure of society or the personality of its members by the educational process; but we have to explain the educational system by the necessities resulting from the social and economic structure of a given society. However, the methods of education are extremely important in so far as they are the mechanisms by which the individual is molded into the required shape. They can be considered as the means by which social requirements are transformed into personal qualities. While educational techniques are not the cause of a particular kind of social character, they constitute one of the mechanisms by which character is formed. In this sense, the knowledge and understanding of educational methods is an important part of the total analysis of a functioning society.

What we have just said also holds true for one particular sector of the whole educational process: the *family.* Freud has shown that the early experiences of the child have a decisive influence upon the formation of its character structure. If this is true, how then can we understand that the child, who—at least in our culture—has little contact with the life of society, is molded by it? The answer is not only that the parents—aside from certain individual variations—apply the educational patterns of the society they live in, but also that in their own personalities they represent the social character of their society or class. They transmit to the child what we may call the psychological atmosphere or the spirit of a society just by being as they are—namely representatives of this very spirit. *The family thus may be considered to be the psychological agent of society.*

. . . While it is true that man is molded by the necessities of the economic and social structure of society, he is not infinitely adaptable. Not only are there certain physiological needs that imperatively call for satisfaction, but there are also certain psychological qualities inherent in man that need to be satisfied and that result in certain reactions if they are frustrated. What are these qualities? The most important seems to be the tendency to grow, to develop and realize potentialities which man has developed in the course of history—as, for instance, the faculty of creative and critical thinking and of having differentiated emotional and sensuous experiences. Each of these potentialities has a dynamism of its own. Once they have developed in the process of evolution they tend to be expressed. This tendency can be suppressed and frustrated, but such suppression results in new reactions, particularly in the formation of destructive and symbiotic impulses. It also seems that this general tendency to grow—which is the psychological equivalent of the identical biological tendency—results in such specific tendencies as the desire for freedom and the hatred against oppression, since freedom is the fundamental condition for any growth. Again, the desire for freedom can be repressed, it can disappear from the awareness of the individual; but even then it does not cease to exist as a potentiality, and indicates its existence by the conscious or unconscious hatred by which such suppression is always accompanied.

We have also reason to assume that, as has been said before, the striving for justice and truth is an inherent trend of human nature, although it can be repressed and perverted like the striving for freedom. In this assumption we are on dangerous ground theoretically. It would be easy if we could fall back on religious and philosophical assumptions which explain the existence of such trends by a belief that man is created in God's likeness or by the assumption of a natural law. However, we cannot support our argument with such explanations. The only way in our opinion to account for this striving for justice and truth is by the analysis of the whole history of man, socially and individually. We find then that for everybody who is powerless, justice and truth are the most important weapons in the fight for his freedom and growth. Aside from the fact that the majority of mankind throughout its history has had to defend itself against more powerful groups which could oppress and exploit it, every individual in childhood goes through a period which is characterized by powerlessness. It seems to us that in this state of powerlessness traits like the sense of justice and truth develop and become potentialities common to man as such. We arrive therefore at the fact that, *although character development is shaped by the basic conditions of life and although there is no biologically fixed human nature, human nature has a dynamism of its own that constitutes an active factor in the evolution of the social process.* Even if we are not yet able to state clearly in psychological terms what the exact nature of this human dynamism is, we must recognize its existence. In trying to avoid the errors of biological and metaphysical concepts we must not succumb to an equally grave error, that of a sociological relativism in which man is nothing but a puppet, directed by the strings of social circumstances. Man's inalienable rights of freedom and happiness are founded in inherent human qualities: his striving to live, to expand and to express the potentialities that have developed in him in the process of historical evolution.

At this point we can restate the most important differences between the psychological approach pursued in this book and that of Freud. The first point of difference . . . [is that] we look upon human nature as essentially historically conditioned, although we do not minimize the significance of biological factors and do not believe that the question can be put correctly in terms of cultural *versus* biological factors. In the second place, Freud's essential principle is to look upon man as an entity, a closed system, endowed by nature with certain physiologically conditioned drives, and to interpret the development of his character as a reaction to satisfactions and frustrations of these drives; whereas, in our opinion, the fundamental approach to human personality is the understanding of man's relation to the world, to others, to nature, and to himself. We believe that man is *primarily* a social being, and not, as Freud assumes, primarily self-sufficient and only secondarily in need of others in order to satisfy his instinctual needs. In this sense, we believe that individual psychology is fundamentally social psychology or, in Sullivan's terms, the psychology of interpersonal relationships; the key problem of psychology is that of the particular kind of relatedness of the individual toward the world, not that of satisfaction or frustration of single instinctual desires. The problem of what happens to man's instinctual desires has to be understood as one part of the total problem of his relationship toward the world and not as *the* problem of human personality. Therefore, in our approach, the needs and desires that center about the individual's relations to others, such as love, hatred, tenderness, symbiosis, are the fundamental psychological phenomena, while with Freud they are only secondary results from frustrations or satisfactions of instinctive needs.

The difference between Freud's biological and our own social orientation has special significance with regard to the problems of characterology. Freud—and on the basis of his findings, Abraham, Jones, and others—assumed that the child experiences pleasure at so-called erogenous zones (mouth and anus) in connection with the process of feeding and defecation; and that, either by overstimulation, frustration, or constitutionally intensified sensitivity, these erogenous zones retain their libidinous character in later years when in the course of the normal development the genital zone should have become of primary importance. It is assumed that this fixation on the pregenital level leads to sublimations and reaction-formations that become part of the character structure. Thus, for instance, a person may have a drive to save money or other objects, *because* he sublimates the unconscious desire to retain the stool. Or a person may expect to get everything from somebody else and not as a result of his own effort, *because* he is driven by an unconscious wish to be fed which is sublimated into the wish to get help, knowledge, and so forth.

Freud's observations are of great importance, but he gave an erroneous explanation. He saw correctly the passionate and irrational nature of these "oral" and "anal" character traits. He saw also that such desires pervade all spheres of personality, man's sexual, emotional, and intellectual life, and that they color all his activities. But he mistook the causal relation between erogenous zones and character traits for the reverse of what they really are. The desire to receive everything one wants to obtain—love, protection, knowledge, material things—in a passive way from a source outside of oneself, develops in a child's character as a reaction to his experiences with others. If through these experiences the feeling of his own strength is weakened by fear, if his initiative and self-confidence are paralyzed, if hostility develops and is repressed, and if at the same time his father or mother offers affection or care under the condition of surrender, such a constellation leads to an attitude in which active mastery is given up and all his energies are turned in the direction of an outside source from which the fulfillment of all wishes will eventually come. This attitude assumes such a passionate character because it is the only way in which such a person can attempt to realize his wishes. That often these persons have dreams or phantasies of being fed, nursed, and so on, is due to the fact that the mouth more than any other organ lends itself to the expression of this receptive attitude. But the oral sensation is not the cause of this attitude; it is the expression of an attitude toward the world in the language of the body.

The same holds true for the "anal" person, who on the basis of his particular experiences is more withdrawn from others than the "oral" person, seeks security by making himself an autarchic, self-sufficient system, and feels love or any other outgoing attitude as a threat to his security. It is true that in many instances these attitudes first develop in connection with feeding or defecation, which in the early age of the child are his main activities and also the main sphere in which love or oppression on the part of the parents and friendliness or defiance on the part of the child, are expressed. However, overstimulation and frustration in connection with the erogenous zones by themselves do not lead to a fixation of such attitudes in a person's character; although certain pleasurable sensations are experienced by the child in connection with feeding and defecation, these pleasures do not assume importance for the character development, unless they represent—on the physical level—attitudes that are rooted in the whole of the character structure.

For an infant who has confidence in the unconditional love of his mother, the sudden interruption of breast-feeding will not have any grave characterological consequences; the infant who experiences a lack of reliability in the mother's love may acquire "oral" traits even though the feeding process went on without any particular disturbances. The "oral" or "anal" phantasies or physical sensations in later years are not important on account of the physical pleasure they imply, or of any mysterious sublimation of this pleasure, but only on account of the specific kind of relatedness toward the world which is underlying them and which they express.

Only from this point of view can Freud's characterological findings become fruitful for social psychology. As long as we assume, for instance, that the anal character, as it is typical of the European lower middle class, is caused by certain early experiences in connection with defecation, we have hardly any data that lead us to understand why a specific class should have an anal social character. However, if we understand it as one form of relatedness to others, rooted in the character structure and resulting from the experiences with the outside world, we have a key for understanding why the whole mode of life of the lower middle class, its narrowness, isolation, and hostility, made for the development of this kind of character structure.[2]

The third important point of difference is closely linked up with the previous ones. Freud, on the basis of his instinctivistic orientation and also of a profound conviction of the wickedness of human nature, is prone to interpret all "ideal" motives in man as the result of something "mean"; a case in point is his explanation of the sense of justice as the outcome of the original envy a child has for anybody who has more than he. As has been pointed out before, we believe that ideals like truth, justice, freedom, although they are frequently mere phrases or rationalizations, can be genuine strivings, and that any analysis which does not deal with these strivings as dynamic factors is fallacious. These ideals have no metaphysical character but are rooted in the conditions of human life and can be analyzed as such. The fear of falling back into metaphysical or idealistic concepts should not stand in the way of such analysis. It is the task of psychology as an empirical science to study motivation by ideals as well as the moral problems connected with them, and thereby to free our thinking on such matters from the unempirical and metaphysical elements that befog the issues in their traditional treatment.

[2] F. Alexander has attempted to restate Freud's characterological findings in terms that are in some ways similar to our own interpretation. (Cf. F. Alexander, "The Influence of Psychological Factors upon Gastro-Intestinal Disturbances," *Psychoanalytic Quarterly*, Vol. XV, 1934.) But although his views constitute an advance over Freud's, he has not succeeded in overcoming a fundamentally biological orientation and in fully recognizing interpersonal relationships as the basis and essence of these "pregenital" drives.

Finally, one other point of difference should be mentioned. It concerns the differentiation between psychological phenomena of want and those of abundance. The primitive level of human existence is that of want. There are imperative needs which *have* to be satisfied before anything else. Only when man has time and energy left beyond the satisfaction of the primary needs, can culture develop and with it those strivings that attend the phenomena of abundance. Free (or spontaneous) acts are always phenomena of abundance. Freud's psychology is a psychology of want. He defines pleasure as the satisfaction resulting from the removal of painful tension. Phenomena of abundance, like love or tenderness, actually do not play any role in his system. Not only did he omit such phenomena, but he also had a limited understanding of the phenomenon to which he paid so much attention: sex. According to his whole definition of pleasure Freud saw in sex only the element of physiological compulsion and in sexual satisfaction the relief from painful tension. The sexual drive as a phenomenon of abundance, and sexual pleasure as spontaneous joy—the essence of which is not negative relief from tension—had no place in his psychology.

What is the principle of interpretation that this book has applied to the understanding of the human basis of culture? Before answering this question it may be useful to recall the main trends of interpretation with which our own differs.

1. The "psychologistic" approach which characterizes Freud's thinking, according to which cultural phenomena are rooted in psychological factors that result from instinctual drives which in themselves are influenced by society only through some measure of suppression. Following this line of interpretation Freudian authors have explained capitalism as the outcome of anal eroticism and the development of early Christianity as the result of the ambivalence toward the father image.[3]

2. The "economistic" approach, as it is presented in the misapplication of Marx's interpretation of history. According to this view, subjective economic interests are the cause of cultural phenomena, such as religion and political ideas. From such a pseudo-Marxian viewpoint,[4] one might try to explain Protestan-

---

[3] For a fuller discussion of this method, cf. E. Fromm, *The Dogma of Christ*, Holt, Rinehart, and Winston, Inc., New York, 1964.

[4] I call this viewpoint pseudo-Marxian because it interprets Marx's theory as meaning that history is determined by economic motives in terms of the striving

tism as no more than the answer to certain economic needs of the bourgeoisie.

3. Finally there is the "idealistic" position, which is represented by Max Weber's analysis, *The Protestant Ethic and the Spirit of Capitalism.* He holds that new religious ideas are responsible for the development of a new type of economic behavior and a new spirit of culture, although he emphasizes that this behavior is never exclusively determined by religious doctrines.

In contrast of these explanations, we have assumed that ideologies and culture in general are rooted in the social character; that the social character itself is molded by the mode of existence of a given society; and that in their turn the dominant character traits become productive forces shaping the social process. With regard to the problem of the spirit of Protestantism and capitalism, I have tried to show that the collapse of medieval society threatened the middle class; that this threat resulted in a feeling of powerless isolation and doubt; that this psychological change was responsible for the appeal of Luther's and Calvin's doctrines; that these doctrines intensified and stabilized the characterological changes; and that the character traits that thus developed then became productive forces in the development of capitalism which in itself resulted from economic and political changes.

With regard to Fascism the same principle of explanation was applied: the lower middle class reacted to certain economic changes, such as the growing power of monopolies and postwar inflation, with an intensification of certain character traits, namely, sadistic and masochistic strivings; the Nazi ideology appealed to and intensified these traits; the new character traits then became effective forces in supporting the expansion of German imperialism. In both instances we see that when a certain class is threatened by new economic tendencies it reacts to this threat psychologically and ideologically; and that the psychological changes brought about by this reaction further the development of economic forces even if those forces contradict the

---

for material gain, and not as Marx really meant, in terms of objective conditions which can result in different economic attitudes, of which the intense desire for the gain of material wealth is only one. A detailed discussion of this problem can be found in E. Fromm's "Über Methode und Aufgabe einer analytischen Sozialpsychologie," *Zeitschrift für Sozialforschung,* Vol. I, 1932. P. 28 ff. Cf. also the discussion in Robert S. Lynd's *Knowledge for What?,* Princeton University Press, Princeton, 1939. chap. II.

economic interests of that class. We see that economic, psychological, and ideological forces operate in the social process in this way: that man reacts to changing external situations by changes in himself, and that these psychological factors in their turn help in molding the economic and social process. Economic forces are effective, but they must be understood not as psychological motivations but as objective conditions: psychological forces are effective, but they must be understood as historically conditioned themselves; ideas are effective, but they must be understood as being rooted in the whole of the character structure of members of a social group. In spite of this interdependence of economic, psychological, and ideological forces, however, each of them has also a certain independence. This is particularly true of the economic development which, being dependent on objective factors, such as the natural productive forces, techniques, geographical factors, takes place according to its own laws. As to the psychological forces, we have indicated that the same holds true; they are molded by the external conditions of life, but they also have a dynamism of their own; that is, they are the expression of human needs which, although they can be molded, cannot be uprooted. In the ideological sphere we find a similar autonomy rooted in logical laws and in the tradition of the body of knowledge acquired in the course of history.

We can restate the principle in terms of social character: The social character results from the dynamic adaptation of human nature to the structure of society. Changing social conditions result in changes of the social character, that is, in new needs and anxieties. These new needs give rise to new ideas and, as it were, make men susceptible to them; these new ideas in their turn tend to stabilize and intensify the new social character and to determine man's actions. In other words, social conditions influence ideological phenomena through the medium of character; character, on the other hand, is not the result of passive adaptation to social conditions but of a dynamic adaptation on the basis of elements that either are biologically inherent in human nature or have become inherent as the result of historic evolution.

20 *The Negro Dilemma*

E. U. ESSIEN-UDOM

The question, then, is posed whether this
unparalleled alienation and our partial
entrance into what is termed the mainstream
of American life precludes our exploration of
our identity as a minority of African descent
and our recourse to the African heritage as a
fructifying source of our creative endeavor.[1]

SAMUEL W. ALLEN

Reprinted from *Black Nationalism* by E. U. Essien-Udom by permission of the
University of Chicago Press. Copyright 1962 by The University of Chicago.

[1] *The American Negro Writer and His Roots* (New York: American Society of
African Culture, 1959), p. 14.

A century after the Emancipation, nineteen million black Americans, robbed of their traditions and of a pride in their past, are still seeking acceptance by the white majority but are continuing to live in semibondage on the fringes of American society. They are groping for a way out of this dilemma, but no way is clear, certain, or easy.

Few middle- and upper-class Negroes[2] have escaped the cultural subordination and degradation of the Negro masses. Some have striven to become "white middle class," believing and acting as if they were exempt from the open contempt in which whites hold their race. Their world view and philosophy is a naive individualism. The road to success for the majority of them lies in trying to escape psychologically from their identity as Negroes and in practicing an unmitigated opportunism.

Until the early part of this century, most Negro leaders and many individuals among the first generation of educated Negroes proudly styled themselves "race men" who were above all concerned with reconstructing the economic, moral, and cultural life of their people. Today, however, such a reference is not only shunned but repudiated. The identification of middle-class Negro leaders with the masses of their race has grown increasingly tenuous and weak. They appear no longer to be seeking the dignity and the integrity of their race in America, but rather the political rights of Negroes as American citizens—a valuable goal but only one aspect of the Negro's experience and goals in American life.[3] The bonds of race which bind them to the masses are increasingly loose and involuntary. They are no longer the leaders of their race, for they have arrived, i.e., gained entrance into white middle-class society.[4] They cannot, however, take the millions of other Negroes along with them. They reject and despise the Negro masses, whom they deem responsible for what they know

---

[2] For a most illuminating study of the Negro middle class, see E. Franklin Frazier, *Black Bourgeoisie* (Glencoe, Ill.: Free Press, 1957).

[3] For a good discussion of "race values" and "race ends" among Negroes, see James Q. Wilson, *Negro Politics: The Search for Leadership* (Glencoe, Ill.: The Free Press, 1960), chap. XIII, "Goals of Negro Leaders." See also Gunnar Myrdal, *An American Dilemma* (New York: Harper, 1944) for the ambivalences in Negro behavior concerning "race ends"; Frazier, *op. cit.,* pp. 216 ff.; R. Kinzer and E. Sagarin, *The Negro in American Business: The Conflict Between Separation and Integration* (New York: Greenberg, 1952); St. Clair Drake and Horace Cayton, *Black Metropolis* (New York: Harper, 1945), pp. 716–754.

[4] The term "white middle class" is used here as the norm of individual social attainment in the United States.

to be a continuing rejection by the whites, into whose society they are not really assimilated.[5]

White middle-class society, in reality, is not, and for a long time to come may not be, open to the millions of black Americans. But, in fact, neither is Negro middle-class society open to them. The inferior material and cultural standards of the Negro masses prevent them from entering either society. Their economic status, their moral habits, and the image they have been given of themselves, condemn them to live and die trapped in the Negro ghettos of the urban centers of America. In all probability, most will remain members of the lower class, despised by white and Negro middle-class society alike. The overwhelming objective limitations placed on their cultural, economic, and political aspirations make it impossible for them to escape from their community; they cannot wish away their racial identity. Whether they view it positively or negatively, they cannot be indifferent to it. It is the stuff of their lives and an omnipresent, harsh reality. For this reason the Negro masses are instinctively "race men."[6]

This feeling of being "race men" as opposed to racists is an inarticulate but common one among the Negro masses. It was particularly exemplified in the lives and teachings of the Negro leaders of the nineteenth and early twentieth century, for these men identified themselves with, and were continuously involved in, the fate of the Negro masses without developing a racist ideology. The intelligentsia of the present, however, have lost touch with this concept in their concern over the legitimate importance of integration. In their anxiety not to appear racist in their thinking, they have repudiated all racially conscious movements and organizations, but at the same time, they find themselves, because of this repudiation, powerless to move the Negro masses toward their professed goals. Their attempt to be at once Negro and non-Negro is an insoluble dilemma. To some extent it accounts for their disdain and rejection of the black nationalist movements.[7] It also explains their failure to appreciate the as yet

---

[5] We do not deny that there is greater social mobility among Negroes at the present time than in any other time in their history. In fact, it is for this reason that class distinction within the Negro group is acquiring new social significance. It makes the disparity obvious between the "fortunes" of the lower classes and those of the middle and upper classes.

[6] Cf. David Riesman, *Faces in the Crowd: Individual Studies in Character and Politics* (New Haven: Yale University Press, 1952), p. 91.

[7] For attitudes of middle-class Negro leaders and intellectuals toward the Garvey movement, the only truly nationalist movement among American Negroes during

imprecise and conflicting yearnings of the Negro masses for racial definition and integrity.

The nationalist leaders contend that the Negroes must become consciously aware of their identity as a group in America; they must realize their degradation and strive by individual and collective effort to redeem their communities and regain their human dignity. The Negro masses, unlike the middle and upper class, are seeking a way out of a sociocultural environment, a spiritual and psychological impasse, fostered by the stubbornly lingering mores of slavery and complicated during the present century by the urbanization of American society. The vast majority of black Americans, however, do not know how to liberate themselves. They look forward to that day when they will find themselves in the "promised land" without making any effort to bring it about.

This book attempts to record the striving of thousands, and perhaps unrecorded millions, of American Negroes to reclaim for themselves and their group the normal self-pride and confidence which their history in America has denied them. It is an account of their struggle to recover, even to reconstruct, a world in which they can enjoy an unashamed sense of identity and to vindicate their honor as black Americans.

The focus of the study is the Nation of Islam, a movement led by Georgia-born Elijah Muhammad, who is known to his followers as the Messenger of Allah and whom they believe to be divinely chosen and divinely inspired to unite American Negroes under the Crescent of Islam. In the early nineteen-thirties, the Nation of Islam was led by Prophet W. D. Fard, who is said to have come from Arabia. His organization first concentrated on Detroit Negroes and gained an estimated membership of perhaps 8,000 during the critical years of the depression. Late in 1933 he disappeared and Elijah Muhammad became the leader of the movement. Prophet Fard is acknowledged by Muhammad and his followers as the Mahdi. He is "Allah in the Person of Master Wallace Fard Muhammad."[8] (The Mahdi occupies the same position of Messiahship in Islam as the person of the Christ in Christianity.) Between 1934 and 1946 Elijah Muhammad also organized followers in Chicago, Milwaukee, and

---

the twenties, see Edmund D. Cronon, *Black Moses* (Madison, Wisc.: University of Wisconsin Press, 1957), pp. 113 ff.; Frazier, *op. cit.*, pp. 121–123.

[8] The title "Mr." preceding the present leader's name distinguishes him from "Allah in the Person of Wallace Fard Muhammad," for whom the title "Master" is reserved.

Washington, D.C. Prophet Fard's initial success in Detroit, however, was not matched at that time by comparable successes in any other large city. In fact, in 1942, when Muhammad and his followers were indicted and imprisoned for violations of the Selective Service Act, the total membership of the movement came to only a few hundred. Today, it is estimated at a quarter of a million, and followers are organized in twenty-one states and the District of Columbia.[9]

The movement is organized about Temples, each known as "Muhammad's Temple of Islam."[10] By December, 1959, there were said to be fifty such Temples in various parts of the United States. Each Temple is under the direction of a minister who is directly responsible to Muhammad. The present study is based on an intensive examination of Muhammad's Temple No. 2, in Chicago, which was established in 1934 and now has a regular membership of nearly 1,000 adults. It functions also as the headquarters—"the Mecca"—of the movement.

For more than two decades the Nation of Islam was a small, highly secretive group known to few Negroes. Its activities and influence expanded immensely during the years 1954–61, however, and Muhammad now bids openly for the allegiance of the Negro masses of the country. His name is widely known among Negroes, not only because of the activities of the Muslims,[11] but also because of weekly columns which he writes for nationally circulated Negro newspapers; and he has also come to public notice through alarmist white newspaper, radio, and television publicity. The movement is under police surveillance in every city where there is a Temple, and the Federal Bureau of Investigation is said to have closely watched it for possible subversive tendencies. In 1959 the American white public became aware, to some extent, of this movement's existence and of the name

[9] Membership has been estimated variously by the following publications: at 70,000 (*Time,* August 10, 1959, p. 25); at 200,000 (*Sepia,* November, 1959, p. 21). Muhammad is quoted in *Time* as claiming a total membership of 250,000. *U.S. News and World Report* notes that "other sources place its size at anywhere from 10,000 to 70,000" (November 9, 1959, p. 112).

[10] Renamed "Muhammad's Mosque" in 1960. However, they shall be designated as "Temples" throughout this study, the name by which these organizational units are widely known.

[11] Followers of Muhammad profess faith in Islam as they understand it. They refer to themselves as "Muslims." In order to avoid confusion with other believers in Islam who go by the same name but whose creed is different, the English spelling "Moslem" is used to distinguish these other believers from Muhammad's followers.

of its spiritual leader. It can be asserted with some confidence that the Nation of Islam is now the most important black nationalist movement in the United States.

Elijah Muhammad claims that "Allah in the Person of Master Wallace Fard Muhammad," or Prophet Fard, confronted him in 1930 and for the following three years explained to him the history and significance of the "Black Nation." He taught Muhammad his beliefs concerning the Caucasian race, the religions of Islam and Christianity, as well as the "truth" about the beginnings of creation, the "impending" destruction of the Caucasian race and its civilization, and the final overthrow of white rule over the black peoples. Furthermore, Allah revealed to him that the United States would be destroyed in 1970. After this apocalypse, the Black Nation—the entire world population of the "black, brown, yellow, and red" races—would emerge as the sole ruler of the world under Allah's benign and righteous guidance.

The Nation of Islam, however, is distinguished from the Black Nation in that it is a chosen people within the Black Nation, elected by Allah as His special instrument for the entire redemption of the Black Nation. In theory the Nation of Islam consists of the Negro population of the United States; but in practice and for the time being, it is confined to the followers of Elijah Muhammad. Muhammad proclaims that his mission on earth is to deliver this message to the "so-called American Negroes," who until the coming of Master W. F. Muhammad had no knowledge of themselves or of their enemy (the Caucasian race and its Christianity), their religion (Islam), or of their God (Allah). For the present he is concerned with organizing them so that they may return to their own religion and their own kind in fulfillment of the covenant which he believes Allah made with their "patriarch," Abraham of the Old Testament. But he is also bent on moral reform and dedicated to the cultural and economic advancement of his followers. Present membership in the Nation of Islam, which is strictly limited to non-whites, consists almost entirely of American Negroes. Belief in Allah and acceptance of Islam as taught by Muhammad are minimum requirements for membership.

The concept of nationalism, which is germane to this study, may be thought of as the belief of a group that it possesses, or ought to possess, a country; that it shares, or ought to share, a common heritage of language, culture, and religion; and that its heritage, way of life, and ethnic identity are distinct from those of other groups. Nationalists believe that they ought to rule themselves and shape their own destinies, and that they should therefore be in control of their social, economic, and political institutions. Such beliefs among American Negroes, particularly among the followers of Muhammad, are here called black nationalism.

It must be admitted at the outset that neither the Nation of Islam nor any other black nationalist organization wholly conforms to this definition. Nonetheless, it may be helpful, in comprehending certain patterns of behavior among the black nationalists, to observe the degree to which they incorporate nationalist symbols, and in re-marking deviations from the ideal type. Although black nationalism shares some characteristics of all nationalisms, it must be considered a unique type of separatist nationalism seeking an actual physical and political withdrawal from existing society. Apart from the unifying symbols of race and religion, it employs the heritage of abuse and indignity to which the Negro people in the United States have been subjected and, perhaps more importantly, their common desire for self-improvement. Although most nationalisms involve the idea of race, they are able to develop historically within a definite geographi-cal territory and can therefore easily evoke the common traditions and symbols of that region. The Nation of Islam, however, lacks both a territorial base and the symbolism drawn from either the Negro's past in the United States or from his African origins. This peculiar nationalism has placed its antecedents in what it believes to be "Arabian civilization," the highest development of which was reached in Egypt. It is also extraordinary that its belief in itself as a definite nation of people has produced absolutely no political pro-gram for the establishment of a national home. Rather, the final na-tional homeland is guaranteed solely through eschatological beliefs taken from Old Testament prophecies.[12]

The ideas of an eventual return to a national homeland and of black redemption after the apocalypse (the latter a version of the Armageddon of the Book of Revelation) lend the movement two forceful ideological dynamics and inform it with an abstract world view. Both ideas have inspired religious zeal, loyalty to the movement and its leader, and personal sacrifices for the common good. The

[12] For an excellent discussion of eschatology, see Norman Cohn, *The Pursuit of the Millennium* (London: Secker and Warburg, 1957), p. xiii. In Christian doc-trine, the final struggle is to be between the hosts of Christ and the hosts of anti-Christ. In Muhammad's teaching, the struggle is to be between the Black Nation and the Caucasian race—the world of Islam and the world of Christianity.

Muslims' sense of expectancy aids them in persevering and in sustaining their hopes.

However, the religious teachings of Muhammad do not fully explain the behavior patterns of the Muslims. *Esoteric* in nature, centered upon eschatological and apocalyptic hopes, they are too removed from the present realities of the Muslims' lives to account for the sincerity of their practices, their ethical and cultural prescriptions. Although extremely important as a psychological factor of unity and hope, they must be distinguished from the *exoteric* teachings of Muhammad, with which they of course interact. The exoteric forms of the religion stem directly from Muhammad's attempt to cope with the social, cultural, and psychological environment in which the Negro finds himself. They offer the believer a set of incentives and a definite discipline which enable him to transcend the common plight and degradation of the Negro masses, and they impart to the movement an active, cohesive, and expanding existence. Foremost among these incentives is the belief that they, the Muslims, are laying the foundation for a nation, even though it is now only a "nation within a nation." Second, they believe that in Islam, and particularly in the Nation of Islam, they now enjoy freedom, fraternity, justice, and equality under their own government. Third, they affirm that their lives have been morally and materially bettered since they accepted Islam as a way of life. As shall be shown in later chapters, this last belief is an immeasurably strong motivation.

Muhammad's exoteric teachings emphasize the techniques for attaining the good life in the "sweet here and now" and not in the "sweet bye and bye." Heaven and hell are thought to be "two conditions on earth which reflect one's state of mind, his moral condition and actions." Knowledge of one's identity—one's self, nation, religion, and God—is considered the true meaning of the Resurrection, while ignorance of it is the meaning of hell. An interplay between the esoteric religious beliefs and the techniques for rising above the environment and attaining the good life has significantly limited the lack of discipline and the other-worldliness which the Muslims deplore as characterizing the religious life of the Negro masses. Similarly, it serves as an antidote to the intense messianic expectancy which often informs chiliastic movements. The Muslims have gained an enthusiasm for acting together to achieve their ends without necessarily sacrificing the mood of "watchful waiting."

The history of the alienation of Africans from their homeland

and of their subsequent subordination and humiliation in the New World for over two centuries is well known. Equally familiar is the contribution of slavery to family disintegration and to cultural disorientation.[13] The result is that Negroes have acquired what appears to be an appalling sense of inferiority and even of hatred for their "Negro-ness." This heritage of slavery, as well as their continuing subjection to abuse and indignity, must be fully recognized and appreciated before the problem which black nationalism seeks to resolve can be understood.

Elijah Muhammad makes his appeal primarily to the urban lower-class Negroes, who are for the most part migrants from southern rural sections where they had been accustomed to a way of life markedly different from that encountered in the city. In common with the white working class, they share the frustrations, anxieties, and disillusionments of contemporary urban life; but the Negroes' experience in adjusting to city life is additionally complicated and aggravated by their special status in American society. Black nationalism has its roots in these urban tensions and in the hopeless frustration which the Negroes experience in trying to identify themselves and their aspirations with white society. Compelled by segregation, discrimination, poverty, and ignorance to remain on the periphery of white society and to live and die within the subculture of the Negro ghettos, the Negro masses have had to disassociate themselves from white society. At the same time, however, they are compulsively attracted to it, since power, status, security, even beauty remain white priorities, white possessions. This conflict in Negro thinking is further disturbed by the demand of white society that the Negroes conform to its material, cultural, and moral standards while denying them the economic and social resources for so doing. Thus, the burden of a final irony is added to the Negro's dilemma.

White society assumes that the Negro will almost always act in accordance with the stereotypes of Negro behavior which it has evolved. Thus, in its view, the Negro will always act as a paragon of almost supine patience and reasonableness; he will not be subject to the human emotions of hatred, anger, and love, nor of personal and group pride. He will be content with employment which does not challenge his intelligence and which pays him only a subsistence wage; he will be happy to live and raise his family in patently inade-

[13] See E. Franklin Frazier, *The Negro Family in the United States* (Chicago: University of Chicago Press, 1939).

quate housing within a congested ghetto; and send his children to schools which add to confusion and frustrations rather than elevating human intelligence, talent, and dignity.[14]

Faced with these stereotypes and rebelling against them because of their untruth and hostile intent, the Negro also unconsciously rejects the standards of the ruling white society which has foisted them upon him. In doing so, he succeeds merely in perpetuating the stereotypes and in incurring the added opprobrium of white society, which sees in this rejection a confirmation of its unflattering views.

This dilemma, so fraught with paradox, is responsible for the attempt by middle-class Negroes to conform in detail to white standards and to separate themselves from the Negro masses. The black nationalists, however, though they too seek to differentiate themselves from the Negro subculture, have eschewed all *rapprochement* with white society.

However, the majority of Negroes accept their "place" in white society and in the Negro subculture as inescapable while at the same time unconsciously rejecting the subculture because of its low prestige, insecurity, and futility. Consequently, most Negroes live and die without ever achieving a unified consciousness of their membership in the Negro community or in the larger American society;

> It is a peculiar sensation, this double-consciousness, this sense of always looking at one's self through the eyes of others, of measuring one's soul by the tape of a world that looks on in amused contempt and pity. One ever feels his two-ness—an American, a Negro; two souls, two thoughts, two unreconciled strivings; two warring ideals in one dark body, whose dogged strength alone keeps it from being torn asunder.[15]

The Negro cannot choose both the dominant white culture and his own subculture. This sense of suspension between two societies and of dual membership presents enormous impediments to the process of adjustment. Negroes are involved, subconsciously though it may be, in assertion of membership in one and in denial of membership in the other, or in a feeble assertion of both, or in the denial of their affinity with both. In consequence no Negro "ethos" has de-

[14] Cf. James B. Conant, *Slums and Suburbs: A Commentary on Schools in Metropolitan Areas* (New York: McGraw-Hill Book Company, 1961), pp. 2, 3, 18–27.
[15] W. E. B. DuBois, *The Souls of Black Folk,* 7th ed. (Chicago: A. C. McClurg, 1907), pp. 3–4.

veloped, no ethnic and institutional loyalty aiding Negroes in pursuing common goals.[16] Involved only peripherally in the American ethos, they are thus only partially inspired by it.

Black nationalists have in general attempted to deal with the problem of the Negro's ethnic identity by insisting that "what the Negro needs" is complete separation from the white majority and the establishment of a national home. Unlike the vast majority of American Negroes, the nationalists maintain that a positive identification with their "Negro-ness," or with their ancestral homeland, is a prerequisite to both personal dignity and effective social action. There is, however, no agreement among them as to what their ethnicity is. They are not even agreed upon a name for themselves. Some prefer "Afro-Americans," others "Aframericans," "Africans Abroad," "Persons of African Descent," "Asiatics," or simply "black people."[17] Thus, when the word "Negro" is used by the Muslims, which is rarely, it is qualified by "so-called" or used contemptuously to differentiate Negroes not belonging to the movement from themselves. They are also careful about the word "race" because they believe themselves to constitute a "nation." It is the Caucasians, they believe, "racing with time," who form a "race."

This lack of consensus about the Negro's ethnicity appears also among non-nationalists. Although the majority of Negroes accept their American nationality and patiently and hopefully await the day when their citizenship will neither be qualified nor left in doubt, there is no consensus as to the terminology by which they wish to be known. They are still ambivalent toward the term "Negro," even though both "colored" and "Negro" are most widely used. The intellectuals as well as the ordinary Negroes frequently assert that since there is

---

[16] W. G. Sumner defines the word "ethos" as: "the sum of the characteristic usages, ideas, standards, and codes by which a group was differentiated and individualized in character from other groups." *Folkways* (Boston: The Athenaeum Press, Ginn and Co., 1906), p. 36. The writer is especially indebted to Professor Edward C. Banfield's application of this concept in his analysis of an Italian community. See *The Moral Basis of a Backward Society* (Glencoe, Ill.: Free Press, 1958).

[17] Although the controversy over the use of the word "Negro" or "colored" is now less frequently voiced, the use of either word in addressing different Negro audiences continues to evoke a lively agreeable or disagreeable emotional reaction. The controversy finds guarded expression in print. See J. A. Rogers, *Africa's Gift to America* (New York: Futuro Press, Inc., 1959). Although Rogers prefers to use all the prevailing names, such as Negro, colored, black, African-American, he has suggested that the "correct" term would be "African-European-American-Indian."

no complete biological unity within the group, the very term "Negro" is a social rather than a racial classification in the United States.[18]

Some emphasize the fact that historical circumstances have made Negroes a "nation within a nation," and have evolved an indigenous "Negro culture" based upon their experiences in America or on their African origin, or on both.[19] Dr. W. E. B. DuBois has been foremost among those who emphasize this dualism (Negro-Americanism) in Negro thought—a nation without a polity, nationals without citizenship. His writings, strongly tinctured with nationalism, represent the effort of a highly sophisticated man to resolve these dilemmas and, in effect, they parallel efforts of others who seek resolution in black nationalism. Negro fraternal, philanthropic, and business associations are practical responses to the dualism of loyalty arising from the tensions of black-white relationships.

Black nationalists insist that these dilemmas, confusions, and the absence of internal cohesion are largely responsible for the failure of Negroes to exert concerted pressure for the things that they demand from society.[20] They claim that the solution to the problem of the

---

[18] James W. Ivy, "Le fait d'être Nègre dans les Amériques," *Présence Africaine* (Paris), No. 24–25, Fev.–mai, 1959, pp. 123–124; also E. Franklin Frazier, "What Can the American Negro Contribute to Africa?" in *Africa as seen by American Negroes*, Special Issue of *Présence Africaine*, ed. J. A. Davis, August, 1959, pp. 275–276. Cf. W. E. B. DuBois, *An Appeal to the World* (New York: N.A.A.C.P., 1947), p. 1.

It is interesting to note that Dr. DuBois again discussed the problem of terminology for the Negro in a speech before the Seventh Annual Conference, the All-African Student Union of the Americas, Inc., held at the University of Chicago, June 18–21, 1958 (mimeographed), pp. 2–3. See also George S. Schuyler, "The Caucasian Problem," *What the Negro Wants*, ed. Rayford W. Logan (Chapel Hill: The University of North Carolina Press, 1944), p. 284: "The term Negro itself is as fictitious as the theory of white racial superiority on which Anglo-Saxon civilization is based, but it is nevertheless one of the most effective smear devices developed since the Crusades. It totally disregards national, linguistic, cultural and physical differences between those unable to boast a porcine skin, and ignores the findings of advanced sociologists and ethnologists. . . ."

[19] Cf. *The American Negro Writer and His Roots* for this subject in general.

[20] Aside from their antagonism toward the National Association for the Advancement of Colored People, the nationalists point out that it does not receive the support of the Negro masses. The NAACP, which is the most "militant" organization seeking full citizenship for Negroes, can only boast a total membership of 334,000 as of December 15, 1959. The increase over the previous year is said to be a little over nine per cent. Considering the importance of the objectives of the organization, this is a rather small number out of a total population of Negroes estimated at nearly 19 million. It should be added that the membership also in-

Negro's identity and to internal constraints which arise from it is a prerequisite of all other solutions. They seem to believe that these internal constraints are overlooked by many Negroes (especially the middle class) and, consequently, that most Negroes tend to perceive their problems as well as their communities *solely* as the creation of white society. They come to the inevitable conclusion that their efforts must be directed to making white society recognize and assume full responsibility for the solution of these problems. The nationalists admit that attitudes and actions of white society are powerful obstacles to their solution, but they point out that the level of community involvement among the urban Negro masses—other than for "funerals, food, and fun"—is either nonexistent or absolutely minimal.

The writer has been impressed by the absence of internal cohesion and the low level of community involvement among the urban Negro masses. These explain in part the inability of Negroes to have a significant say concerning the economic and political norms of their communities. Furthermore, the Negro community provides few or no criteria by which its members can meaningfully interpret and relate the dominant white culture and the realities of American society to their specific experiences. The Negro masses cannot participate fully and responsibly in their communities. Perhaps more than is generally admitted, the internal constraints account for the Negroes' general lack of a sense of common need.[21]

It is no wonder that so many Negroes resort to mere opportunism and become totally preoccupied with immediate survival values (shelter, clothing, food, and recreation) or that they are easily swayed to seek salvation in escapist or purely diversionary activities such as alcoholism, drug addiction, gambling, spiritualism, and conspicuous display. Many Negroes, however, hope that eventually the American Dream will be fulfilled for them as individuals, if not through their own efforts, then by "good luck."

Black nationalism has brought these problems into sharp focus, especially those internal constraints and divisions which prevent Negroes from acting in unison or even in seeking individual self-improvement. Although it would be hard to determine how much of Muhammad's effort is deliberate and how much is unconscious, the impression

---

cludes whites. See the *Chicago Daily Defender*, January 11, 1960, p. 7, for membership figures.

[21] Although this view does not deny the meagreness of material resources available within the Negro community, it emphasizes the absence of a psychological "leverage" necessary for mobilizing whatever resources there may be.

is given that he is trying to create a Negro ethos and hence a self-consciously unified Negro community. Examining his exoteric teachings reinforces this impression.

Because it symbolizes the oppression of the Negro, the white culture's political and religious basis is rejected: the Muslims do not vote in local or national elections; they resist induction into the United States military services; and they categorically reject Christianity as the "graveyard" of the Negro people. The Negro subculture is as well rejected as "uncivilized," and as impeding their material, cultural, and moral advancement.

In order to create, to fashion a unified community, Muhammad first directs his attack against those forces which have so disastrously atomized and weakened Negro society. He seeks to provide the Negro with a spiritual and moral context within which shaken pride and confidence may be restored and unused or abused energies directed toward an all-encompassing goal; to heal the wound of the Negro's dual membership in American society. Specifically, Muhammad denounces the matriarchal character of Negro society; the relative lack of masculine parental authority which makes the enforcement of discipline within the family difficult; the traditional lack of savings- and capital-accumulation habits; and the folk belief that "white is right," which leads to a dependence upon the initiative of the white man. Personal indolence and laziness are sternly deprecated. Habits of hard work and thrift are extolled.

The Muslims disapprove of the expression of undisciplined, spontaneous impulses. The pursuit of a "righteous" life as prescribed by the "Laws of Islam" and by Muhammad's directives is seen as the major purpose of existence. These laws and directives prohibit the following: extra-marital sexual relations, the use of alcohol, tobacco, and narcotics, indulging in gambling, dancing, movie-going, dating, sports, long vacations from work, sleeping more than is necessary to health, quarreling between husband and wife, lying, stealing, discourtesy (especially toward women), and insubordination to civil authority, except on the ground of religious obligation. Maintaining personal habits of cleanliness and keeping fastidious homes are moral duties. The eating of pork, cornbread, collard greens, and other foods traditional among southern Negroes is strictly proscribed. No one is permitted to straighten his hair. Women may not dye their hair or conspicuously use cosmetics. Intemperate singing, shouting, laughing loudly are forbidden. Violation of any of these or other rules is punished immediately by suspension from the movement for periods ranging from thirty days to a maximum of seven years, depending on the gravity of the offense. The most important sanctions which appear to regulate the behavior of Muslims are loss of membership in the movement and the chastisement from Allah.

Muhammad's effort to inculcate a sense of self-esteem in the Muslims by encouraging them to practice and assimilate habits that we associate with the middle class is obvious in his teachings. The quest for respectability within and without the Negro community is a primary goal. Their enthusiastic desire to be independent of white control is demonstrated partly by their willingness to overstretch their resources in order to maintain private elementary and high schools in Chicago and Detroit. The effort to strengthen the Muslims' sense of pride is apparent in Muhammad's emphasis on the "glorious" past of the Black Nation: the special relationship between the Muslims and Allah and their connection with "Arabian-Egyptian" civilization.

It should be stressed, however, that Islam is not offered to Negroes merely as a divisive symbol. To the believers it is a living faith and a positive way of life, enabling them, in unacknowledged ways, to follow with devotion moral values reminiscent of the New England Puritans and to aspire to a style of life usually associated with the middle class.[22] The Muslims, being the elect of God, are obligated to pursue a righteous life which would justify their special status in His sight. The pursuit of wealth is good only in so far as it enhances the common good—the elevation of the Nation of Islam and, in general, the masses of American Negroes. The Muslims are determined to rise on the scale by their own efforts. Imbued with a common purpose, the Muslims appear to drown their fears, frustrations, anxieties, and doubts in the hope of attaining a national home and in the promise and assurance of redemption *now* in the "New World of Islam," purged of the suffering and corruption of the world about them. Such is the sense of "tragic optimism" which has characterized the organized effort of the Negro nationalists to assert their identity and to discover their human worth and dignity in American society.

[22] Cf. Max Weber, *The Protestant Ethic and the Spirit of Capitalism,* trans. Talcott Parsons (New York: Charles Scribner's Sons, 1958), chap. V, on the relationship between "Asceticism and the Spirit of Capitalism." Elsewhere (p. 39), Weber notes that "National or religious minorities which are in a position of subordination to a group of rulers are likely, through their voluntary or involuntary exclusion from positions of political influence, to be driven with peculiar force into economic activity." Although Negroes have not been able to make a serious inroad into the economy, a few Negro leaders from Frederick Douglass to Muhammad have urged economic independence as a means to their "salvation."

21 *James Forrestal: An Appraisal*

ARNOLD A. ROGOW

"Who was James Forrestal?" was the question asked many pages ago, with the expectation that the following chapters would attempt to provide a tentative answer. Of course, those who insist on simplicity and certainty in biography will not like the word *tentative,* and those who liked or admired Forrestal, and those who hated him, will be reluctant to accept the answer that has emerged. Everyone agrees that Forrestal was complex, even enigmatic; beyond that

Reprinted with permission of The Macmillan Company from *James Forrestal: A Study of Personality, Politics and Policy* by Arnold A. Rogow. © Arnold A. Rogow 1963. Published in England by Rupert Hart-Davis, Ltd.

there is no agreement about the man who was James Forrestal, and there may never be agreement.

Perhaps the nub of the problem is that "man" should be written "men," for Forrestal was, to vary an old expression, all men to all men. Consider the matter of his politics. He considered himself an enlightened conservative, or a "liberal conservative," as he once termed himself. To Forrestal these labels—a word he disliked—referred to something more than the fact that he placed himself somewhere between New Deal Democrats and Hoover Republicans. Once, in reading a review of a book about William Hazlitt, Forrestal was struck by Hazlitt's statement, "I believe in the theoretical benevolence and the practical malignity of man." Forrestal underlined the sentence and pasted the review, which was entitled "William Hazlitt, a Man Not Made for Love," in one of his scrapbooks.[1] The application to governmental problems of man's "theoretical benevolence" and "practical malignity" was, for Forrestal, the foremost task of "liberal conservatives" like himself.

"Moderate" and "middle-roader" are terms Forrestal also found acceptable as self-references, but they are not terms that everyone would regard as accurate. To many liberals Forrestal was and is a symbol of reaction—the word "Fascist" is occasionally used—and by them he is remembered as a dangerous man who might have become, had he lived, a malevolent man of destiny. But Walter Millis, also a liberal, has described Forrestal's career as "great and singularly selfless," and he has praised Forrestal's "courage, insight . . . firmness of his counsel . . . high abilities . . . unswerving integrity of purpose."[2]

Many conservatives, while using similar language in paying tribute to Forrestal; are inclined to emphasize Forrestal's role in alerting the nation to the threat of Communism. "He clearly saw," writes James F. Byrnes, "the menace of communism before his colleagues recognized it. Frequently he warned of their plans for world domination and the dangers of relying upon promises made by them."[3] According to General Albert C. Wedemeyer, Forrestal was one of the few men after the war who "understood the full implications of communism. . . ." As a "reward for his prescience and honesty," Wede-

[1] The Hazlitt biography was Catherine Macdonald Maclean's *Born under Saturn: A Biography of William Hazlitt* (New York: The Macmillan Company, 1944). It was reviewed by Clara G. Stillman in the *New York Herald Tribune* of April 16, 1944.

[2] *Diaries*, p. 555.

[3] Letter to the writer, March 12, 1962.

meyer alleges, "Forrestal was actually hounded into suicide."[4] Former Major General Edwin A. Walker, the subject of considerable controversy in 1962 with reference to military education and propaganda activities, has gone even further than Wedemeyer in associating Forrestal with other distinguished opponents of a "no-win" policy toward the communist world. Walker, a member of the John Birch Society, testifying in April, 1962, before a subcommittee of the Senate Armed Services Committee, declared that

> General MacArthur, Senator Joseph McCarthy, Secretary James Forrestal, Syngman Rhee, Chiang Kai-shek, Tshombe, myself, and others, with more to come, as well as untold thousands who have not made the headlines, have all been framed by this hidden policy.[5]

Forrestal has also been eulogized in at least one novel, the hero of which is charged with mental incompetence because of his efforts to combat communist subversion.[6]

Although it is doubtful that Forrestal would have been sympathetic to either former Major General Walker or the John Birch Society, his evident appeal to the extreme or radical right in America merits analysis, and we shall return to the phenomenon shortly. It is already clear, however, that Forrestal the political man is someone who defies the simple and conventional political labels. Forrestal the human being is also someone to whom the usual categories do not apply. Many of his associates, for example, think of him as a cold individual who was sparing of his emotions—as a man, in short, "not made for love." But one friend who knew him better than most puts the point somewhat differently. Forrestal, he recalls,

> was gregarious and yet frightened of people. He had a quality which inspired people to treat him with great loyalty and want to know him, and yet he always kept them and everyone else at arm's length.
>
> He never had many close friends. I had a great many friends, and once I had a large number of them over for a party. He asked me if they were *really* all friends, and when I said I wouldn't have asked them if they weren't friends, he seemed somewhat surprised. His own experience, he said, was that you only had a few close friends, and that he himself only had three or four. He felt that

---

[4] General Albert C. Wedemeyer, *Wedemeyer Reports!* (New York: Holt Rinehart and Winston, Inc., 1958), p. 430.
[5] *Hearings Before the Special Preparedness Subcommittee of the Committee on Armed Services,* United States Senate, 87th Congress, Second Session, Part 4, April 5, 1962, p. 1524.
[6] Colonel Victor J. Fox, *The Pentagon Case* (New York: Freedom Press, 1958).

every man only has a certain amount of himself to give to others and it should not be squandered.

Certainly he did not squander what *he* had to give, and as is often the case with those who hoard or repress their emotions, he was in many respects a lonely man. His aides recall a number of Christmas eves and New Year's days when Forrestal worked in his office, and he sometimes appeared oblivious of the fact these were occasions most men spent with their families or friends. "I recall one Christmas morning," a colleague reports,

> when Forrestal telephoned to ask me to play golf with him around noon at the Chevy Chase club. I risked a serious argument with my wife when I accepted, but after some discussion she agreed that I should do so if Forrestal felt the need for that kind of activity and companionship on Christmas day when most of us would think only in terms of being at home with the family. After the game, as I remember it, he went to the office, and I went home.

There is a pathetic quality about this story, but it is important to keep in mind the many occasions when Forrestal did not want companionship and was tactless in rejecting it. More than one Washington hostess can remember a dinner party that Forrestal promised to attend but at which he never appeared. And there was one abortive yacht cruise on the Potomac that did not endear him to a number of his government colleagues and their wives. Forrestal preferred to entertain guests on the yacht available to the Secretary of Defense partly because, as he once put it, a yacht party did not require him to "wait around" until the guests were ready to depart. "When the boat docks," he confided to a friend, "the party's over." On the occasion referred to, however, the yacht never sailed. Although the guests were aboard at the time scheduled—there were several Supreme Court Justices and Cabinet members among them—Forrestal himself was absent. When an aide was finally able to locate him, Forrestal declared flatly that he would not join his guests and that the yacht should sail without him. "Tell them I'm tied up at the office and can't get away," he instructed the aide. The aide did so, and the guests walked off the yacht, some of them making no secret of their displeasure with Forrestal's behavior.

Yet he could also be charming, thoughtful, and capable of inspiring loyalty and affection. The wife of a distinguished newspaper correspondent recalls that she was prepared to dislike Forrestal; she had heard that he was cold, ruthless, and reactionary. But when she met him she found him one of the most attractive men she had ever met. Other friends, belying his reputation for parsimony, remember his usually anonymous gifts of money to friends and college classmates whose luck had turned bad, and it is beyond question that he gave financial assistance, also anonymously, to a number of deserving Princeton students. A former butler in the Forrestal household testifies to his generosity in dealing with the servants; they were paid well, and there was at least one occasion when Forrestal offered to lend a valet the money required for a business venture. During the war he made it a point to write consoling letters to old Beacon and Wall Street friends whose sons or husbands had become casualties, and when he himself was abroad he took pains to visit a medical ward where someone from Beacon was receiving treatment.

Parsimony and generosity, rudeness and thoughtfulness, above all keeping people "at arm's length" and reaching out to them—Forrestal's personality was peculiarly dichotomous; it is almost as if he never was able to decide what sort of man he wanted to be. As a result, any given characterological statement or interpretation can be contradicted, whether the statement pertains to a large or small detail of his life. One would expect, for example, that those who saw him regularly would be in agreement about the manner of his dress, a small detail and because small, a detail that should provoke minimal controversy. But while some friends and associates remember him as a man who dressed in perfect taste, others argue, with some photographic evidence to support them, that Forrestal preferred "flashy" combinations that frequently succeeded in being garish. Forrestal, one colleague recalls,

> went in for loud, pin-striped suits, striped shirts, and two-tone shoes. The shoulders were usually overpadded, and the pin-stripes a bit too conspicuous. It was expensive stuff, all right, but not really in good taste. I think it was his way of rebelling against the dull blues and grays of bureaucratic clothing in Washington, but later his taste also became more conservative. When he was Defense Secretary he usually went in for flannel suits, sports jackets, button-down collars, and so forth.

This comment and many others suggest the essential truth in the statement of one business friend that Forrestal

> was a strange mixture. I never met anybody exactly like Forrestal or even remotely like him. But everybody who knew him at all respected and admired him, and the comparative few who were close to him had real affection for him. In business some people might

have called him a slavedriver, but I don't think they would have done so if they realized that he drove himself much harder than he did other people. All through the time that I knew him he worked at least sixteen hours a day. I don't think he ever quite understood why everybody else didn't do the same. . . .

Did Forrestal understand why *he* worked sixteen hours a day? Putting the question in a larger frame, Did Forrestal know he was "a strange mixture," and if so did he know why? Probably no one now living can answer this question with any certainty, but one friend of almost thirty years' standing is convinced that Forrestal was caught in a variety of conflicts into some of which he had a good deal of insight. "The story of James Forrestal," he comments,

> is in many ways an American tragedy; the stuff of a Dos Passos or Dreiser novel. It contains much that need be said about the social and moral structure of America. . . .
>
> It is not just the Irish Catholic boy who never stopped thinking of himself as a "Mick." It is the man who thought Princeton and Wall Street spelled grace, charm, success and strength; the man who embraced the American dream and found it wanting.
>
> The fault does not lie just with a deeply religious mother who wanted her son to join the priesthood, which he rejected. It is the society in which he lived which saw the Racquet Club as a social nirvana. The tragedy was that Forrestal was aware of it all. He lived his life as a conflicted man, walking a tightrope held taut by a concept of original sin at one end, the American dream of success and recognition at the other.
>
> There is still another tragedy. Forrestal came close to being a caricature. Deeply sensitive, uncertain, afraid of intrusions upon his soul, he solved his dilemma by becoming a caricature of the Rational Man. Functioning almost entirely on a rational level, he could never allow himself to enter the world of childhood, for to do so would have meant shedding the self-woven cocoon by which he protected his vulnerability. Above all else, Forrestal was vulnerable. He smothered himself in his own highly developed art of self-protection as few men have.

The "rational face" Forrestal chose to present to the world, continues the friend, was also "that of the physical man." To Forrestal

> strength of character and body were synonymous. He was the man with the broken nose who exercised daily, stressed independence, and allowed no contact with his interior.
>
> He was a character Hemingway would have loved, but not understood.

"He lived his life as a conflicted man"—a perceptive comment. But to speak of the "original sin at one end" of the tightrope and the "American dream of success" at the other is to speak of only one strand of the "tightrope." There were the other strands—Forrestal's lifelong struggle to appear stronger and tougher than he actually was, and his efforts during the Washington years to impress others as the very model of a philosopher-king. For a good part of his life Forrestal was also the agnostic who was never able to free himself entirely from the moral strictures of Catholicism, and in Princeton and New York he was the Irish Catholic or "Mick" who was never completely at ease in an Anglo-Saxon Protestant environment. The Wall Street Forrestal never quite overcame a suspicion of the rich and well-born although he envied and emulated them, and the Washington Forrestal distrusted liberals although he served in the administrations of two of the most liberal Presidents in history. Indeed, it is one of the major paradoxes of his life that he was appointed to the highest position he achieved in government by a President for whose personality and principles he felt an active dislike.

It would be plausible but not very profound to suggest it was ambition that brought a conservative investment banker to a liberal Washington, and that it was ambition that had earlier transported the Irish Catholic to Protestant Princeton, and the smalltown Democrat to Republican Wall Street. It would be equally plausible but not very profound to attribute Forrestal's work habits—the sixteen-hour days and seven-day weeks—to ambition. But what is meant by ambition, and why was Forrestal, apparently, more ambitious than most of his contemporaries in Wall Street and Washington?

In answer to the latter question, many of his friends believe that the unhappy marriage played a large role in Forrestal's striving for success. As one of them puts it:

> Everyone who knew Forrestal was aware that his family life was unhappy, and I always thought this was the main reason he worked so hard. He found in work some of the satisfactions that other men find in their family relations. If he had been a happier man I doubt that he would have driven himself—and others—as hard as he did. There really wasn't much for him to go home to at the end of the day, so why not stay at the office and get a headstart on the next day's business?

This interpretation is not without merit, but it neglects the point that Forrestal worked long hours, and was inclined to expect subordinates to work long hours, before his marriage in 1926. No one who knew him, in fact, including the surviving Beacon friends of his youth, can remember a time when Forrestal was without ambition and a stubborn resolve to succeed. While still an adolescent, he concluded that sheer determination and hard work were the twin keys to success in life, always provided that one possessed a modicum of intelligence. Those activities that were simply relaxing or playful or merely fun he was rarely able to enjoy; instead he converted them into purposeful enterprises that, to some degree, functioned as outlets for determination and work. Thus golf, tennis, handball, and other sports were approached, not as forms of relaxation, but as body-building exercises, and most of the books, jokes, and anecdotes he enjoyed were appreciated less for their entertainment value than for their capacity to instruct and enlighten. Forrestal, in other words, was too driven a man to enjoy, much less indulge in, those aspects of the human experience that are purely frivolous.

This fatal flaw in his personality undoubtedly owes much to his childhood and adolescence. In general, these years provide support for the thesis that in Forrestal's case, as in the case of many another political man, the quest for fame and power was a response to early psychic deprivation.[7] The early home life did not nurture a personality that was self-confident and outgoing, but one that was insecure and withdrawn. Forrestal's father, the more permissive of his parents, was less important than his mother in his own and his brothers' upbringing, and it is clear that Mary Toohey Forrestal did not welcome open demonstrations of affection, assertions of independence, and violations of rather strict household rules. Ultimately her youngest son rebelled, but by that time the essential form of his personality had been cast, and it was a form that was not broken until the last months of his life. The Forrestal who, as a child, had been deprived of love and understanding would not, as an adult, be able to give much love and understanding to others. The Forrestal who, in his youth, was uncertain of his abilities and lacking in confidence would, in his mature years, work harder and longer than most men, and would also attempt to prove himself by becoming first richer, and then more powerful than most men. The young Forrestal who was often ill, ashamed of his physique, and perhaps uncertain of his masculinity, would, all his life, exercise strenuously, emphasize body-contact sports, and try to appear "tough."

[7] The relationship between power-seeking and personality development has been most fruitfully explored in the works of Harold D. Lasswell. See especially his *Power and Personality* (New York: W. W. Norton and Company, 1948).

The early home life may also have been reflected in his personal and professional relations. To what extent, for example, was his decision to marry Josephine influenced by conscious or unconscious feelings about his mother? If we assume, as do all his friends, that Josephine was never really "his type," the reasons for the marriage must have involved something more than mutual attraction or even simple convenience. Certainly it can be argued that Forrestal should never have married in the first place; it is still more certain that he should never have married Josephine, and that the marriage had tragic consequences for both of them.

Forrestal's father, it appears, was less significant than his mother during the childhood years, and partly for that reason we know little about his relations with his youngest son. Those in Beacon who remember him suggest that most of his energies went into his business activities, local politics, church affairs, the militia, and related areas. If, as one Beaconite indicates, it was his wife who "wore the pants" in the family, we can infer that to Forrestal his father must have appeared weaker than his mother, perhaps even less masculine. How did he feel about this father who cast a somewhat flickering male image or manly model for his sons to imitate? One can imagine that Forrestal may have felt a good deal of ambivalence toward a father who marched in parades at the head of the column but who walked very softly around the house. If the accounts of old family friends can be trusted, Mary Forrestal's bark was much more to be feared than James Forrestal's bite.

Mary Forrestal may also have helped define her son's later concepts of strength and masculinity. While Forrestal came to reject much that his mother represented, his dependence upon her during childhood undoubtedly contributed to a certain passivity in his own nature of which he became increasingly aware in the adolescent and early adult years. Regarding such passivity as a feminine attribute, Forrestal may have felt, consciously or unconsciously, that he would have to struggle more than most men to establish his essential masculinity. If the quest for a male indentity frequently led him to a gym or other sports arena, it more significantly influenced his attitude toward a variety of Cold War issues. In Forrestal's world of foreign policy and military problems involving the Soviet bloc, to be militant was to be masculine.

It is possible that Harry Truman, many years later, activated some of the ambivalence that Forrestal felt toward his father. Both Truman and the senior Forrestal had been small-town businessmen, and there were other similarities between the former AEF artillery captain and the one-time major in the New York National Guard. Truman could bluster, swagger, and swear on public occasions, but it seemed to Forrestal that he was weak and even timid in dealing with party politicians, Zionists, air-power lobbyists, and others who placed narrow interest above national interest. From Forrestal's point of view Truman as President and free-world leader left something to be desired, but it is fair to remark that all his life Forrestal had difficulty relating to and accepting authority. For those in authority whom he regarded as weak he generally had contempt; those who were strong he tended to dislike and resent. The former category may have included his father; there can be no doubt it included certain business associates and a large number of politicians, chief among them Truman. In the latter group were one or two professors at Princeton, various employers after he left Princeton, including some of his superiors at Dillon, Read, Admiral King, and Franklin D. Roosevelt. Priding himself on his own independence, he regarded dependence upon others as a form of weakness, and he was also inclined to avoid people who were or would become dependent on him.

Forrestal's personality, in other words, was one that never fully matured, if maturity be defined as the ability to emerge from a bleak childhood with a minimum of emotional scar tissue. But paradoxically, it was a personality that could and did function with great success much of the time Forrestal held office. Whatever its roots, the compulsion to work, to be grim, to flex the muscles and jut the jaw suited the national temper during World War II. A taut personality could be understood to reflect the conviction that the defeat of the Axis would be followed by Soviet efforts to exploit the victory over Germany and Japan. In May, 1944, when the Allied invasion of France was still a month away, Forrestal exclaimed to George Earle, "My God, George, you and I and Bill Bullitt are the only ones around the President who know the Russian leaders for what they are."[8] When one considers that those "around the President" included Stimson, Patterson, McCloy, Admirals Leahy and King, and General Marshall, considers further that Harriman was serving as ambassador in Moscow and Hurley as our emissary to China, the statement can be viewed as evidence that Forrestal was almost obsessed by the idea that he was indispensable in the prosecution of the Cold War. Knowing "what they are" and strongly inclined to believe that the

---

[8] Wedemeyer, *op. cit.*, p. 417.

Second World War would surely be followed by a third, Forrestal did not have to justify to his associates the seven-day weeks and sixteen-hour days. If the nation was to win *both* wars, all citizens, and not merely the Secretary of the Navy, would need a continuing dedication to preparedness no matter what the personal sacrifice.

Unfortunately for Forrestal, his mood of tense toughness was less suitable after 1945, when the nation, despite his warnings, sought to relax and return to "normalcy." The mothers, wives, and children wanted the men back, and the men, despite the lures—and there were many—dangled before them by the Services, wanted to get out of uniform and into civilian clothes. A soldiery determined to return to the college, the office, the factory, and the farm as soon as possible, and a citizenry eager to splurge on consumer goods, could not be easily persuaded that Stalin was not only another Hitler but also far more dangerous. The attitude favoring business-as-usual gradually changed, but it did not change either fast enough or far enough to suit Forrestal and those who saw the world as he did. He especially lamented the fact that there were almost as many in the Truman Administration as there had been in the Roosevelt Administration who were, not to put too fine a point on it, naïve with regard to Soviet intentions and tactics. At various times he expressed reservations about Truman, Byrnes, Harriman, Marshall, Leahy, Stimson, in addition, of course, to his particular *bête noir* Henry A. Wallace.

In the context of postwar affluence and "togetherness," Forrestal could be and was made to appear a warmonger by those who disliked him or who disagreed, for whatever reason, with his views. In certain respects, he was an easy target for all those who favored "peaceful coexistence"—and it would be foolish to pretend that Stalinist sympathizers were not among them. Insights and understandings based on psychology are not common in political discourse, and hence it was relatively simple for fellow travelers, liberals, and pacifists to attribute Forrestal's Cold War militancy to his Dillon, Read background. In the simplest expression of this formula, Forrestal was *against* the Soviet Union and Communism because he was *for* Wall Street and capitalism. Few if any of his critics suggested that his position may have been much more a reflection of his Matteawan background than of his years as an investment banker.

His friends and admirers, on the other hand, dismiss both Matteawan and Wall Street in their assessment of his role in the Cold War. Forrestal, in their view, was guided solely by objective considerations, namely, the true and factual nature of the threat posed to the free world by Soviet Communism. In the simplest expression of their formula, Forrestal was one of the great heroes and patriots in American history; indeed, some of them believe that he was the only hero and patriot of high rank in postwar Washington. For those on the far Right, like former Major General Walker, the number of patriots during the Truman era was exceedingly small including, in addition to Forrestal, only General MacArthur and Senator Joseph R. McCarthy.

It is doubtful that either of these appraisals is correct. Forrestal would hardly have avoided being influenced by the twenty years spent on Wall Street, but that does not mean that he was purely and simply a "Wall Street imperialist." And while it is true that Forrestal was both conservative and a deeply committed man in the struggle against Soviet Communism, he was not a reactionary and not, until he became ill, a fanatic. In short, the man who functions as villain for many liberals and radicals is not the real Forrestal but a gross caricature. And the man who is hero-worshiped by the John Birch Society is not the well Forrestal but the sick one.

These conclusions emerge from any careful examination of Forrestal's own prescriptions for American foreign and defense policy. To be sure, Forrestal was willing to "go to the brink" far more often than most other members of the Truman Administration. He also thought it essential to spend more on defense, even if such spending required some regimentation of the economy. He was even willing, in the name of national defense, to restrict certain freedoms that in peacetime had never before been curtailed. In 1945, for example, he proposed that all radio and cable services be merged into one privately owned corporation operating under limited government supervision. The merger, he thought, would facilitate the reliability and security of communications.[9] In February, 1949, he urged on newspaper, radio, and movie executives the necessity of their practicing "voluntary" censorship in all cases which directly or indirectly involved national security. Almost all those he approached, including publishers Arthur Hays Sulzberger of *The New York Times* and Roy Howard of the Scripps-Howard chain, were opposed to the proposal, and he did not pursue it further during the remaining weeks he held office.

Forrestal also believed that the United States could not afford to be scrupulous in the tactics employed to combat communist in-

[9] *The New York Times*, March 20, 1945.

fluence internally and externally. In addition to favoring the utmost extension of counterintelligence activities engaged in by the FBI, CIA, and other agencies, he was an early advocate of training in clandestine or guerrilla warfare of the type that has since become almost conventional in Southeast Asia. Thus in October, 1947, he endorsed a memo from William J. Donovan urging that magazine articles be written to inform the public of "the nature of irregular war and the manner in which the Soviet Union has employed it." Enclosing an article of his own, Donovan wrote Forrestal, "There is no one who can take the lead in this but you" and "Jim, we must not let this get away from us." Crossing out the first statement, Forrestal circulated copies of Donovan's memo to others in the government, including Lovett, with the notation ". . . there is plenty of obvious sense in what he says. . . ."[10]

But while Forrestal placed great stress on the nation's security and military capabilities, he was hardly unaware of the political and economic aspects of the Cold War. This awareness is particularly evident in a memorandum sent to the President via Clark Clifford on March 6, 1947. The day before Forrestal had discussed with Clifford the opportunity for the United States to exercise world economic leadership; indeed, he emphasized, if most of the world was to remain free, the United States could not escape "responsibility for leadership." The memo of the following day put in writing the points Forrestal had developed in his discussion with Clifford, and because it constitutes a fairly complete statement of what he meant by "responsibility for leadership," it is worth quoting in full. "For a long time now," Forrestal began,

> it has been clear that there is a serious, immediate and extraordinarily grave threat to the continued existence of this country. These are the facts:
>
> **1.** The present danger which this country faces is at least as great as the danger which we faced during the war with Germany and Japan. Briefly stated, it is the very real danger that this country, as we know it, may cease to exist.
>
> **2.** From 1941 to 1945 we won a war by enlisting the whole-hearted support of all our people and all our resources. Today we are losing a comparable struggle without ever having enlisted the strength of our people and our resources—and the consequences

[10] Memo to Lovett, October 9, 1947. "But what [Donovan] forgets," he added, "is the wide gap between the genial attitude of Congress toward his activities during the war and the present short rations."

of our loss will be the same consequences that would have followed if we had lost the war of 1941–45.

3. Of the strategic battlegrounds of the present struggle, we have already lost Poland, Yugoslavia, Romania, Bulgaria, and a number of others; Greece is in imminent peril; after Greece, France and Italy may follow; and after France and Italy, Great Britain, South America, and ourselves.

4. We lost strategic battlegrounds in the war of 1941–1945, also—but even while we were losing some battlegrounds, we were planning the offensives by which we were to win the ultimate victory. And we won the victory by pressing home our attacks— by landing our troops at Guadalcanal, North Africa, Guam, Iwo Jima, Normandy, the Philippines, and a host of other places.

5. This country cannot afford the deceptive luxury of waging defensive warfare. As in the war of 1941–45, our victory and our survival depend on how and where we attack.

6. By providing outstanding economic leadership, this country can wage its attack successfully—and can thereby build the foundations of a peaceful world. For the only way in which a durable peace can be created is by world-wide restoration of economic activity and international trade.

7. In order to be successful, our product—our economic leadership—will have to prove its superiority to the commodity which Russia has lately been so successful in peddling. Russia has a product which is skillfully tailored to appeal to people who are in despair—and thanks to German and Japanese aggression, Russia has had a wealth of customers who are sufficiently desperate to turn to anything. Moreover, the accomplishment of Russia's aims has been greatly simplified by the fact that we have heretofore offered the world no practical antidote for the Russian poison.

8. What we must do is create the conditions under which a free world society can live. With that as our object, a group of our most competent citizens should be called together in order to enlist the full support of all elements of our economy in the accomplishment of this basic American task. For only by an all-out effort on a world-wide basis can we pass over from the defense to the attack. In making our all-out effort, we will be forwarding not only world stability but also our national interest— which includes, of course, business interest, labor interest, and public interest.

9. As specific examples of the sort of thing which we must do, the following may be enumerated:

  a. Japanese assets amounting to some $137,000,000 are presently impounded. If these assets were set up as a revolving fund with which Japan could import raw materials for its industries, Japanese exports could again enter the channels of world trade—and Japanese workers would have employment and something to eat.

b. A similar revolving fund could be set up for Germany, for a durable peace can rest only upon a Germany that, while militarily impotent, is industrially active.

c. Financial support should be provided for local enterprises in those countries where a struggling economy needs a helping hand—but the furnishing of such support should in every case be handled by competent American personnel, in order to assure that the money goes into *productive* enterprises that are of direct use both to the country involved and to world trade. (Wherever possible, *private capital* in this country should render the necessary financial assistance—for this is essentially a business task, in which government's greatest contribution is the creation of favorable conditions under which business can work.)

10. The group referred to above should be called together promptly. It should consist of our best brains—from management, from labor, from both the executive and the legislative side of the government, from any source that has a contribution to make—for the issues to be faced are crucial, and we must attack if we are to survive.

The actions taken during 1947 and 1948 did not convince Forrestal that Truman fully understood the relationship between foreign policy and defense needs, and in his speeches and writings he sought to persuade the public, if not the President, that our "responsibility for leadership" required a stronger military establishment. With many friends in the newspaper and magazine world, Forrestal could always be certain that his own point of view, with or without his name attached, would be accorded a hearing. The Luce publications, especially *Fortune* magazine, had occasionally devoted space to Forrestal's views, and in October, 1948, he was given another opportunity to build support for an increase in military spending beyond the amount fixed by the President. Asking Forrestal to talk with Robert Elson and Roy Alexander of the *Fortune* staff, publisher Henry Luce requested Forrestal to give them his "prescription" for

how much defense we need in order to carry out foreign policy. Of course, for what we say there we will take entire responsibility . . . what we'd like to have is—confidentially or what not—your prescription, which in all probability we would adopt.

In its December, 1948, issue *Fortune* published an article titled "The Arms We Need" that was almost entirely based on Forrestal's "prescription." While most people knew Communism could not be contained without military force, the article commented, "only a tiny fraction" was able to judge how much military strength was required. "For two months," continued the article,

> FORTUNE has gone to school on this problem, both with responsible military experts and with leading foreign policy strategists. As a result of this study, FORTUNE has come to the unpleasant conclusion that if the US intends to continue its present foreign policy, it will in all probability need greater military force than it now possesses . . . (costing) $18 billion for fiscal 1950.

The $18 billion, *Fortune* suggested, would not buy a "war force" but a

> force strong enough to:
> 1. Convince the Politburo that we mean business.
> 2. Make us a desirable, reliable partner in alliances.
> 3. Provide a shield behind which our allies can recover their morale, rebuild their governments and rally their forces.

Such a "barebone outline" of a military program was worthless, however, unless it related to both American foreign policy and Soviet military strength. There were, of course, no absolute guarantees of security, but the United States "must and can be prepared to secure and maintain certain geographical footholds from which we can operate to check the advance of Communism." *Fortune* did not identify these "footholds," but it implied that Truman's $14.4 billion ceiling on military expenditures would have an adverse effect on their maintenance. To illustrate its point that the budget ceiling was "politically expedient but strategically unwise," the article noted that the ceiling had been imposed

> at the moment when the US had challenged the Soviet power in Europe by inaugurating the air lift. In effect, the gesture was to raise the Soviet bid and, at the same time, by limiting the military budget, give the tip-off that we were betting only a few white chips. It is conceivable that these contradictory actions may have undermined all efforts to settle the Berlin crisis on favorable terms.

Strength in foreign and military policies, *Fortune* indicated, would be achieved only if appropriations for their support took precedence over programs "of political interest." Increased spending on arms was possible without rationing and higher taxes provided the Administration limited spending "on social objectives." Conceding that such restraint would require "remarkable self-denial," *Fortune* never-theless emphasized that

> Mr. Truman, confirmed in his own right and in his own power as President, has never been in a better position to put the national interest ahead of partisan politics. . . . He, more than any other American, should now understand that the only way to avoid having American foreign policy dominated by crisis is to live in crisis—pre-pared for war.

The necessity "to live in crisis—prepared for war" was, for Forres-tal, so far beyond dispute that he was inclined to question the intelli-gence and motivations of those who disagreed with him. It may well be that future historians will endorse his approach to crisis and pre-paredness and that some of them will even entertain similar suspicions of certain officials who made policy in the United States between 1940 and 1950. But whatever the judgment of history, it is difficult to avoid the conclusion that Forrestal's personality needs and policy recommendations were closely related. The Cold War, no matter how inevitable, provided him with an arena for the play of transference and projection. Anxieties and insecurities, regardless of personal source, could become focused on Soviet behavior and be partially appeased by a stubborn insistence on a "tough" foreign and military policy. Suspicions of all sorts readily attached themselves to real or alleged communist conspiracies at home and abroad, and fears di-rected at the Soviet Union could appear wholly sane and rational. Until the last few months of his life, Forrestal could impress almost everyone as a "reasonable" man because it was "reasonable," in the context of the Cold War, to feel anxious, insecure, suspicious, and fearful. Above all, it was "reasonable" to appear "tough," to warn against compromises and concessions, and to talk of "forcing the issue" and the necessity of "showdowns."

The reality of Forrestal's personality, however, whether or not it was also the reality of our foreign policy, was not essential tough-ness but essential weakness. A stronger man, it is plausible to suppose, would have been less oriented toward power and more able to accept rebuffs and ultimate rejection. A more confident man would have been more flexible in his attitude toward foreign and domestic issues, and a more self-sufficient man would have retired from office, as others have done, perhaps a trifle bloody and bowed, but unbeaten. Unfortunately and tragically, Forrestal was none of these men, and when he found his power sapped and his ambition thwarted, he could not command their resources.

It needs also to be said that even at the height of his career Forrestal was never quite able to resolve contradictions in his professional life, some of which partook of the nature of "double-binds," that is, splittings of personality caused by a pulling and tugging in opposite directions. To the conflicts of his personal life, which were numerous, were added the sharp and frequently bitter policy conflicts between warring factions in both the Roosevelt and Truman Administrations. More often than not, Forrestal found himself on the conservative side, but there were occasions when he thought of himself as a man-in-the-middle who was caught not between friends and enemies but between friends.

This was especially the case after the war in certain economic policy areas. As a Cabinet officer Forrestal was in the position of having to embrace the Truman economic program, or at least maintain a public silence on issues where he was in disagreement. Many of his Wall Street and business associates, however, called upon him again and again to intervene in policy areas involving business regulation, antitrust suits, and labor legislation. On several occasions Forrestal was strongly urged to exert influence on behalf of the oil industry, some sections of which, during and after the war, thought themselves threatened by nationalization. Forrestal, although sympathetic, was sometimes reluctant to interfere in policy areas that were not his concern, and he also knew that such intervention risked the displeasure of other Administration officials and invited charges that he was a Wall Street "front man." Yet he usually resolved the conflict of loyalties in favor of his friends. It was generally true, as one oil executive put it many years later, that "I could always count on Jim when Ickes or some other damn fool was trying to make trouble. All I had to do was pick up the phone." It is doubtful that this friend and others similarly placed ever realized what price in torn loyalty and career tension Forrestal paid for their assurance that they "could always count on Jim. . . ."

In the end, of course, Forrestal paid with psychosis and suicide, in effect paid with his life for an accumulation of guilts, tensions, frustrations, and conflicts that finally became overwhelming. But is it possible to say that this price need not have been paid, that Forrestal on March 1, 1949, might have been enabled to bear the burden of what amounted to "a dismissal under fire"?[11] These questions raise a variety of difficulties, not the least of which is a difficulty, perhaps

[11] Millis in *Diaries,* p. 553.

inherent, in psychiatric biography. And that difficulty, in brief, is that such study is more productive of hindsights than foresights. Many personality and situational characteristics that contributed to Forrestal's illness and suicide developed during the early years of his life history, and it is therefore possible to "account" for the terminal tragedy, at least in part. But at what points in his life could that tragedy have been predicted, assuming that Forrestal made no effort to exploit the resources of psychiatry? When he left Matteawan for Hanover and Princeton? When he ceased to regard himself as a believing Catholic? When he was married and far advanced on his Wall Street career? When he went to Washington in 1940, or when he became Defense Secretary, or when his immediate resignation was requested?

No certain answers are possible, but it is certain that no one close to Forrestal advanced such predictions, even as late as March, 1949. Although some friends and associates suspected he was ill late in 1948, it does not appear that they urged him to consult a psychiatrist, much less enter a "rest home" or private sanitarium. And when the President became aware that his Defense Secretary was experiencing a breakdown, it did not occur to him to recommend anything more than a lengthy vacation followed by a fact-finding trip around the world that would include visits to our defense installations. Even on March 29, when there could hardly be any doubt that Forrestal was suffering from a psychosis, the official recommendation involved nothing more than an extended visit to Hobe Sound, Florida. His ailment, it was believed, would quickly succumb to a therapy of golf, swimming, sunshine, and rest.

Had his friends and associates been more sensitive to his condition during the last months of 1948, Forrestal might have been restored by measures less drastic than confinement at Bethesda. But they were not sensitive, despite a variety of cues provided by the sick man. The apparent suicide of Czechoslovak Foreign Minister Jan Masaryk on March 10, 1948, made a deep impression on Forrestal, and he referred to it often, both in public and private, as a key turning point in the Cold War. The frequency of reference, however, suggests that Masaryk's death may have had for him a more personal meaning. It was also in 1948 that Forrestal began to make numerous allusions to the physical and mental health of other officials. Thus on one occasion, in September, 1948, discussing with John McCone a certain episode involving Vannevar Bush, Forrestal suggested that Bush's behavior "reflects a certain amount of nervous and physical instability. I mean—not his mind but just he's drawn pretty fine,

I think."[12] Forrestal, no doubt, would not have welcomed suggestions that he, too, was revealing "a certain amount of nervous and physical instability," for the relief of which psychiatric counseling was imperative. Indeed, it is probable that he would have regarded such counseling as, on his part, a confession of weakness. In any event, there is no evidence that he was advised by anyone to see a psychiatrist until early in April at Hobe Sound. It also appears that apart from William Menninger, he was not acquainted with any psychiatrist in Washington or elsewhere; he was also inclined to minimize the importance of psychiatry as both theory and therapy.[13]

---

[12] Forrestal, who himself was always "drawn pretty fine," had long been aware of this quality in others, but his sensitivity to it sharply increased during 1948. Two years before the discussion with McCone, Forrestal had visited General Clay in Berlin and had concluded that Clay was beginning to show the strains of the tense USA-USSR confrontation in Germany. In a memo to Patterson in July, 1946, Forrestal wrote, "I think you should order General Clay to take a ten-day or two-week holiday—nothing else will make him do it—and if he doesn't get some break he runs the risk of blowing up entirely. . . ."—*Diaries*, p. 133.

[13] Many years before, when Forrestal was still with Dillon, Read, some one close to him had gone to a psychiatrist to seek a cure for alcoholism. The alcohol problem remained unsolved, and it is possible that Forrestal's distrust of psychiatry and psychiatrists owed something to this experience.

Suggested Further Reading

In addition to the footnotes to the editors' introductions and to the selections themselves, the following sources may be helpful for their relevance, recency, and suggestiveness. For convenience, they are coordinated with the sections of this volume. As in the case of the text selections, many of these items are applicable to several sections.

I. THE RELEVANCE OF PERSONALITY FOR POLITICS

Arendt, Hannah, *The Human Condition*. Chicago: University of Chicago Press, 1958.

Bowlby, John, "Psychology and Democracy," *Political Quarterly*, 17 (1946), pp. 61–76. Also Bobbs-Merrill Reprint PS-312.

Bronfenbrenner, Urie, "Personality and Participation: The Case of the Vanishing Variables," *Journal of Social Issues*, 16 (1960), pp. 54–63.

Christiansen, Bjørn, *Attitudes toward Foreign Affairs as a Function of Personality*. Oslo: Oslo University Press, 1959.

de Grazia, Sebastian, *The Political Community: A Study of Anomie*. Chicago: University of Chicago Press, 1948.

Freud, Sigmund, *Civilization and its Discontents*, ed. and trans. James Strachey. New York: W. W. Norton, 1961.

Greenstein, Fred I., "Personality and Politics: Problems of Evidence, Inference, and Conceptualization," *American Behavioral Scientist* (November–December, 1967), pp. 38–51.

Hoffer, Eric, *The Ordeal of Change*. New York: Harper and Row, 1963.

Kelman, Herbert C., "Social-Psychological Approaches to the Study of International Relations: The Question of Relevance," in Herbert C. Kelman, ed., *International Behavior: A Social-Psychological Analysis*. New York: Holt, Rinehart and Winston, Inc., 1965, pp. 565–607.

Levinson, Daniel J., "The Relevance of Personality for Political Participation," *Public Opinion Quarterly*, 22 (1955), pp. 3–10.

McClosky, Herbert, "Personality and Attitude Correlates of Foreign Policy," in James N. Rosenau, ed., *Domestic Sources of Foreign Policy*. New York: The Free Press, 1967, pp. 51–109.

Marx, Karl, *Selected Writings in Sociology and Social Philosophy*, in T. B. Bottomore and M. Rubel, eds. and trans. London: Watts and Co., 1956.

Scott, William A., "International Ideology and Interpersonal Ideology," *Public Opinion Quarterly*, 24 (1960), pp. 419–435.

Wallas, Graham, *Human Nature in Politics*. Lincoln: University of Nebraska Press, 1962.

II. SOCIALIZATION: THE ACQUISITION OF POLITICAL DISPOSITIONS

Dawson, Richard E., "Political Socialization," in James A. Robinson, ed., *Political Science Annual*, Vol. 1. Indianapolis: Bobbs-Merrill, 1966, pp. 1–84.

Easton, David, and Jack Dennis, "The Child's Acquisition of Regime Norms: Political Efficacy," *American Political Science Review*, 61 (1967), pp. 25–38.

Hess, Robert D., and Judith Torney, *The Development of Attitudes in Children*. Chicago: Aldine, 1967.

Jennings, M. Kent, and Richard G. Niemi, "The Transmission of Political Values from Parent to Child," *American Political Science Review*, 62 (1968), pp. 169–184.

Keniston, Kenneth, *The Uncommitted: Alienated Youth in American Society*. New York: Dell, 1967.

Keniston, Kenneth, *The Young Radicals: Notes on Committed Youth*. New York: Harcourt, Brace, & World, 1968.

Kornberg, Allan, and Norman Thomas, "The Political Socialization of National Legislative Elites in the United States and in Canada," *Journal of Politics*, 27 (1965), pp. 761–775.

Langton, Kenneth P., "Peer Group and School and the Political Socialization Process," *American Political Science Review,* 61 (1967), pp. 751–758.

Newcomb, Theodore M., "The Persistence and Regression of Changed Attitudes," *Journal of Social Issues,* 19 (1963), pp. 3–14.

Sigel, Roberta S., "Images of a President: Some Insights into the Political Views of School Children," *American Political Science Review,* 62 (1968), pp. 216–226.

III. INDIVIDUAL POLITICAL BEHAVIOR

Agger, Robert E., Marshall Goldstein, and Stanley Pearl, "Political Cynicism: Measurement and Meaning," *Journal of Politics,* 23 (1961), pp. 477–506.

Brown, Roger, *Social Psychology.* New York: The Free Press, 1965, chapter 10, "The Authoritarian Personality and the Organization of Attitudes," pp. 477–546.

Eysenck, Hans J., *The Psychology of Politics.* London: Routledge & Kegan Paul, 1954.

Froman, Lewis A., Jr., and James K. Skipper, Jr., "Factors Related to Misperceiving Party Stands on Issues," *Public Opinion Quarterly,* 26 (1962), pp. 265–272.

Hoffer, Eric, *The True Believer.* New York: New American Library, 1958.

Janda, Kenneth, "A Comparative Study of Political Alienation and Voting Behavior in Three Suburban Communities," in *Studies in History and the Social Sciences: Studies in Honor of John A. Kinneman.* Normal, Ill.: Illinois State University Press.

Janowitz, Morris, and Dwaine Marvick, "Authoritarianism and Political Behavior," *Public Opinion Quarterly,* 17 (1953), pp. 185–201.

Key, V. O., Jr., and Frank Munger, "Social Determinism and Electoral Decision: The Case of Indiana," Eugene Burdick and Arthur J. Brodbeck, eds., *American Voting Behavior.* Glencoe, Ill.: The Free Press, 1959, pp. 281–299.

Kornhauser, William, *The Politics of Mass Society.* New York: The Free Press, 1959.

Krugman, Herbert E., "The Appeal of Communism to American Middle Class Intellectuals and Trade Unionists," *Public Opinion Quarterly,* 16 (1952), pp. 331–355.

Lane, Robert E., and David O. Sears, *Public Opinion*. Englewood Cliffs, N. J.: Prentice-Hall, 1964.

Levin, Murry B., *The Alienated Voter*. New York: Holt, Rinehart and Winston, Inc., 1960.

Litt, Edgar, "Political Cynicism and Political Futility," *Journal of Politics*, 25 (1963), pp. 312–323.

Rokeach, Milton, *The Open and Closed Mind*. New York: Basic Books, 1960.

Rosenberg, Morris, "The Meaning of Politics in Mass Society," *Public Opinion Quarterly*, 15 (1951), pp. 5–15.

Rosenberg, Morris, "Self-Esteem and Concern with Public Affairs," *Public Opinion Quarterly*, 26 (1962), pp. 201–211.

Salisbury, Robert H., and Gordon Black, "Class and Party in Partisan and Non-Partisan Elections," *American Political Science Review*, 57 (1963), pp. 584–592.

Sigel, Roberta S., "Effect of Partisanship on the Perception of Political Candidates," *Public Opinion Quarterly*, 28 (1964), pp. 483–496.

IV. COMPONENTS OF PERSONALITY AND POLITICAL SYSTEMS

Brown, Roger, *Social Psychology*. New York: The Free Press, 1965, chapter 9, "The Achievement Motive," pp. 423–476.

Freud, Sigmund, and William C. Bullitt, *Thomas Woodrow Wilson: Twenty-Eighth President of the United States*. Boston: Houghton Mifflin, 1967.

Fromm, Erich, *The Sane Society*. New York: Holt, Rinehart and Winston, Inc., 1955.

Inkeles, Alex, "National Character and Modern Political Systems," in Francis L. K. Hsu, ed., *Psychological Anthropology: Approaches to Culture and Personality*. Homewood, Ill.: Dorsey Press, 1961, pp. 172–208.

Riesman, David, "From Morality to Morale," in Alfred H. Stanton and Stewart E. Perry (eds.), *Personality and Political Crisis*. Glencoe, Ill.: The Free Press, 1951, pp. 81–101.

Schaar, John H., *Escape from Authority: The Perspectives of Erich Fromm*. New York: Basic Books, 1961.

Wolfenstein, Victor, *The Revolutionary Personality: Lenin, Trotsky, Gandhi*. Princeton, N. J.: Princeton University Press, 1967.

Index
of Authors
and Titles

Index
of Authors
and Titles